The Legacy of Charles W. Mills and The Racial Contract in Educational Justice

Race is everywhere and pretending not to see it only does more damage than good. This book delves into the work of Charles Mills and how his underlying philosophies of race still play out in today's economic, educational, political, and sociological arena.

Charles Mills left a legacy of philosophical racial analyses needed to better understand race, racism, whiteness, and white supremacy worldwide. From the Racial Contract to global issues of colonial whiteness and epistemological racial ignorance, Mills' theories still resonate in the research that race scholars conduct today. Needless to say, despite his passing, Charles' work lives on. To honour Mills' scholarship, this book draws on interdisciplinary studies (e.g., sociology, political science, Black studies, and education) to excavate the racial landscape of the United States post Trump, anti-CRT bans, #BLM, and global racial reckonings. Within this volume prominent scholars of race worldwide and, from a variety of disciplines, discuss Mills' theories as applied to contemporary discourses of race, whilst also offering very personal vignettes that best illuminate who Charles was to us all. Essentially, the man behind the theories. Filled with both deep theoretical analyses and personal stories of Charles, this book will liven the spirits, hearts, and hope for racial justice and those who work endlessly toward it.

This book is a key resource for scholars, researchers, and practitioners in the fields of education, sociology, political science, racial and ethnic studies, development studies, and philosophy. It was originally published as a special issue of the journal *Race Ethnicity and Education*.

Cheryl E. Matias is a full professor in the School of Leadership and Education Sciences at the University of San Diego who earned several awards, including the 2020 Mid-Career Award for her work on racial justice in teacher education at American Educational Research Association. She researches the emotionality of whiteness in teacher education and motherscholarship that supports women of color and motherscholars in the academy. She has several books: *Feeling* White, *Surviving Becky(s)*, *The Handbook on Critical Theoretical Reseach Methods in Education*, and *The Other Elephants in the (Class)room*. She is a motherscholar of three, including boy-girl twins.

Photograph by Cheryl E. Matias

The Legacy of Charles W. Mills and The Racial Contract in Educational Justice

His Work Lives On

Edited by
Cheryl E. Matias

Routledge
Taylor & Francis Group

LONDON AND NEW YORK

First published 2025
by Routledge
4 Park Square, Milton Park, Abingdon, Oxon OX14 4RN

and by Routledge
605 Third Avenue, New York, NY 10158

Routledge is an imprint of the Taylor & Francis Group, an informa business

© 2025 Taylor & Francis

British Library Cataloguing in Publication Data
A catalogue record for this book is available from the British Library

ISBN13: 978-1-032-86959-9 (hbk)
ISBN13: 978-1-032-86963-6 (pbk)
ISBN13: 978-1-003-53018-3 (ebk)

DOI: 10.4324/9781003530183

Typeset in Minion Pro
by Newgen Publishing UK

Publisher's Note
The publisher accepts responsibility for any inconsistencies that may have arisen during the conversion of this book from journal articles to book chapters, namely the inclusion of journal terminology.

Disclaimer
Every effort has been made to contact copyright holders for their permission to reprint material in this book. The publishers would be grateful to hear from any copyright holder who is not here acknowledged and will undertake to rectify any errors or omissions in future editions of this book.

To Charles, your scholarship, swag, and heart will never be forgotten.
Thank you and rest in peace.

Contents

Citation Information

The following chapters in this book were originally published in *Race, Ethnicity, and Education*, volume 26 issue 4 (2023). When citing this material, please use the original page numbering for each article, as follows:

Introduction

Dancing with Charles: A man, scholar, legacy
Cheryl E. Matias
Race, Ethnicity, and Education, volume 26 issue 4 (2023), pp. 419–425

Chapter 1

We will greet our enemy with rifles and roses: Charles Mills and the perpetual impact of the Racial Contract
David Stovall
Race, Ethnicity, and Education, volume 26 issue 4 (2023), pp. 426–435

Chapter 2

The Racial Contract and white saviorism: centering racism's role in undermining housing and education equity
Ann M. Aviles
Race, Ethnicity, and Education, volume 26 issue 4 (2023), pp. 436–455

Chapter 3

White racial ignorance and refusing culpability: how the emotionalities of whiteness ignore race in teacher education
Michalinos Zembylas and Cheryl E. Matias
Race, Ethnicity, and Education, volume 26 issue 4 (2023), pp. 456–477

Chapter 4

Expectations as property of white supremacy: the coloniality of ascriptive expectations within the racial contract
Daniel D. Liou
Race, Ethnicity, and Education, volume 26 issue 4 (2023), pp. 478–496

For any permission-related enquiries please visit:
www.tandfonline.com/page/help/permissions

Notes on Contributors

Ann M. Aviles, Department of Human Development and Family Sciences, College of Education and Human Development, University of Delaware, Newark, DE, USA.

Bryant O. Best, Department of Teaching and Learning, Peabody College of Education and Human Development, Vanderbilt University, Nashville, TN, USA.

Wyatt Driskell, Educational Policy Studies & Evaluation, University of Kentucky, Lexington, KY, USA.

Tyrone A. Formana, Black Studies and Sociology, University of Illinois Chicago, Chicago, IL, USA.

Margaret A. Hagerman, Department of Sociology, Mississippi State University, Starkville, MS, USA.

Amanda E. Lewis, Black Studies and Sociology, University of Illinois Chicago, Chicago, IL, USA.

Daniel D. Liou, Mary Lou Fulton Teachers College, Arizona State University, Tempe, AZ, USA.

George Lipsitz, University of California Santa Barbara, Santa Barbara, CA, USA.

Cheryl E. Matias, School of Leadership and Education Sciences, University of San Diego, CA, USA.

H. Richard Milner IV, Department of Teaching and Learning, Peabody College of Education and Human Development, Vanderbilt University, Nashville, TN, USA.

David Stovall, Department of Black Studies; Department of Criminology, Law and Justice University of Illinois at Chicago, Chicago, IL, USA.

Michalinos Zembylas, Programme of Educational Studies, Open University of Cyprus, Latsia, Cyprus.

Introduction – Dancing with Charles: a man, scholar, legacy

Cheryl E. Matias

Abstract

Scholars like Leonardo (2009) or Yancy (2006) regularly apply, otherwise, dance with Charles Mills' concepts like the Racial Contract (Mills 1997), epistemology of ignorance (Mills 2007), and white Marxism and Black Radicalism (Mills 2003). By extension, when other educational scholars apply Leonardo or Yancy they inadvertently dance with Charles too. Partner dancing, such as bachata, is about a continual ebb and flow between dance partners, taking turns leading and following. So, whether directly engaging Charles's conceptualization like the Racial Contract or entangling with his work vis-à-vis scholarly concepts derived from his original conceptualization we, as scholars, continue to dance with Charles, letting him lead at times, following at others. Essentially, Charles's scholarship and his legacy never skip a beat in the academic cadence of educational research on race, ethnicity, and education. This piece pays homage to his legacy.

May I have this dance?

Much like the rest of the world I, too, received the news of Charles'[1] passing in October 2021. Though initially numb due to the increasing death rates during the COVID-19 pandemic, the numbness quickly wore off, forcing me to feel the full weight of this loss. You see, the loss was not simply about his foundational scholarship that has undergirded many of today's most notable scholars advancing racial justice (many of whom authored here), it was about Charles himself: always jovial, critical, and full of life. I remember trying to teach him how to use Marco Polo[2] so we could send videos to each other during the pandemic shutdown. He had me rolling with laughter when his videos appeared showing only his forehead on the screen. Despite the 'forehead show', his analysis on the colonial project of academic egos was ever on point. Or the times I would turn to him seeking advice in academia, especially regarding whether I should take on more administrative roles, one in which he would call me out, knowing all too well I only turned to him to coach me out of it. His most convincing argument was reminding me that one of his greatest accomplishments in life was 'never being chair of the department'. *That* was Charles. He could stick a one liner with such complexity and nuance, capturing race, capitalism, and gender in ways no one ever could; in doing so, he left people laughing yet critically pondering.

One of the most memorable remembrances of Charles was taking him out clubbing ... yes, I said clubbing! I am an avid salsa and bachata dancer. So, during one conference, Critical Race Studies in Education Association (CRSEA), together with other colleagues and doctoral students, we sought to teach Charles how to bachata in Albuquerque, New Mexico. The rhythmic beats of old and new bachata, with its easy four step dance moves and hip swaying, could not have been a greater metaphor for Charles himself. For much like his playful protests claiming he was *Jamaicanizing* bachata – that is, infusing his Jamaican culture and moves onto the Dominican dance – Charles and his scholarship were always infused into our scholarship.

Dancing with Charles

Major ideas like whiteness in education, per education scholar Zeus Leonardo (2009, 2015), to conceptualizations of the white gaze by philosopher George Yancy (2017) regularly applied Charles's concepts like the Racial Contract (Mills 1997), epistemology of ignorance (Mills 2007), and white Marxism and Black Radicalism (Mills 2003). And yet, by extension, when educational scholars apply concepts of whiteness qua Leonardo (e.g. Linley 2017; Matias and Boucher 2023; Philip and Benin 2014, etc.) or the white gaze qua Yancy (e.g. Coloma 2012; Matias 2016; Paris 2019; Stewart and Gachago 2022), they inadvertently dance with Charles too. In fact, partner dancing, such as bachata, is about a continual ebb and flow between dance partners, taking turns leading and following. So, whether directly engaging Charles's conceptualization like the Racial Contract (e.g. Leonardo 2013; Liou 2019; Liou and Rojas 2020; Mueller 2022) or entangling ourselves with his work vis-à-vis scholarly concepts derived from his original conceptualization (e.g. Cabrera and Corces-Zimmerman 2017; Menashy and Zakharia 2022) we, as scholars, continue to dance with Charles, letting him lead at times, following at others. Essentially, Charles's scholarship and his legacy never skip a beat in the academic cadence of educational research on race, ethnicity, and education.

Thus, it becomes acutely appropriate to honor Charles's legacy in *Race, Ethnicity, and Education* (REE) because this journal continually 'explores the dynamics of race, racism and ethnicity in education policy, theory, and practice', by inviting old and new theorizations of race, racism, and white supremacy. Instead of simply calling out racism, like Charles's work, REE interrogates race, racism, and white supremacy simply because 'We want to know what went wrong in the past, is going wrong now, and is likely going to *continue* to go wrong in the future if we do not guard against it' (original italics, Mills 1997, 92). Essentially, REE and Charles are great dance partners in fighting against racial injustice.

The beat of *this* dance: our special issue

This special issue revisits, honors, and extends Charles Mills' scholarship whilst paying homage to the man himself. Many of the authors in this issue have had personal relationships with Charles and weave in the man behind the scholarship. Carefully dancing between theory, scholarship, and personal anecdotes, the articles in this special issue journal edition draw on Charles's works to create understanding of how race, racism, whiteness, and white supremacy play out in today's arena. With anti-CRT bans, rise of white nationalism, increasing awareness to #BlackLivesMatter, and the erroneous attempt towards *eracism*—erase racism (see Matias-Padua 2010) there is no time better than now to reinvestigate the Racial Contract.

Though most of the authors in this special issue are in the field of education (e.g. David Stovall, Ann M. Aviles, Daniel D. Liou, Wyatt Driskell, Michalinos Zembylas, Richard H. Milner, Bryant O. Best, and myself), others hail from different social science disciplines like Sociology (e.g. Amanda Lewis, Tyrone Forman, and Margaret Hagerman) and Black Studies & Sociology (e.g. George Lipsitz). Despite the field or discipline, all the authors came together to commemorate, reminisce, and honor Charles' scholarship and the man he was in the eight articles of this special issue.

There are four major sections in this Special Issue: The Racial Contract: Then and Now (Stovall); The Racial Contract Applied to Educational Justice (Aviles, Zembylas & Matias; Liou; Driskell); The Racial Contract Applied to Educationally Just Methods (Best & Milner); and, The Racial Contract Beyond (Lipsitz, Lewis, Forman & Hagerman). After my Special Issue Opening, the issue opens with 'The Racial Contract: Then and Now' wherein Dr. Dave Stovall writes 'We Will Greet our Enemy with Rifles and Roses: Charles Mills and the Perpetual Impact of the Racial Contract'. Stovall's article flows between the 'rifles' and 'roses' of Mills's scholarship, and how Charles personally mentored him at the University of Illinois Chicago. Stovall's exhilarating commentary reveals that 'Dr. Mills's lesson for all of us is that we should never be fearful of white supremacy'. Behind those prophetic words are eons of encouragement for continuing racially just scholarship and activism.

Section Two, entitled 'The Racial Contract Applied to Educational Justice', is comprised of four articles. First, Dr. Ann M. Aviles's 'The Racial Contract and White Saviorism: Centering Racism's Role in Undermining Housing and Education Equity' gives a haunting interrogation of the 'structure and function of race in the policies and practices related to education and housing – specifically McKinney-Vento (1987) Education Policy, and the Fair Housing Act of 1968—given the over-representation of Black and Brown individuals and communities that experience housing instability and discrimination, and its parallels to education'. Weaving in her own personal connections with Charles, Aviles dives into his racial contract and its connection to the white savior industrial complex, warning scholars 'Rather than continuing the "epistemology of ignorance" required by the Racial Contract, educators, practitioners, and policy makers must uncompromisingly and unapologetically combat the racial discrimination that is widespread in schools and society, particularly in regards to students and families of color experiencing housing instability'.

I co-author the section's second article with Michalinos Zembylas. 'White Racial Ignorance and Refusing Culpability: How the Emotionalities of Whiteness Ignore Race in Teacher Education' illustrates how the work we do in theorizing the technologies of affect and white emotionalities in teacher education are but extensions of Mills's theorization of epistemology of ignorance. Without Mills's initial conceptualization of how white ignorance actively operates to obscure the racial contract, the scholarship both Dr. Zembylas and I have built on affect theory and white emotionality would be for naught. We end the article with a caution for educationally just researchers: we write, 'As Mills (2007) has shown, racialized habits are deeply engrained affective habits that often obscure the workings of oppression and white privilege, making it difficult to dismantle them. And yet, unless educators, activists, and other stakeholders find ways of intervention that can begin to truly challenge those affective habits, even if the cracks are small, it will be impossible to break the hegemony of the affective economy of whiteness in various social domains, including teacher education'.

The third article, entitled 'Expectations as Property of white Supremacy: The Coloniality of Ascriptive Expectations within the Racial Contract' by Dr. Daniel D. Liou draws on Mills's racial contract 'to reenvision the sociology of expectations in schools and society. Specifically, the article generates insight into how expectations for one's intellectual superiority and inferiority are authored into the racial contract, functioning as a form of coloniality in regulating racial hierarchies within the global systems of white supremacy'. That is, Liou takes to task how something as seemingly innocent as expectations in education are 'ascriptive at their core', i.e. always embedded with whiteness as a colonial polity. Liou posits that until educational researchers 'problematiz[e] expectations', they will not be able to delink 'colonial knowledge from education to transform the interconnecting and intersecting points of ascription'.

The fourth article is written by Wyatt Driskell. 'Naming the Unnamed: A Millsian Analysis of the American Educational Contract' reveals how, by understanding Mills's racial contract, one can better 'understand the political, historical, and philosophical context surrounding the current controversy over CRT'. Driskell demonstrates how the racial contract rears its ugly head in educational movements, indicating that 'the white polity's efforts to distort the social world can be unscrambled and the tenets of the Racial Contract are laid bare before the reader'. Driskell warns educational researchers that therefore, instead of ignoring the Racial Contract, we must name it so to 'share in the responsibility to resist it'.

'The Racial Contract Applied to Educationally Just Methods' entitles the third section, with the featured article 'Too Much Talking, Not Enough Listening: The Racial Contract Made Manifest in a Mixed-Race Focus Group Interview' by Bryant O. Best and Dr. Richard H. Milner, IV. Here, the authors demonstrate 'the importance of researchers to build and practice analytic lenses to identify when the Racial Contract manifests in and through interviews and a research process'. Inasmuch as the Racial Contract structures a society, it also underscores the very methods we, as researchers, employ to study that society. The authors caution that 'espousing to do liberal work does not equate to having liberal beliefs and practices' and can instead 'be harmful to Black and Brown people'; therefore, 'social and racial justice researchers must be mindful of and deliberate as they make decisions about addressing conflicts that arise in studies', especially as the Racial Contract continues to operate.

Section Four, entitled 'The Racial Contract Beyond', features two articles. First, Dr. George Lipsitz's 'Rejecting the Racial Contract: Charles Mills and Critical Race Theory' reveals how 'the Racial Contract as Mills theorizes it contains important yet often overlooked implications for understanding social movement mobilization as a key crucible of oppositional knowledge and as a mechanism through which the Racial Contract has been both implemented and resisted'. Diving into the birth of and resistance to CRT, Lipsitz asserts that the anti-CRT campaign in K-12 schools 'replicates a longstanding social pedagogy designed to preserve the epistemology of ignorance as part of a century's old whiteness protection program', and the Racial Contract thus provides 'a lens that reveals social mobilizations and autonomous learning centers to be key sites for racial justice struggles'.

To drive this Special Issue home, sociologists Amanda Lewis, Tyron Forman, and Margaret Hagerman's present the article 'Charles Mills Ain't Dead!: Keeping the Spirit of Charles Mills's Work Alive by Understanding and Challenging the Unrepentant Whiteness of the Academy'. In this gut-wrenching testimony of the lives of professors in academia, the authors weave in their personal connection to Charles, his scholarship, the ideas from each of the articles in this special issue, and what must be considered for racial justice to ensue. Or as they so humbly write, 'We learned so much from him and we hope to use this essay to share some of those lessons'. Drawing from their personal stories and tying it in with the articles in this special issue, the authors demand that 'As scholars we must do more than just theorize power, race, and inequality, we should also commit to utilizing our scholarly lens to describe, undermine, and ultimately dismantle the informal and formal habits, processes, and policies that reproduce white supremacy in the "hallowed" halls of academia'. In essence, they assert, academics 'must show up for each other intellectually and personally', and only until that happens can the spirit of Charles's love and commitment truly be felt.

The beat goes on

Charles Mills had a way with words. From a complex point made by a mere one-line question like, 'If there is a backlash against affirmative action, what would the response be to the demand for the interest in the unpaid forty aces and a mule?' (1997, p. 39) to a complex sentence which, had so many commas, lasted almost a paragraph long, and was so profoundly intricate that to this day I still struggle with its meaning – and this is after asking Charles if he could better explain it, to which he chuckled, 'I don't know what I wrote'.[3] He brought a smile to us all, both by his charming and funny personality – in fact, he used to call he and me the 'Jamaican-Filipino Decolonizers Unite'—and by the depth of his thought process regarding race in the United States and beyond. After reading a work of Charles's, you could not help but feel your heart and soul smile precisely because his words gave us our words, his dance aligned with our steps. Meaning, as Black, Indigenous, People of Color we have felt these lashing for so long it was so hard to name. No longer an invisible lashing, Mills' theorizations of race, whiteness, and coloniality called out that which was rarely spoken before and, in doing so, unapologetically demanded for better. Suffice it to say that his heart beats on within us. His words live on within our scholarship. And his legacy lives on in the struggle for racial justice. So, continue everyone dancing with Charles.

Notes

1. I purposely use Charles not out of disrespect. Instead, 'Charles' is how I often referred to him in our personal communique and I want readers to know the man behind the Mills scholarship.
2. Marco Polo is a video chat app https://www.marcopolo.me/.
3. See the first two lines of his chapter 'White Ignorance' in Sullivan and Tuana's (2007) *Race and Epistemologies of Ignorance*.

Special Note

To my colleague, mentor, and friend, thank you for all you have done. Please rest in peace now; we will take it from here.

Disclosure statement

No potential conflict of interest was reported by the author.

References

Cabrera, N. L., and C. Corces-Zimmerman. 2017. "An Unexamined Life: White Male Racial Ignorance and the Agony of Education for Students of Color." *Equity & Excellence in Education* 50 (3): 300–315. doi:10.1080/10665684.2017.1336500.

Coloma, R. S. 2012. "White Gazes, Brown Breasts: Imperial Feminism and Disciplining Desires and Bodies in Colonial Encounters." *Paedagogica historica* 48 (2): 243–261. doi:10.1080/00309230.2010.547511.

Leonardo, Z. 2009. *Race, Whiteness, and Education.* New York: Routledge.

Leonardo, Z. 2013. "The Story of Schooling: Critical Race Theory and the Educational Racial Contract." *Discourse: Studies in the Cultural Politics of Education* 34 (4): 599–610. doi:10.1080/01596306.2013.822624.

Leonardo, Z. 2015. "Contracting Race: Writing, Racism, and Education." *Critical Studies in Education* 56 (1): 86–98. doi:10.1080/17508487.2015.981197.

Linley, J. L. 2017. "Teaching to Deconstruct Whiteness in Higher Education." *Whiteness and Education* 2 (1): 48–59. doi:10.1080/23793406.2017.1362943.

Liou, D. D. 2019. "Disrupting the Ideology of Settled Expectations: Forging New Social Movements to Dismantle the Educational Racial Contract." *Berkeley Review of Education* 9 (1): n1. doi:10.5070/B89146424.

Liou, D. D., and L. Rojas. 2020. "The Significance of the Racial Contract in teachers' College Expectancies for Students of Color." *Race Ethnicity and Education* 23 (5): 712–731. doi:10.1080/13613324.2018.1511529.

Matias, C. E. 2016. "Whiteness as Surveillance: Policing Brown Bodies in Education." *Feeling White: Whiteness, Emotionality, and Education* 115–126.

Matias, C. E., and C. Boucher. 2023. "From Critical Whiteness Studies to a Critical Study of Whiteness: Restoring Criticality in Critical Whiteness Studies." *Whiteness and Education* 8 (1): 64–81. doi:10.1080/23793406.2021.1993751.

Matias-Padua, C. E. 2010. *Where are you REALLY from? Raced curriculum, racial identity, and a project for a fuller humanity* [Dissertation]. University of California, Los Angeles.

Menashy, F., and Z. Zakharia. 2022. "White Ignorance in Global Education." *Harvard Educational Review* 92 (4): 461–485. doi:10.17763/1943-5045-92.4.461.

Mills, C. W. 1997. *The Racial Contract.* New York: Cornell University Press.

Mills, C. W. 2003. *From Class to Race: Essays in White Marxism and Black Radicalism.* Maryland: Rowman & Littlefield.

Mills, C. W. 2007. "White Ignorance." In *Epistemology of Ignorance*, edited by S. Sullivan and N. Tuana, 1 13–38. New York: State University of New York Press.

Mueller, J. C. 2022. ""Imagine an Ignorance That Fights back": Honoring Charles Mills, Our Inheritance and Charge." *Sociology of Race and Ethnicity* 8 (4): 443–450. doi:10.1177/23326492221119889.

Paris, D. 2019. "Naming Beyond the White Settler Colonial Gaze in Educational Research." *International Journal of Qualitative Studies in Education* 32 (3): 217–224. doi:10.1080/09518398.2019.1576943.

Philip, T. M., and S. Y. Benin. 2014. "Programs of Teacher Education as Mediators of White Teacher Identity." *Teaching Education* 25 (1): 1–23. doi:10.1080/10476210.2012.743985.

Stewart, K. D., and D. Gachago. 2022. "Step into the Discomfort: (Re)orienting the White Gaze and Strategies to Disrupt Whiteness in Educational Spaces." *Whiteness and Education* 7 (1): 18–31. doi:10.1080/23793406.2020.1803760.

Sullivan, S., & Tuana, N., Eds. 2007. Race and epistemologies of ignorance. Suny Press.

Yancy, G. 2017. *Black Bodies, White Gaze: The Continuing Significance of Race in American.* 2nd ed. Maryland: Rowman & Littlefield.

PART I

The Racial Contract: then and now

We will greet our enemy with rifles and roses: Charles Mills and the perpetual impact of the Racial Contract

David Stovall

ABSTRACT

The following article positions the work of Charles Mills (1951–2021) as seminal to the development of critical race theory (CRT) in education. His groundbreaking contribution, The Racial Contract, has served as the foundation for understanding the myriad ways that white supremacy is central in the social contract championed by scholars of the Western European Enlightenment period. It is a 'rifle' in that it offers an unapologetically Black interruption to the necessity of refusal and resistance. The 'rose' of Dr. Mills' work is always represented in his humor and commitment to joy in the face of violence and extreme hostility. The article names the genesis of my relationship with Dr. Mills as a newly hired professor at the University of Illinois at Chicago and through his mentorship of founding members of the Critical Race Studies in Education Association (CRSEA).

If I fall in the struggle, take my place

Gaze at my lips as they stop the wind's madness

I have not died.

I can still call you from beyond my wounds

Bang your drum so that the people might hear your call to battle.

-Muin Tawfiq Bseiso, 'Al-Ma'raka'

Serving as a rifle in the struggle

The words of Palestinian poet and freedom fighter Muin Tawfiq Bseiso are particularly fitting as I remember the lessons delivered so graciously by Dr. Charles Mills (1951–2021). As we are now called to fill the void left by Dr. Mills' presence in the long struggle for liberation and self-determination, I am assured that his soul is still with us. Because we are still banging our drums, the hope remains that our people will heed the call to fight in the perpetual struggle against white supremacy. Because Dr. Mills was forever giving in his time here on earth, he remains the quintessential example of what it means to work humbly and unapologetically. In countless ways, Dr. Mills' work is a valued weapon in the larger struggle. I refer to it as a rifle in the larger spirit of self-defense, where the rifle is not meant for a frontal attack, but is serves as the lasting reminder that critical, community-engaged scholars will be protected, no matter the adversary. In the case of Dr. Mills, detractors were clear that if you approached his work with derision or misinformation, you had better be prepared for the smoke that came in response to the attack. I truly appreciated this as a person entering academia because it demonstrated the need for clarity. In this sense, clarity is an inward-facing responsibility, in that it is not the attempt to be validated by the rules of the academy. Instead, it is a commitment to be clear about what you are doing and why you are doing it. Dr. Mills was always willing to share his time and energy with the understanding that it is of the utmost importance to provide tangible examples of the possibilities of scholarship rooted in the radical tradition. Despite his transition, it is important to note that while not here in physical form, the commitments and understandings brought forward by Charles Mills *are still with us*. To paraphrase an African proverb, you are only forgotten when your name stops to be spoken amongst the living. The vision and clarity of his writings allows for students and faculty to know that you are not by yourself if you make the conscious decision to break from the orthodoxy of academia. In the current moment, Mills' unflinching scholarship continues to stand in the face of detractors, challenging the ridiculous and outright absurd claims against critical race theory (CRT) or any scholarship that intentionally names, challenges and works against racism/white supremacy.

Instead of eulogizing the work of Dr. Mills, the hope of this contribution is to put his seminal text *The Racial Contract* in conversation with the current moment as k-20 educators and researchers find themselves in a struggle that was long prophesized. As some were taken off guard, many critical race theorists prepared for this day. Despite the surprise of some, the lessons of *The Racial Contract* live through our commitments and attempts to support each other, despite the feeling that everything is unraveling. In approaching the 25th anniversary of *The Racial Contract*, the article is divided into five sections. The first section is my recollection of my first interactions with Dr. Mills and how he provides an explicit example of how to resist the psychic violence of the academy. The second section provides a moment when he shared the origin story of *The Racial Contract* as a text. Section three speaks to his support of junior scholars in the Critical Race Studies in Education Association. Section four speaks to praxis, in an attempt to use *The Racial Contract* with a group of high school students. Concluding the account are thoughts on the necessity of refusal, as a new cadre of scholars continue the work of Dr. Mills in written and physical form.

A joyous approach, despite the hostility and violence of the academy

I was hired at the University of Illinois at Chicago in the summer of 2000. Over the last twenty-two years I have come to know the hostility and violence of the academy as observer, survivor and unwilling participant (i.e. promotion and tenure committees, graduate student reviews, grading, etc.). The welcoming smiles quickly disappear once you tell people that you study white supremacy and work with others to defeat it. Especially in education, where there is often a concerted effort to make things 'nice' and 'acceptable' to mainstream white society. I have become quite used to the open-mouthed smiles and frantic head nodding of nervous colleagues when I explain what I do and what my commitments are. Nowadays I quietly laugh at the 'oh, that's so nice' replies or the quick smiles that I used to get in the hallways. All of it is understood as the ancillary actions that the academy takes with the hope that I will capitulate and accept its project of colonization. In my refusal of these norms, my approach to the academy has been a strange mix of belligerence, disgust and resistance. Dr. Mills, in his unwavering acceptance of those who are rooted in refusal, always provided the affirmation that it is not only good to refuse the academy, but it is mandatory in preserving your physical, mental and spiritual health.

In one of my first experiences with Dr. Mills, he and I were walking down the street with a number of other faculty members as part of a break between conference presentations. I had just become aware of *The Racial Contract* through a couple of colleagues. As we were walking to the next venue, he briefly introduced himself as Charles Mills, and I said to him 'Charles Mills who wrote *The Racial Contract?*' He nodded and said, 'that's me' and we walked over to the next conference session. From that day on, we would run into each other at various meetings across campus and he was always kind and would invite me to talk with him about how things were going as a new faculty. From then on, I was deeply inspired by his sincerity and his willingness to engage me beyond extractive, transactional exchanges so common in the academy.

A contract origin story

Dr. Mills was deeply involved in the community of Black philosophers. One year he hosted a conference of Black philosophers, highlighting the oft-ignored contributions of Black people in the discipline and outside of traditional philosophy. His running joke was that there was 'no need to worry because there aren't that many of us in the first place'. During one of the conference presentations, he told the genesis story of *The Racial Contract*. He explained to the group that he patterned the concept after Carole Pateman's book *The Sexual Contract* (Pateman 1988). Mills appreciated her critique of Locke, Hobbes and Rousseau's interpretation of the social contract and felt as if he could make a similar argument with regards to race. If the assumed social contract put forward by enlightenment philosophers ignored gender and the contribution of women, then it should also be critiqued for its lack of a discussion of race. Mills makes a shift however, providing the assertion that despite the omission or recognition of race in the social contract, white supremacy remains 'the unnamed system that has made the modern world what it is today' (Mills 1997, 1). It is thereby 'contractual', as 'theory that founds government on the popular consent of individuals taken as equals' (ibid, 2). If we couple it with the set of agreements rationalized by protestant Christian rationales an early capitalist formation founded in exploitation, we gain a deeper understanding of the actions of the colonizer and nation-state.

Dr. Mills continued his story by telling us that he originally sent a shorter version of the manuscript as an article to the philosophy journal *Ethics*. As one of the top journals in social, legal, and political philosophy, he thought the concept was one that was in line with what the journal was publishing at the time. Unfortunately, his submission was rejected. When he told one of his friends that it was rejected, his comrade told him, 'Don't worry about it, turn it into a book'. Dr. Mills pondered the idea and went ahead and lengthened the manuscript and submitted it as a book soon after the rejection. In a strange twist of irony, the editors of *Ethics* offer praise for the book in the form of a promotion blurb that appears on the first pages of the manuscript. I guess it wasn't good enough to get in the journal but was good enough to get a blurb. Where we will never know if the rejection was due to the inability of the editors to come to grips with Mills critique of the enlightenment cannon, the rejection itself becomes an important narrative on how to move forward, despite the inherent roadblocks and barriers. In the same vein, the multitude of critical scholars remain overjoyed that Dr. Mills utilized his navigational capital to create *The Racial Contract* (Yosso 2005).

Roses as support in word and deed

I am a founding member of the Critical Race Studies in Education Association (CRSEA). As scholars who were deeply influenced by the lies of Dr. Charles Mills, Gloria Ladson-Billings, Margaret Montoya, Angela Harris, Francisco Valdez, Adrienne Wing, Daniel Solórzano, Laurence Parker, Eric Yamamoto, and David Gillborn, we started as a small collective of early scholars and graduate students who engaged CRT and the intersectional disciplines that allow us to engage education. Our early wishes were to create a space for critical race scholars in education could see each other, with the hope of exchanging ideas and figuring out ways to best support each other, given the hostility of the academy. We thought the best way to do this was to create a small gathering where people would be able to present their work while receiving constructive support by others in the field. In our early days of the conference (even before we had an actual name), Dr. Mills was always supportive of our work. We would have two panels that were always the highlight of the conference, one that was a panel of senior scholars and the other that would feature teachers, community organizers and youth workers. For the first two years of the gathering, Dr. Mills would participate on the senior scholar panel and offer some of the most poignant commentary on the necessity of understanding white supremacy ideologically and materially.

One year, Mills opened his comments on the panel as to why philosophers will always be employed at universities. He told the crowd 'philosophers will always have a job at the university because we're the cheapest to employ – all we need to do our work is a paper and pencil'. It was this type of humor that opened us up to how he saw the world with both levity and candor, reminding us never to take the academy too seriously while always understanding our work critically. His epic battles with William Watkins on the schisms between scholars from the Marxist/structuralist tradition and critical race theorists were always deeply insightful. In these discussions he would demonstrate what interdisciplinary scholarship looked like in word and deed, explaining that the structuralists are correct in naming a capitalism as a totalizing system. Often in the same breath, he would remind them that like capitalism, white supremacy is also a totalizing system where people should be challenged to understand how race is always intertwined in a discussion with class, gender, age, (dis)ability and sexual orientation. The ease and dexterity of his conversation was invigorating in that he wasn't into debate for the sake of debate. Instead, he was committed to a process that did not discourage disagreement, while turning the issue to how to work together with folks who are willing to challenge white supremacy.

The 2018 CRSEA conference in Albuquerque, New Mexico is a particular memory that I hold dear. Instead of a panel of scholars, the conference held a session that was a conversation between Dr. Mills and legal scholar Margaret Montoya. In their conversation he returned to his conversation about being influenced by Carole Pateman, to the point that they connected with each other to write *Contract and Domination*, speaking to the conjoined relationship between race and gender in critique of the social contract. Dr. Montoya spoke to the necessity of centering gender and praxis in CRT and why the work is never static. I appreciated the way the conversation bounced between both of them, oscillating between how theory informs the practical and the responsibility of not solely resting on the theoretical construct. People in the audience appreciated the open and deeply human conversation between them as they laughed and reminded us that our loyalty should never be to academia. Instead, they reminded us that the critical scholar is one that works with and in communities, making sure to interrupt the colonial project of higher education. The audience of mostly grad students and new faculty asked questions that allowed for all in attendance to understand what a broader and deeper commitment to struggle looks like in real time. I keep a picture from the conversation between them at the conference in my phone as a constant reminder of what is always possible and necessary. Keeping true to his deep sense of humility, directly after their conversation, he asked myself and a group of graduate students if he could join us for lunch. It is a moment that remains lucid in my mind's eye, as the quintessential example of what it means to never succumb to the belief that anyone is beneath you and the best we can ever do is to do right by the people we care about. Being employed as an academic for more than twenty years, I try my best to emulate what I saw and felt from Dr. Mills by doing what I can to support up-and-coming scholars in their journey through the madness/wilderness of the academy. From Dr. Mills I am affirmed that the academy will never be the site of liberation. More in tune with the musings of Drs. Fred Moten and Stefano Harney, the best relationship with the university should be a criminal one, where we reappropriate the abundance of resources afforded to academic institutions and return them to the places like the ones we come from (Harney and Moten 2013). Mills lived this in thought and deed, as he gave us wisdom to be shared with others as duty and responsibility to work with others to change our conditions. Instead of deeply exclusionary institutions that often thrive in practices of exploitation, this work will take place on the ground with the people who have been with us long before we were granted the permission to put strange letters behind our names and refer to ourselves as 'experts'.

Roses as understanding the Racial Contract through praxis

For the last twenty-five years I've worked in a sub-field of critical race theory known as critical race praxis (CRP). I was always attracted to the idea that scholars operating from the radical imaginary should spend 'less time with abstract theorizing and more time on the ground people who are experiencing injustice' (Yamamoto 1997, 830). It's especially important to me in that it is intentional about bringing praxis (action and reflection in the world in order to change it) and CRT in the same space to push our thoughts and actions. I was immediately drawn to CRP due to my initial frustration with the academy and its call to academics to get out of their own heads and to get with people who are trying to figure out how to build conditions for justice with people who have joined them in struggle. When I was introduced to *The Racial Contract*, it also allowed me to connect the practical, political and personal.

At the same time of this realization, I was involved with a community effort to demand quality education in an area that had been ignored by the city despite being promised a school to service young people and families in the neighborhood. When community members were victorious in their efforts to secure the school for their community, I was invited to be a member of the design team. Instead of approaching the community with a CRP project, I spent more time listening to the issues and concerns of the community in terms of what they wanted in a school. As I spent more time as an active listener and participant in the design team process, CRP became more apparent to me as the design team process challenged me to incorporate the four tenets of the construct (conceptual, material, performative and reflexive). Yamamoto's (1997) call to spend less time with abstract theorizing was happening in real time as I worked with the design-team. I was challenged to suspend the notion of 'expertise' in the Western European tradition of research, understanding that the actual experts were the people who were able to identify concerns in their community while working with others to change the condition. CRP tenets came to mind first in my reflections on the design team process, as they spoke clearly to what people engaged in the process were trying to accomplish in creating a school.

With regard to the conceptual tenet of CRP, the idea was to develop a high school curriculum that reflected the needs and desires of the community in terms of quality education. The material tenet required us to secure the resources necessary to develop a justice-centered curriculum. As a performative endeavor, this tenet required us to create and enact plans that brought the idea of a justice-centered curriculum to life. The final reflexive tenet was the one that pushed faculty, staff and students to identify what was going well and where we needed to improve. It required us to come to grips with what was not going well in our process, while building strategies and practice that would improve the areas we identified as needing immediate attention.

After a few years at the high school, when the inaugural group of students were in their senior year, myself and another university comrade who was also on the design team created a couple of classes for the students. Earlier in the process to create the school on the design team, we wrote in the initial proposal to the school district that both of us as university faculty would create a series of classes that would give students early college credit. My course was called *Education, Youth and Justice*. Along with the other classes, it met the general education requirements at most four-year universities. Because the high school has a social justice focus, the class was meant to pair concepts of social justice with current and historical interpretations of social movements to enhance our understandings of the purpose of education. In terms of the design of the course, we wanted to put a number of theoretical constructs in conversation with each other (specifically CRT, contract theory, cycle of critical praxis) to provide students with examples of critical analysis.

The Racial Contract was of particular importance in the creation of the class, given Dr, Mills' seminal reframing of the social contract proposed by Western European enlightenment philosophers. The class started with Mill's interpretation of racism as a political system.

> What is needed is a global theoretical framework for situating discussions of race and White racism, and thereby challenging the assumptions of White political philosophy, which would correspond to feminist theorists' articulation of the centrality of gender, patriarchy, and sexism to traditional moral and political theory. What is needed, in other words, is a recognition that racism ... is *itself* a political system, a particular power structure of formal or informal rule, socioeconomic privilege, and norms for the differential distribution of material wealth and opportunities, benefits and burdens, rights and duties (Mills 1997, 2–3).

Because a contract is an agreement between two or more parties for the doing or not doing of something specified, we utilized Mills' challenge to understand the racial contract to be a signed one, in the sense that life for people of color in the Western Hemisphere is reflective of a set of decisions that operate on the premise of dehumanization. If people are dehumanized or thought of as less than human, the laws that govern the land concretize the idea, often resulting in further marginalization and isolation.

Our discussion of *The Racial Contract* allowed us to move into our larger researcher assignment of explaining how the racial contract affects the nine areas of human life and activity (Education, Economics, Entertainment, Labor, Law, Religion, Sex (Gender), War and Politics) identified by social theorist Neely Fuller (Fuller 1984). Once students began to grapple with the idea of a racial contract existing in the United States, some of the chosen topics were immigration, gentrification, school discipline policies for LGBTQ youth of color, reproductive rights, and health care. From their chosen topics, I would provide additional resources while contacting people in my network of schools, organizations, and researchers to secure relevant information for their research assignments.

In addition to an individual research paper, students were also required to develop a public presentation to be presented to a group of researchers at a local university. The idea was to get students to develop an assignment similar to the ones students would get in college. The assignment was to pick an area of interest, articulate its connection to one of the nine areas of human life and activity and demonstrate its connection to *The Racial Contract*. Students drew from a broad-range of topics, including immigration, video games and police brutality. We also took students to the university to present their work to college faculty and to the Dean of the College of Education. We also invited Professor Mills to the presentation. Due to a scheduling conflict, Dr. Mills was unable to attend, but was very pleased that a group of high school students were engaging his work. As the students thrived in their individual projects and group presentations, we owe a great debt of gratitude to Dr. Mills for laying the groundwork for a critical unit in the course. Without *The Racial Contract*, I am certain that we would not have the type of interest from students in class. Their ability to connect their daily lives to the totalizing power of white supremacy was reflective of their deep understanding of the contractual relationship between race and polity.

Rifles and roses: heads up and eyes open for our enemy

As we find ourselves trudging through the three pandemics of white supremacy, capitalism, and COVID-19, *The Racial Contract* stands as a prophetic account. Alerting to all of us that the use of violence and ideological conditioning is critical in perpetuating white supremacy and is instrumental in explaining the current set of attacks on CRT and any attempt to provide critical analysis in k-20 classrooms. As conservative pundits moved on former president Donald Trump's executive order 13,950, banning the use of CRT in federal trainings, the landslide of events have triggered a maelstrom of subsequent attacks on CRT and the use of critical analysis in classrooms. Manhattan Institute fellow Christopher Ruffo has outwardly named his association attack on CRT and his desire to rebrand the construct 'to have the public read something crazy in the newspaper and immediately think "critical race theory"' (https://www.washingtonpost.com/education/ 2021/06/19/critical-race-theory-rufo-republicans/). While not unusual in the bevy of attacks on the capacity of people to name white supremacy and its functions, the current moment has been heightened by the protests in the Summer of 2020. As the masses of white people across the planet realized that state-sanctioned violence targeting Black people and other people of color is normalized and approved, there were some factions of the country that understood that there was nothing they could do to quell the protests after the deaths of George Floyd and Breonna Taylor. Because more people began to ask questions about centuries of violence against people of color in the name of 'law and order', *The Racial Contract* offers a solemn reminder.

> . . . the model of the Racial Contract shows us that we need another alternative, another way of theorizing about and critiquing the state: the *racial*, or white-supremacist state, whose function inter alia is to safeguard the polity *as* a white or white-dominated polity, enforcing the terms of the Racial Contract by the appropriate means and, when necessary, facilitating its rewriting from one form to another (Mills 1997, 82).

Mills' reminder that this moment is not new is an important one, given the surprise by some at the vehement attacks on people of color since the pandemic. If the function of the state is to protect its white inhabitants, we see the vestiges of the racial contract daily. The arrival of new legislation banning curriculum that makes (white) children feel bad about themselves is a frontal attack on anything that challenges the myths of a meritocratic society. American ahistoricism and historical amnesia create a formidable wall that operates as a failsafe against any challenge to it. The racial contract makes sure that discussions concerning race, class, gender, age, (dis)ability, and sexual orientation will always be challenged and chided as disingenuous, divisive, and hate-mongering. Again, people miss the point – talking about race doesn't make the conversation racist. If we come to grips that the United States of America, according to its own laws and regulatory systems, is a land founded on enslavement, genocide and wrongful land appropriation in the form of settler colonialism, the conversation would have less sting and could potentially bring about discussions on how to make sure those founding tenets are permanently abolished. Instead, we find ourselves in a most bizarre moment, where the vast majority of CRT detractors have either never read CRT or have wrongly assumed critical philosophers to be critical race theorists.

Despite the ridiculousness of the moment, it is one that should not be taken lightly. The lack of education from a critical perspective has created a bevy of disinformation hoarders and influencers that have led to tragic results. K-12 teachers are losing their jobs for the mere mention of race or racism in their classrooms (https://www.brook ings.edu/blog/fixgov/2021/07/02/why-are-states-banning-critical-race-theory/).

University professors are facing sanctions for teaching classes that they were hired to teach. Certain texts have been banned and historical accuracy has been outlawed in many states (https://www.edweek.org/policy-politics/map-where-critical-race-theory-is-under-attack/2021/06). However, a text like *The Racial Contract* reminds us that we've been here before. The problem is that white power structures are doing all they can to force some people to forget while making it possible for scores of generations to never know.

I remain deeply thankful for the rifles and roses offered by Dr. Mills in his unflinching interrogation of white supremacy. It remains my hope that those who come after him will understand the seriousness of the current moment, realizing that the choice to fight is an easy one if we pay attention to what's at stake. Dr. Mills' lesson for all of us is that we should never be fearful of white supremacy. Especially since it has told us its function and purpose for time immemorial. It should never catch us off guard. If it does, we are still confused. Instead, we should be guided by the words of poet, educator and freedom fighter Haki Madhubuti in his poem *Earthquakes*.

> *when the smiles quit when the laughter quiets*
> *conflict beckons hearts hurt blood rushes*
> *hands sweat*
> *spine strengthens & brothers comprehend.*
> *catch the sun & get on up*
> *rise on the run. open eyed*
> *ready & expecting danger*
> expecting earthquakes (Madhubuti 1984, 113).

Dr. Mills reminds us that sometimes the earth may shake beneath our feet, but if we remain committed, we will soon be on solid ground.

Disclosure statement

No potential conflict of interest was reported by the author(s).

References

Fuller, N. 1984. *The United Compensatory Code/System/Concept: A Textbook/Workbook for Thought, Speech And/Or Action for Victims of Racism (White Supremacy)*. Chicago: Third World Press.

Harney, S., and F. Moten. 2013. *The Undercommons: Fugitive Planning and Black Study*. New York: Minor Compositions.

Madhubuti, H. 1984. *Earthquakes and Sunrise Missions: Poems and Essays of Black Renewal 1973-1983*. Chicago: Third World Press.

Meckler, L., and J. Dawsey. 2021. "Republicans, Sparked by an Unlikely Figure, See Political Promise in Targeting Critical Race Theory." *The Washington Post*, June 21. https://www.washingtonpost.com/education/2021/06/19/critical-race-theory-rufo-republicans/.

Mills, C. 1997. *The Racial Contract*. London: Cornell.

Pateman, C. 1988. *The Sexual Contract*. London: Polity.

Pateman, C., and C. Mills. 2007. *Contract and Domination*. London: Polity.

Ray, R., and A. Gibbons. 2021. *Why are States Banning Critical Race Theory?*. Brookings Institute. November. https://www.brookings.edu/blog/fixgov/2021/07/02/why-are-states-banning-critical-race-theory/

Schwartz, S. (June 11, 2021). Map: Where Critical Race Theory is Under Attack. *Ed Week*. https://www.edweek.org/policy-politics/map-where-critical-race-theory-is-under-attack/2021/06

Yamamoto, E. 1997. "Critical Race Praxis: Race Theory and Political Lawyering in Post Civil-Rights America." *Michigan Law Review* 95 (4): 821–900. doi:10.2307/1290048.

Yosso, T. 2005. "Whose Culture Has Capital? A Critical Race Theory Discussion of Community Cultural Wealth." *Race Ethnicity and Education* 8 (1): 69–91. doi:10.1080/1361332052000341006.

PART II

The Racial Contract applied to educational justice

The Racial Contract and white saviorism: centering racism's role in undermining housing and education equity

Ann M. Aviles ⓘ

ABSTRACT

Homelessness disproportionately impacts communities of color. The Racial Contract is employed to examine and understand the limited influence of educational, and social policies/practices that were developed to combat and/or ameliorate housing instability among students and communities of color experiencing homelessness. The White-Savior Industrial Complex is incorporated to account for the dispositions and/or approaches taken by many white teachers and human service professionals; specifically aiming to illuminate the ways in which many teachers and human service providers perceive, treat, and respond to students and families of color experiencing housing instability. To more appropriately address the racial inequities negatively impacting students, families and communities of color experiencing housing instability, a disruption or voiding of the Racial Contract via structural, curricular, and relational systems/social agreements are necessary.

Introduction

The first time I heard Dr. Charles Mills speak, I was taken by his candor, humor, and intellectual integrity regarding education and race. I was early in my graduate school career and he was the keynote speaker for the American Educational Studies Association, giving the George Kneller Lecture in 2004 on Race, Racism and Education Policy. He was soft spoken, yet fierce and assured in the delivery of his remarks. As a third-year graduate student in an Education Policy Studies in Urban Ed program, his critical epistemological framing and stance were illuminating as I was seeking out various theories, concepts and approaches to unpacking my research topic – an examination of the over-representation of Black and Brown students experiencing homelessness/housing instability[1] in Chicago Public Schools (CPS). This initial exposure to his work captured my interest, and I was encouraged by my advisor to read his text *From Class to Race: Essays in White Marxism and Black Radicalism* (Mills 2003); a text which deeply informed my understanding and analysis of the racial dynamics at play in schools required to ensure educational access for students identified as housing insecure, specifically given the racial composition of said students (at the time, Black students comprised 90% of students experiencing homelessness in CPS, yet were 40% of the entire CPS population). Pointedly, Mills (2003) describes race as 'explicitly seen in terms of political economy: the systemic domination and exploitation of one group by another, brought about through European expansionism and racial capitalism' (p. 200). While much of the research I was reading at the time focused on economic arguments – poor people were more likely to experience housing instability (acute and chronic)—there was a noticeable pattern of Black and Brown communities in Chicago being more heavily impacted.

Mills (2003) cogent argument that the denial of equal opportunity in its various forms (e.g. housing, job discrimination) is predicated on racial exploitation reflected the disproportionate number of Black and Brown students and families experiencing housing instability. Mills (2003) reasoning uncovers that 'they were *not* entitled to equal rights and protections, equal treatment under the law and equal political input' (Mills 2003, 210). This status continues to be a prominent part of US hierarchy and culture, it is so embedded into the fabric of society that as noted by Mills (2003) ' . . . the moral economy of the white nation is still comfortable with a disrespect for people of color that is not even seen and realized to be such' (p. 217). It is this inherent or invisible structure that really spoke to me. While I have never experienced housing instability, my identity as an Afro-Latina led me to reflect on the myriad of ways that I, and/or my family/friends of color continue to be unprotected or conditionally protected under the law and socio-political context of the US. As such, I wanted to further understand and explore the over-representation of students of color comprising students experiencing housing instability within the CPS System. As I continued my work in this area, I found Mills' seminal text, *The Racial Contract* (Mills 1997), to be instructive in shaping my understanding of the structure and function of race in schools and society.

Being an admirer of his work, I was thrilled to learn he had been chosen as one of two winners of the 2018 Derrick Bell Legacy Award (DBLA); an award presented on behalf of the Critical Race Studies in Education Association (CRSEA) to honor scholars who advance issues of social justice, equity, and activism in education research, theory, and practice. Being a part of the CRSEA leadership team for that academic year, I was ecstatic that he would be providing remarks to the association members and conference participants. Beyond expectations, he provided keen insights on the political and social conditions that continue to uphold the Racial Contract in society. Rightly so, his remarks were revered by conference participants who responded with a standing ovation. It was a momentous experience of which I am so grateful to have witnessed. Dr. Mills, in his modesty, humbly bowed in acknowledgement and appreciation for the audience response. His kindness and generosity for participants was evident as he stayed long after his talk to take pictures with participants, sign books, and continue the conversation with students, faculty and community members alike. What also stood out to me was his humility, his willingness to patiently and attentively listen as various conference participants engaged him in conversations regarding race and racism in education. I am so appreciative that I was present to observe his brilliance and thoughtfulness; and even more honored to have been able to correspond with him regarding the DBLA award and other logistics surrounding his presence at CRSEA that year.

When I heard the news of Dr. Mills' passing I was surprised by the way it 'hit' me, I was deeply saddened. I went through my email and found the letter he was sent on behalf of CRSEA informing him of his award, as well as the photos we were able to capture during his talk. I recall thinking this was not just a loss to academia, but even more significantly, a loss to humanity. The few interactions I was able to have with him, and my engagement with his body of scholarship have, and continue to inform and shape my thinking, discourse, and approach to examining issues of race and racism in the areas of housing and education. In this paper I aim to engage in a 'conversation' with Mills' work to further explore and consider what does it mean to engage the Racial Contract in this current moment? Given my personal experiences, research interests, and concern for equity in education, housing, and social policy, I also draw on Cole's (2012) notion of the White-Savior Industrial Complex (WSIC), engaging a concept, that I hope to demonstrate in this essay to be one of the many ways that the Racial Contract continues to be upheld in society.

This paper highlights the structure and function of race in the policies and practices related to education and housing – specifically McKinney-Vento (1987) Education Policy, and the Fair Housing Act of 1968—given the over-representation of Black and Brown individuals and communities that experience housing instability and discrimination, and its parallels to education. First, I include an examination that utilizes the operative frames of the Racial Contract (Mills 1997), and The White-Savior Industrial Complex (Cole 2012) to unpack the 'normative' assumptions undergirding the understanding and application of these policies in practice, next, I explore the everyday approaches to addressing the racial disparities found in education and housing, specifically for students, families, and communities of color facing housing instability as identified by McKinney-Vento. Finally, I provide considerations that seek to inform discourse and praxis surrounding the fields of education, and family science/human services.

This ongoing scholarly endeavor stems from an early experience I had as a graduate student when presenting my research to a group of educators and social workers – a conference presentation that was met with resistance and denial. The primarily white, female audience pushed back on my framing of homelessness and its connections to the racial hierarchy of US society, insisting that homelessness was the result of economic differences and had little, if anything, to do with the racial status of students and families. While there has been some shifts in the literature (see Olivet et al. 2018; Aviles de Bradley, 2015a; Aviles de Bradley, 2015b; Edwards 2021), many still argue that economic factors supersede those of race when seeking to remedy or 'eliminate' homelessness (e.g. job training programs, financial coaches). While there is more recognition of the racial dynamics embedded in society and their connection to housing and educational outcomes for Black and Brown students, the approaches and solutions are often race-neutral, race-evasive or worse predicated on the unspoken racial agreements of society, all of which ultimately fail to incorporate an explicit racial justice framing.

Engaging in dialogue: theoretical frameworks

In this section I seek to outline a few aspects of the Racial Contract, as it frames the context in which an approach such as the White-Savior Industrial Complex (WSIC) is deemed an acceptable and appropriate response to addressing the needs of Black and Brown populations navigating housing instability – both in terms of one's housing and educational status. The Racial Contract contributes to understanding how these approaches to 'solving' or addressing homelessness continue to be rooted in a white supremacist frame. The fields of education and human services are the focus here given their parallels – predominantly white (well meaning) female students are often drawn to these professions and home-lessness is a topic that garners emotions of sympathy, charity, and/or disdain/mistrust – perspectives that are often shaped by the racial identity of those seeking support or services related to their unstable housing situation (see Edwards 2021 for further discussion). Several scholars in both fields have written about the ways in which schooling and family composition/dynamics are often viewed and evaluated through a Eurocentric, middle-income frame (Burton et al. 2010; Olivet et al. 2018; Walsdorf et al. 2020; Matias 2016b; Matias and Zembylas 1997; Picower 2009). Students and families who deviate from white, middle-class traditions and norms are frequently labeled problematic or dysfunctional, subse-quently resulting in teachers and human service practitioners who seek to 'save' or 'fix' students and families rather than addressing the broken systems contributing to inequitable conditions in society. Generally these 'fixes' focus on exposure to, and/or adherence of social norms centered around whiteness. To combat this narrative and approach, the focus of this work is to illuminate the racial under-pinnings embedded in policy and discourse that address housing instability for Black and Brown students and families, with the goal of considering and promot-ing approaches grounded in racial justice.

Racial Contract

The Racial Contract differentiates privileges of whites in relation to non-whites—'... the exploitation of their [non-white] bodies, land, and resources, and denial of equal socio-economic opportunities to them. All whites are *beneficiaries* of the Contract, though some whites are not *signatories* to it' (Mills 1997, 11). More pointedly, white persons all benefit from the concept (and lived realities) of white supremacy in society, whether or not they subscribe to these social agreements. In his book, Mills (1997) asserts the '"Racial Contract" as a theory is explanatorily superior to the raceless social contract in accounting for the political and moral realities of the world...' (p. 120). This is an important social dynamic to acknowledge and comprehend, especially given the majority white students seeking to enter the fields of education and human services, and the current practitioners serving individuals often deemed 'subpersons' by mainstream (white) society.

Moreover, the Racial Contract is most salient in relation to economic systems, and is poignantly aimed at economic exploitation of non-whites. The Racial Contract is omni-present, having political, moral and epistemological threads. Mills (1997) purports that the Racial Contract 'continues to manifest itself ... in unofficial agreements of various kinds ... employment discrimination contracts, political decisions about resource alloca-tion, etc'. (p. 73), and is enforced through 'violence and ideological conditioning' (p. 81). Mills' racialized framing of 'unofficial agreements' allows for the recognition and unpacking of power and privilege embedded in the systems and structures that often lead to policies, practices, and experiences of containment and exclusion amongst unstably housed Black and Brown individuals and communities.

White-savior industrial complex

Mills' Racial Contract emphasizes the unspoken societal agreements shaping housing access, educational opportunities, and outcomes for Black and Brown students and families experiencing housing instability. Further, the neoliberal project in the US manipulates resources, often disguising efforts to address racial equity through white saviorism. Here, Cole's (2012) White-Savior Industrial Complex (WSIC) underscores the approach taken by many in Western society to address social ills – an approach that does little, if any, to dismantle systems and structures that create conditions of housing instability, and the subsequent unfavorable educational outcomes for Black and Brown students, their families, and communities. The concept of the WSIC grew from a series of tweets by Nigerian American writer, Teju Cole (2012) stating,

> the fastest growth industry in the US is the White-Savior Industrial Complex ... The white savior supports brutal policies in the morning, founds charities in the afternoon, and receives awards in the evening ... The White- Savior Industrial Complex is not about justice. It is about having a big emotional experience that validates privilege ... (pps. 1–2).

As identified by Cole, white saviorism is more about validating one's privilege than addressing the needs of those impacted by structural inequities (Matias and Zembylas 1997). Anderson, Knee, and Mowatt (2021), summarize Cole's central thesis which purports 'White hegemonic groups seek to do good while also satisfying their own emotional needs' (p. 531). Further, they outline 'a linear process of White hegemonic practices that, (1) first perpetuate injustices "in the morning", (2) heroically aim to fix them "in the afternoon", and then ultimately, (3) garner recognition for those efforts "in the evening".' (p. 533). The manifestation of these practices and the structural conditions that allow for such approaches will be highlighted and discussed in relation to the fields of education and human services. It is important that we explore, analyze, and critique approaches such as the WSIC as they do little to identify, name, and dismantle the system of white supremacy and its role in perpetuating systems of inequity. Too often, these tactics superficially address the problem of housing instability, simultaneously placing the blame on individuals for not trying 'hard enough' when they 'fail' to escape their unhoused situation.

Manifestations of racialized practices in housing and education: a literature review

Housing status or one's housing stability significantly shapes the developmental, educational, and well-being outcomes of children, families, and communities (Hallett and Skrla 2016; Aviles de Bradley, 2015b). Research demonstrates that housing is an important social determinant of health, as such, a lack of stable housing or poor housing conditions can have a negative impact on one's health and well-being (Rolfe et al. 2020). Further, housing policy has and continues to be strongly shaped by racial factors (e.g. Jim Crow, redlining, blockbusting, discrimination). Scholars have identified a strong connection between housing and education policy (Smith and Stovall 2008; Schwartz 2012; Jargowsky 2018). This includes racially disparate experiences and outcomes for students and families in relation to both housing and education.

In the US, race continues to be a salient factor in shaping and predicting health, education, employment, and housing outcomes. Shapiro (2017) notes "Growing up in a low-income racially segregated neighborhood reduces a child's ability to build financial security, gain an education, and accumulate assets over his or her lifetime (p.46). Each year more than sixty-thousand Black people die prematurely because of inequality (Ansell 2017). Moreover, a person's zip code more closely influences health outcomes than a person's genetic code. This is relevant in the US context as most neighborhoods and communities continue to be racially segregated. Mills' Racial Contract (Mills 1997) underscores the demarcation of space, finding that the reservation of privileged spaces is for its first-class citizens (whites). As such, the continued racial segregation of housing can be understood as the unspoken agreements the Racial Contract has in place. This framework helps uncover the ways in which the sustained exclusion and blocked opportunity experienced by a majority of Black and Brown individuals, families, and communities is woven throughout US housing and education policies.

These structural inequalities are evident when examining the racial and ethnic disparities involving incarceration, education, and housing in the US. Black Americans are incarcerated at nearly 5 times the rate of whites, and Latina/o/x populations are 1.3 times more likely to be incarcerated than non-Latina/o/x whites (Nellis 2021). Moreover, people (mostly Black and Brown boys and men) returning home from prison are more likely to experience homelessness (Couloute 2018). Additionally, neighborhood racial segregation in the US has resulted in school segregation (Massy and Tannen 2016b; Owens 2020). This segregation heavily influences school funding, negatively impacting the quality of education in predominantly Black and Brown schools. Finally, students of color are often in schools with fewer resources, are less likely than white students to have access to 'college-ready' courses, and often attend schools with less qualified teachers (UNCF, n.d.). These racially disparate outcomes reflect the Racial Contract in that Black and Brown persons are deemed *subhuman*, and accordingly, are not entitled to the same protections or access to resources as whites.

While instances or symbols of racial progress can be readily identified (e.g. the election of former President Obama—1st Black President, and more recently the appointment of supreme court justice Ketanji Brown Jackson—1st Black female justice), for the great majority of the 46 million Black, and 62 million Brown folks living in the US (Tamir et al. 2021; Krogstad and Noe-Bustamante 2021), structural violence (Galtung 1969) and discrimination continue to serve as significant barriers to attaining social mobility and overall well-being. The fallacy of hard work and meritocracy ingrained in the discourse of US politics and policies creates the illusion that everyone can access the necessary resources and social capital required to achieve economic stability. Mills (2003) asserts, " ... Left critics see the 'underclass' as the latest entry in this old semantic shell game, a way of talking about blacks (and increasingly, Latinos) without talking about blacks (p. 125). Further, Soss, Fording, and Schram (2011) state,

> In poverty governance today, racial biases are not driven primarily by individuals who are conscious racists. They mostly arise 'behind the backs' of officials whose ordinary interactions and choices are structured by race in ways that (more often than not) run contrary to their own racial values (p. 81).

The quotes above speak to the rationale employed by those engaged in a WSIC – they are there to 'help' those in need. One does not need to specifically recognize or address the racial identity of those in 'need', as it is just the way things are. Society deems it 'normal' that Black and Brown individuals and communities are poor, have less access to education, health care, etc. Often, society is more comfortable with addressing the symptoms of white supremacy, but not the actual causes. Therefore, it is not that they are 'conscious' in their racism, it is so ingrained in the psyche of society that few question *why* the people most impacted by homelessness are Black and Brown. It is the 'invisibility' of the Racial Contract deeply embedded in society that subtly, but significantly shapes practices and policy decisions in the domains of housing and education.

Racial realities of housing and education

Racially explicit state-sponsored US housing policies dictated where Black, Brown, and white populations were able to live, resulting in the segregation of most every metropolitan area in the US (Rothstein 2017). While these housing policies were deemed illegal with the passage of the 1968 Fair Housing Act, housing segregation continues to be a persistent problem in the US (Moore 2019; Jargowsky 2018; Rothstein 2017). Further, racially segregated, disinvested communities often include poor housing conditions consisting of, but not limited to, homes with mold, insect/rodent infestations, lack of heat and/or clean water (Desmond 2016; Hirsch 1998; Kozol 1988; Swope and Hernández 2019). Poor housing conditions contribute to poor health and educational outcomes for families and children exposed to these factors. Ross, Reynolds, and Geis (2017) found that the combined effect of poverty and neighborhood stability increased feelings of distress, as many residents did not have the resources to relocate from communities deemed unsafe. Housing segregation has lasting impacts on the financial state, educational opportunities, and life outcomes for people of color (Martin and Varner 2017).

Families and children that lack access to safe, stable housing are often forced to reside 'doubled up' with family and friends, stay temporarily in hotels/motels, shelters, cars, on the streets, or in other spaces deemed inhabitable for living (Hallett and Skrla 2016). Although Black individuals comprise 13% of the US population, they represent approximately 40% of people experiencing housing instability. Housing instability impacts the physical, psychological, and educational needs of students (National Alliance to End Homelessness 2020; Murphy 2011; Rafferty 1999). Overwhelmingly, those most significantly impacted are Black and Brown students. Of the approximate 1.6 million children in the US categorized as housing unstable, Black school age children comprise 27% of the population, despite being 15% of the overall student body, and Brown students represent 38% of unstably housed youth, yet are 26% of the overall student body (National Center for Homeless Education 2021).

Approximately 3.5 million young people (including those not enrolled in school) experienced homelessness over a twelve-month period in the US. Of these young people, Black youth had an 83% higher risk of homelessness, and Brown youth a 33% higher risk, reflective of racial and ethnic disparities that exist in the form of 'school suspensions, incarceration and foster care placement'. (Morton, Dworsky, and Samuels 2017, 12–13). Discrepancies can be found in educational institutions where approximately 80% of the teacher force is white (Schaeffer 2012). It is well documented that educational experiences and outcomes for students vary across racial lines. Factors such as school funding, advanced placement courses, ancillary resources, and school policy are all embedded in race (Stovall 2015; Gillborn, 2014; Milner, 2013). Therefore, we see schools with high enrollment of students of color having fewer dollars spent per pupil, students more likely to be placed in low-track courses, little or no supplemental resources/services, and youth of color experiencing zero tolerance policies more punitively (Anyon et al. 2021; Berry and Stovall 2013).

Similar to the field of education, research demonstrates that non-profit organizations and institutions serving those impacted by housing instability are overwhelmingly white. The report *Obstacles and Opportunities in Addressing the Nonprofit Racial Leadership Gap* (2020) documents the following regarding non-profit staff racial composition: 59% white, 14% Black, 10% Latino/a/x, 7% Asian American, and 8% multiracial. Further, in terms of non-profit leadership, racial inequities were clearly identified: 45% of organizations have white people comprising 75% of those in top leadership levels, while only 14% of nonprofits had 50% people of color in leadership roles (Building Movement Project 2020). The report concluded that the lack of racial diversity among nonprofit leadership was a result of racialized barriers, including lack of support by white boards of directors and biases of executive recruiters; a key report recommendation finds that nonprofits need to focus their attention on structures of race and racism, simultaneously addressing the concerns and experiences of people of color.

For decades, scholars have identified, examined, and sought to address the racial disparities that exist in K-12 educational spaces. Kohli, Pizarro, and Nevárez (2017) found that racism is a permanent and significant factor shaping the educational experiences and trajectories for students of color. Moreover, they note that race and racism have been an integral part of schools in the US since their inception (Kohli, Pizarro, and Nevárez 2017). These racialized practices can be seen through the over-representation of Black and Brown students relegated to special education (Annamma and Morrison 2018; Artiles 2013), and those that are ensnared in the racial discipline gap (Little and Welsh 2016).

The racial disparities in housing segregation can also be seen in school resources and access. Martin and Varner (2017) note ' … White parents have manipulated their resources within the housing sector to ensure that their children receive the benefits of suburban schooling options where higher tax bases provide a significantly more profound investment in schools' (p. 2). School governance and practices continue to more closely mirror the corporate model or capitalist approach found in the housing sector. Buras' (2015) research documents the neoliberal approach to education in New Orleans, finding that charter schools helped pave the way for the elimination of Black veteran teachers. Those who view both housing and school as commodities, rather than as rights granted to individuals and families, contribute to narratives of meritocracy and to systems and structures of racial hierarchy.

The McKinney-Vento Homeless Assistance Act of 1987 serves to address barriers and challenges faced by students experiencing housing instability. Since it was signed into US law over three decades ago, McKinney-Vento has been amended several times in line with larger federal educational policy changes such as No Child Left Behind (2002) and the Every Student Succeeds Act (2015). McKinney-Vento defines housing instability as the absence of a fixed, regular, and adequate nighttime residence, serving to provide support and eliminate barriers to an equal, free and public education for students identified as experiencing homelessness (McKinney-Vento Homeless Assistance Act of 1987).

Many scholars and advocates continue to view McKinney-Vento policy from a colorblind perspective (it explicitly aims to serve students identified as housing insecure), not fully investigating the disparate outcomes for students of color that experience homelessness (Moser Jones 2016). Conversely, a few scholars recognize and center a racial analysis in their examination of McKinney-Vento and other homeless policies (Edwards 2021; Aviles & Heybach, 2017; Aviles de Bradley, 2015a; Aviles de Bradley, 2015b). Acknowledging race in no way diminishes the economic or material realities for white students and their respective families; it does however include a more complex understanding of the racial dynamics that contribute to poverty, housing instability, and educational disparities amongst Black and Brown students and families. Further, centering race works against the unintended consequence of colorblind policies that limit or prohibit us from seeing racial disparities among subpopulations of housing unstable individuals (Edwards 2021; Gillborn, 2014).

While the US has implemented policies to reduce educational barriers for students experiencing homelessness, and to eliminate housing discrimination and segregation, these policies have fallen short in remedying these ongoing challenges, particularly for Black and Brown populations (Olivet et al. 2018; Morton, Dworsky, and Samuels 2017). Mill's Racial Contract and Cole's WSIC help to unpack and explain the structural conditions, and practices that allow these problems to persist. Cole's notion of the WSIC can be understood as a mechanism that upholds the dynamics outlined in Mills' Racial Contract, recognizing the role 'well-meaning' whites take to inform their approaches to working with poor, Black and Brown populations. The WSIC is an approach rooted in paternalism and misguided notions that people most impacted by housing instability need 'saving'. Practitioners and policy makers alike need to be aware of the insidiousness of racial and ethnic constructs influencing the discourse, practices, and approaches to addressing housing instability and education for Black and Brown students and families.

Connecting concepts: analysis/discussion

The construct of race and its subsequent manifestation in society undergirds all aspects of social life and policy in the US. Mills' Racial Contract serves as the backdrop and/or landscape in which educational and housing policy function. To consider how education and housing policies and practices can be informed by both the Racial Contract, and the WSIC, here I attempt to highlight some of the ways in which they can inform this conversation. In doing so, a critical race hermeneutics (CRH; Allen 2021) was employed. CRH seeks to 'unveil racially normative meaning making in dialogues controlled primarily by whiteness, and secondarily by those with more relative power in racial status hierarchies' (Allen 2021, p. 19). This approach allowed for a critical analysis of the language and discourse of policies and practices employed to address housing instability, specifically the manner in which racial dynamics are minimized, avoided, criminalized, or patronized as a function of the Racial Contract in society.

Given that McKinney-Vento has been advanced as racially benign or neutral, the focus here is on the perspective that, 'when people say 'Justice', they mean 'Just us'"[and] ... the hypocrisy of the racial polity is most transparent to its victims" (Mills 1997, 110). More specifically, 'The "Racial Contract" (henceforth simply the "Racial Contract") as a naturalized account is theoretically superior to the raceless social contract as a model of the actual world and, correspondingly of what needs to be done to reform it' (Mills 1997, 120). The unspoken agreements about the normalcy of whiteness and the marginalization of 'other' helps to inform the context in which the purpose, function, and perpetuation of Cole's (2012) WSIC can be understood and acknowledged. In other words, the Racial Contract presumes it natural that Black and Brown students and their respective families are deemed deficient and in need of 'saving'; and who else to save them but well-meaning, economically stable white folks?

If we understand these dynamics to be integral to the social fabric in the US, this leads to further exploration of how this informs the logic of the WSIC. As noted above, Anderson, Knee, and Mowatt (2021) outline the linear process described by Cole (2012) that is used by whites, or the concept/construct of whiteness as an organizing tool in society – Brutal policies in the morning, Charities in the afternoon, and Awards in the evening – here, I take a similar approach. Now, the focus turns to McKinney-Vento, and The Fair Housing Act to underscore the ways in which the WSIC functions within schools and society.

Brutal policies in the morning

Prior to the Fair Housing Act of 1968, US housing policy explicitly promoted and maintained segregation along racial lines. This is also the case for McKinney-Vento (1987)—students were segregated based on their housing status, often learning in make-shift classrooms within shelters, prohibited from attending traditional public schools. In the US, housing status is racialized, reflected in an over-representation of Black and Brown families that experience poverty and subsequently housing instability; often, their economic standing can be understood to serve as a proxy for their racial/ethnic status. It is important to recognize that housing instability is also experienced by white students and families, yet, as noted previously, Black and Brown students and families dispro-portionately comprise unstably housed populations.

Here it is paramount to recognize federal and state policies/practices concerning housing and schools to make the connection between the subsequent racial segregation. The federal and state sponsored housing policies such as Jim Crow, redlining, restrictive racial covenants, etc. (Rothstein 2017) strengthened institutional racism, perpetually ousting Black families from housing opportunities, relegating them to communities lacking the investment and infrastructure afforded to white families. State sponsored racial segregation was also reflected in schools pre Brown (1954). As de jure policies of segregation began to dissipate in both housing and school spaces, de facto segregation persisted.

While racial segregation was outlawed, it was not until 1987 that school segregation based on one's housing status was deemed illegal (McKinney-Vento, 1987). Further, the over-representation of folks of color making up people experiencing homelessness was not the focus of, or discussion when advocates were pushing for the passage of McKinney-Vento. Despite the over-representation of students of color experiencing housing instability, many advocates of McKinney-Vento ignored these racial realities and remained narrowly focused on a student's housing status. For example, a staunch legal advocate who was acutely aware of the way Black and Brown students are poorly treated by schools, allowed race to fall to the wayside in their analysis of this connection, stating:

> I do not really think that people have thought about using the McKinney-Vento Act as an opportunity to specifically speak about racial disparity, I think that the position of people who work under the Act is, if we fully address the needs of these children as we want to do under this Act, that's the turf for McKinney-Vento Homeless Education provision ... Brown v. Board of Education and the legacy of our schools with respect to racial inequality, that's a long sad story. I don't think the McKinney-Vento Act could solve that. (Ms. Davis, July 11, 2008) (Aviles de Bradley, 2015a).

This advocate, while considerate of society's racial realities, made a distinct and clear demarcation between Brown v. Board and McKinney-Vento, supposing that McKinney-Vento was not the relevant policy to address racial inequality in schools. Knowing that the great majority of students experiencing housing instability are students of color should implore policy makers, advocates, and schools to use McKinney-Vento implementation as an opportunity to address racial inequities that shape and influence a student's experience and trajectory in schools.

The Fair Housing Act, and McKinney-Vento were created (and pushed by community advocates) as responses to the 'brutalities' developed by society to maintain segregation. Despite the passage of these policies, it has been documented that housing and school segregation along racial lines are just as, if not more, prevalent today than in the 1950s and 60s. Even with the passage of The Fair Housing Act, racial segregation in housing persists. Mills (2003) informs this understanding, noting that

> ... American white supremacy has not vanished; rather it has changed from a de jure to a de facto form. The mere formal rejection of white supremacist principles will not suffice to transform the United States into a genuinely racially egalitarian society, since the actual social values and enduring politico-economic structures will continue to reflect the history of white domination (p. 179).

The myriad of brutalities enacted against both Black and Brown students are commonly addressed by white saviorism (e.g. backpack giveaways, clothing donations). Rather than focusing on the political and social structures that determine one's value based on their racial/ethnic standing in society, Cole's (2012) naming of the WSIC can be viewed as a significant ideology and approach contributing to the maintenance of white saviorism —a form of/mainfestation of white supremacy. The response is embedded in practices that continue to marginalize and 'other' the 'deserving' poor – often this sentiment too is racialized, as many Black and Brown folks are blamed for their plight in society (e.g. narratives of laziness, criminality, etc.), which can translate into discriminatory practices, or worse, denial of basic human services—actions that have dire consequences on the lives and livelihood of Black and Brown communities.

McKinney-Vento policy reflects beliefs that are in alignment with white saviorism; its aim is to ensure access to schools and to provide unstably housed students with the same opportunities and support provided to their housed peers. The policy is well-intended and meant to reduce barriers and disparities. Despite its intention, McKinney-Vento policy fails to account for the structural factors that contribute to disparate housing access and the subsequent conditions that create the need for a policy such as McKinney-Vento in the first place. This is not to say that McKinney-Vento has no value – it has and does provide students educational access and support – it is presented here to highlight the shortcomings of a policy that does not fully consider the social and political dynamics of race in a hierarchical society such as the US. Here the Racial Contract aids to inform this understanding; the material realities for Black and Brown students and families are significantly tied to, and shaped by their racial/ethnic standing in society.

Charities in the afternoon

McKinney-Vento and the Fair Housing Act have not been the only approaches to alleviating the financial and emotional burden of racial and class disparities experienced by students and their families. The philanthropic sectors of society have invested deeply in addressing the housing, educational, and financial disparities prevalent in US society. This is evidenced through the many housing shelters, food banks, clothing closets, low-income housing assistance programs, etc. In 2010 public charities reported a revenue of 1.5 trillion dollars, generating *philanthrocapitalist* tactics, or a business-like oriented approach to charity (Giridharadas 2016; Raventos and Wark 2018). Given this significant financial investment, one would presume a decrease in people experiencing various challenges, however this is not the case. For example, in the same year, 2010, the number of youth experiencing homelessness grew by 60% (Raventos and Wark 2018, 104). Further, Giridharadas (2016) points out that the top 10% of the population owns 90% of the planet's wealth. The elites or 'winners' understand social ills from their perspective, and this perspective is often void of experiences with poverty, racism, or other forms of discrimination. As a result, those wishing to 'help' often overlook root problems, and just as important, their involvement in contributing to systems of inequity (Giridharadas 2016). Their 'generosity is substitute for, and means of avoiding the necessity of a more just and equitable system and a fairer distribution of power' (Giridharadas 2016, 164).

As noted earlier, Cole (2012) describes the WSIC as being about 'having a big emotional experience that validates privilege'. Many of the non-profit organizations, and the people within them feel 'good' about working at the local soup kitchen or participating in service days, often in the spirit of prominent historical figures such as Martin Luther King, or through organizations such as Habitat for Humanity, organizations and practices that too frequently center whiteness. A recent example of this is the donation made by Bloomberg Philanthropies in the amount of $200 million dollars to charter schools in New York (Johnson 2022). In his speech Bloomberg stated,

> Harlem Children's Zone and Success Academy have both shown what's possible when we put students first, set high expectations, and hold everyone accountable for results . . . There is nothing more gratifying in life than helping a child grow and fulfill their potential.

Bloomberg's sentiments reflect both white saviorism and the unspoken Racial Contract enmeshed in society. His remarks fail to address the conditions that create a need for philanthropy, and instead focus on ahistorical, neoliberal principles of accountability prevalent in educational discourse. These remarks also embody the 'feel good' emotions that accompany helping the 'less fortunate', (in this case primarily Black and Brown students) as Bloomberg himself identifies the gratification he receives from providing this (and other) donations. During his speech he also explicitly recognizes the over-representation of Black and Brown children in New York who will benefit from said generosity. Here I do not mean to dismiss or denigrate the efforts of those who seek to help communities in 'need'. The point is the people providing the support are often motivated by the good feeling it provides knowing they gave to individuals, families or communities, instead of considering the lack of real impact for sustained changes required to move the racial equity needle forward. Often, those that advance their work from a white savior approach are less willing to engage a perspective or dialogue that explicitly names systems and structures of power that perpetually allow for the marginalization of many, while privileging few (Matias and Zembylas 1997). The wealth accumulation of Bloomberg (and many others) is an example of the connectedness of the economic and racial disparities ingrained in US society, and the ways in which their geneoristy serves as a distraction, allowing them to retain wealth under the guise of charity. These chartiable dynamics not only allow for society to ignore the economic disparity at play, importantly, it fails to adequately address the (unsaid) agreements of the Racial Contract.

The naming of these inequitable structures and social dynamics is decades old. In a 1968 speech given by Martin Luther King (MLK) to a group of philanthropists he voiced this concern, stating that while philanthropy is commendable, it should not overshadow the injustice that makes it necessary. Unfortunately, over fifty-years later the US has not heeded MLK's call to action, continually failing to address deep rooted racial and economic injustices that make philanthropy necessary. Most approaches in the fields of education and human services are perpetuating systems and structures that allow a few people with means to feel good about providing services to the many deemed in 'need'. Concepts and dynamics of paternalism and white supremacy can be implicated in contributing to the continued proliferation of charitable organizations and approaches to addressing social ills such as racial inequity and housing instability. The approaches employed should be focused on exposing and eliminating the conditions, systems, and policies that require the need for such practices in society; this requires scholars, practi-tioners, and policy makers to be honest about the racial agreements that regularly allow for the existence of inequitable conditions.

It cannot be denied that good feelings about helping others are reinforced and awarded by society. This is described by Cole as receiving 'awards in the evening' for one's charitable work. Placing this notion in conversation with Mills' Racial Contract allows for the further examination of how these approaches and practices are racialized.

Awards in the evening

There is an inherent contradiction in much of the research and practices that aim to address racial (and other forms of) inequity. As scholars, practitioners and advocates, we are often tasked with demonstrating the *need* for justice work. Frequently, we are asked to document the disparate experiences, opportunities and outcomes of low-income Black and Brown communities in our efforts to make a case in securing funding to address educational and housing injustices. In our efforts, we run the risk of furthering deficit narratives and contributing to the damage of communities (Tuck 2009) in the name of 'advancing' research. The better the case or argument one can make regarding these disparities, coupled with the need for a particular intervention or program increases the likelihood that our work will be funded and possibly recognized for its 'excellence' or 'impact' through various academic and/or organizational accolades. Here, I want to emphasize that there are individuals, organizations and communities that work tirelessly to address the root causes or in this instance, specifically structural racism permeating society, and folks should be recognized and honored for such efforts. On the contrary, the awards that are the focus here are those related to *philanthrocapitalist* tactics; tactics that are more performative than practical, and continue to view white saviorism as the best and only method worth utilizing or investing in (Matias, 2014; Hayes and Juarez 2009). An approach that continues to view the 'other' as less competent, and sometimes worse – as less human.

Cole (2012) describes how the mentality of white saviorism reflects 'American senti-mentality', leading to 'awards in the evening'; awards that often elevate the status and/or visibility of an individual, organization, program, or school. Cole heeds an important warning to us stating, 'I deeply respect American sentimentality, the way one respects a wounded hippo. You must keep an eye on it, for you know it is deadly' (Cole 2012, 3). Many in the philanthropic sphere are rewarded for their ability to uphold systems and structures of racial hierarchy – a deadly practice for many who continue to endure these intractable dynamics. A prime example of this award structure is elucidated through the Bill and Melinda Gates Foundation. In 2020, the Gates Foundation awarded approxi-mately 5.8 billion in direct grantee support (Bill & Melinda Gates Foundation, n.d.). While many may tout this investment as a commitment to education, the Racial Contract and the WSIC encourage critical questions such as, why does such a disparity exist? What allows for a structure to exist that leads to highly concentrated wealth in the US, so much so, that one foundation (and really, one corporation) has amassed enough money, that it must give some away (while others work 2.5 jobs and still can't afford basics such as housing)? What if children, families, and communities facing poverty and housing instability were provided universal basic income payments (Benshoff 2022; Gringlas 2022), and not simply access to a food pantry? Moreover, what if families were paid a housing wage (NLIHC 2021), instead of their only option being a housing voucher that marks and stigmatizes them in the eyes of many landlords? How might a different distribution or formula of funding (e.g. property taxes) for schools address structural inequities, and the unfair advantage of generations of wealth disparity, rather than relying on systems of charity and philanthropy? And finally, if individuals and organiza-tions were no longer recognized or awarded for their charitable efforts, (and if there were not tax structures and incentives in place that provided financial benefit for said efforts) would they be as invested in, or willing to address the disparities that exist for students, families, and communities of color?

Conclusion

Without engaging and addressing the Racial Contract undergirding society, housing and education disparities will continue. Policies such as McKinney-Vento should be seen as a tool in addressing not only economic disparities for students, but racial ones as well. The Fair Housing Act reminds us that policies alone cannot undue the deficit, discriminatory, or put more bluntly, the dangerous beliefs many in society hold about Black and Brown students, families, and their respective communities. Despite having the Fair Housing Act in place for over 50 years, current research shows that homes in largely Black communities are valued at approximately *half* the price of homes in white communities, even when housing type and area incomes are the same (Johns, Robinson, and Chavez 2021).

Society must contend with the harm racism and racial discrimination – both implicit and explicit forms – wreaks on the lives of far too many. The WSIC will not serve as protection or a solution, it will continue to deepen the chasm between the 'have' and 'have-nots'—of which race is a driving factor. To seriously reckon with housing instability, the role of racism must be at the forefront in understanding how students and families of color are relegated to the margins of society through structural inequities; inequities that repeatedly prohibit communities of color from accessing safe, stable, secure housing, and well-resourced, supportive schools.

People impacted by housing instability have demonstrated their leadership to address these structural inequities. For example, the fierce group of women who make up Moms 4 Housing provide a collective, Black women led approach to combatting housing instability in the Bay Area of California. As noted on their website, 'Moms for Housing is a collective of homeless and marginally housed mothers … We are coming together with the ultimate goal of reclaiming housing for the community from speculators and profiteers' (Moms 4 Housing, n.d. https://moms4housing.org/). Moreover, city officials standing in solidarity with this group shared,

> … we need to rethink our policies profoundly around housing because it isn't working when we have thousands in the streets. The trickle down of a few million a year from the county and the state isn't helping Oakland resolve this crisis … We also need to think about how easy it is for people to label Black working mothers as "criminals" and yet not talk about Wedgewood's [corporate landlord] sordid history in the foreclosure crisis. (Moms 4 Housing n.d. https://moms4housing.org/).

Their understanding, framing, and discussion about housing instability led to an increased awareness of the role race plays in housing (in)stability and access for Black and Brown communities in Oakland (Hahn 2020). Further, this group was able to secure housing for themselves while inspiring others to organize and resist unfair and discriminatory housing practices. Rather than reproducing patterns of white saviorism, human service professionals should look to and learn from groups such as Moms 4 Housing to center the perspectives, stories, and insights of folks who intimately understand housing issues. Moreover, non-profit and community organizations should hire and adequately pay folks who are, or have experienced housing instability to shape policies, and effective practices to addressing housing inequities at the local, state and federal levels.

Resistance to white saviorism can also be seen in school spaces (Matias 2016a). The Racial Contract is a reminder that deficit and Eurocentric ideologies run rampant in society – hence scholars and practitioners must critically question the racial norms accepted by many. Some examples include approaches and orientations such as Abolitionist Teaching (Love 2019), School Abolition (Stovall 2018), and Culturally

Sustaining Pedagogy (Paris 2017). As educators and advocates seeking to create a more fair and just world, we can contribute to racial justice by bringing these conversations, perspectives and curricula into our classrooms, clinics, and communities. The Racial Contract shines light on the challenge of centering the racial dynamics at play, due to the social agreement that the 'worth' afforded to Black and Brown bodies is (and always has been seen as) less than those of white bodies. Moreover, the Racial Contract reminds us of the philosophical and material impacts on people's lives-ones that perpetually contribute to symbolic, spiritual, and physical violence for Black and Brown individuals, families, and communities.

We can also work toward racial justice by investing resources to engage in transformative and liberatory praxes such as Participatory Action Research (Payne 2017); meaningfully and deliberately partnering with community members most impacted by the racial inequities prevalent in housing and education. Further, these participatory efforts should be multi-generational and interdisciplinary to more adequately address the developmental, intersectional, and contextual nuances experienced by sub-populations/groups (e.g. gender, ethnicity, age, sexual identity, etc.) (see Sandwick et al. 2018; Allen-Handy and Thomas-EL 2018; Aviles & Grigalunas, 2018; Payne and Brown 2016). Importantly, impacted community members should be leaders and thought partners in research programs and projects; critically, their time and expertise must be fairly compensated.

As someone working (imperfectly) to interrupt/disrupt discourses, systems, and practices contributing to racial disparities, particularly in housing and education, Dr. Mills' words remind me that, 'Naming this [racial] reality brings it into the necessary theoretical focus for these issues to be honestly addressed' (Mills 1997, 133). Rather than continuing the 'epistemology of ignorance' required by the Racial Contract, educators, practitioners, and policy makers must uncompromisingly and unapologetically combat the racial discrimination that is widespread in schools and society, particularly in regards to Black and Brown students and families experiencing housing instability. Insistently working to subvert the Racial Contract in classrooms, non-profits, and other community spaces serves to honor Dr. Mills, his legacy, and fundamentally, our shared humanity.

Note

1. The term housing instability is the authors preferred term and used where possible to expand notions and understandings of the traditional perspective regarding homelessness (often described as persons who reside in a shelter, abandoned building, car, on the street, etc.), whereas housing instability provides a broader understanding to include temporary housing (staying with friends/relatives, couch surfing, or frequent moves). The impact of housing instability on one's physical, cognitive, and general well-being is the focal point as it shapes a student's ability to remain focused and engaged in their educational pursuits. The terms homelessness, housing instability and housing insecure are used interchangeably to reflect the array of terms used in the literature.

Disclosure statement

No potential conflict of interest was reported by the author.

ORCID

Ann M. Aviles ⓘ http://orcid.org/0000-0002-0032-9848

References

Allen, R.L. 2021. "Critical Race Hermeneutics: A Theoretical Method for Researching the Unconscious of White Supremacy in Education." In *The Handbook of Critical Theoretical Research Methods in Education*, edited by E. M. Cheryl, 15–30. New York: Routledge.

Allen-Handy, A., and S.L. Thomas-EL. 2018. "Be(com)ing Critical Scholars: The Emergence of Urban Youth Scholar Identities Through Research and Critical Civic Praxis." *Urban Education* 57 (8): 1450–1481. doi:10.1177/0042085918814589.

Anderson, K., E. Knee, and R. Mowatt. 2021. "Leisure and the "White-Savior Industrial Complex." *Journal of Leisure Research* 52 (5): 531–550. doi:10.1080/00222216.2020.1853490.

Annamma, S., and D. Morrison. 2018. "Identifying Dysfunctional Education Ecologies: A DisCrit Analysis of Bias in the Classroom." *Equity & Excellence in Education* 51 (2): 114–131. doi:10.1080/10665684.2018.1496047.

Ansell, D.A. 2017. *The Death Gap: How Inequality Kills*. Chicago and London: University of Chicago Press.

Anyon, Y., K. Wiley, C. Samimi, and M. Trujillo. 2021. "Sent Out or Sent Home: Understanding Racial Disparities Across Suspension Types from Critical Race Theory and Quantcrit Perspectives." *Race Ethnicity and Education* 1–20. doi:10.1080/13613324.2021.2019000.

Artiles, A.J. 2013. "Untangling the Racialization of Disabilities: An Intersectionality Critique Across Disability Models." *DuBois Review: Social Science Research on Race* 10 (2): 329–347. doi:10.1017/S1742058X13000271.

Aviles de Bradley A. 2015a. "Homeless Educational Policy." *Urban Education* 50 (7): 839–869. doi:10.1177/0042085914534861.

Aviles de Bradley, A.M. 2015b. *From Charity to Equity: Race, Homelessness and Urban Schools*. New York, NY: Teachers College Press.

Aviles A M and Grigalunas N. 2018. ""Project awareness:" Fostering social justice youth development to counter youth experiences of housing instability, trauma and injustice." *Children and Youth Services Review* 84: 229–238. doi:10.1016/j.childyouth.2017.12.013.

Aviles A M and Heybach J A. 2017. "Seeking stability in Chicago: School actions, (c)overt forms of racial injustice, and the slow violence of neoliberal rationality." *EPAA* 25: 58. doi:10.14507/epaa. 25.2634.

Benshoff, L. (31 Jan 2022). Philly to Pilot a Guaranteed Income Experiment, Giving Cash to Some Needy Residents. *National Public Radio*. https://whyy.org/articles/philly-to-pilot-a-guaranteed-income-experiment-giving-cash-to-some-needy-residents/

Berry, T.R., and D. Stovall. 2013. "Trayvon Martin and the Curriculum of Tragedy: Critical Race Lessons for Education." *Race Ethnicity and Education* 16 (4): 587–602. doi:10.1080/13613324. 2013.817775.

Bill & Melinda Gates Foundation. Foundation Facts. https://www.gatesfoundation.org/

Brown, V. 1954. *Board of Education, 347*, 483. U.S.

Building Movement Project 2020. *Race to lead revisited: obstacles and opportunities in addressing the nonprofit racial leadership gap.* https://docs.google.com/viewerurl=https%3A%2F%2Fbuildingmovement.org%2Fwpcontent%2Fuploads%2F2020%2F07%2FRTLRevisitedNational-ReportFinal.pdf

Buras, K. 2015. "Race, Charter Schools, and Conscious Capitalism: On the Spatial Politics of Whiteness as Property (And the Unconscionable Assault on Black New Orleans)." *Harvard Educational Review* 81 (2): 296–330. doi:10.17763/haer.81.2.6l42343qqw360j03.

Burton, L. M., E. Bonilla-Silva, V. Ray, R. Buckelew, and E. Hordge-Freeman. 2010. "Critical Race Theories, Colorism, and the Decade's Research on Families of Color." *Journal of Marriage and Family* 72 (3): 440–459. doi:10.1111/j.1741-3737.2010.00712.x.

Cole, T. (21 March 2012). The White-Savior Industrial Complex. *The Atlantic.* https://www. theatlantic.com/international/archive/2012/03/the-white-savior-industrial-complex/254843/

Couloute, L. 2018. *Nowhere to Go: Homelessness Among Formerly Incarcerated People.* Prison Policy Initiative. https://www.prisonpolicy.org/reports/housing.html.

Desmond, M. 2016. *Evicted: Poverty and Profit in the American City.* New York: Broadway Books.

Edwards, E. 2021. "Who are the Homeless?: Centering Anti-Black Racism and the Consequences of Colorblind Homeless Policies." *Social Sciences* 10 (9): 340. doi:10.3390/socsci10090340.

The Fair Housing Act, Title VIII of the Civil Rights Act of 1968, *42 U.S.C. §§* 3601-19.

Galtung, J. 1969. "Violence, Peace and Peace Research." *Journal of Peace Research* 6 (3): 167–191. doi:10.1177/002234336900600301.

Gillborn, D. 2014. "Racism as Policy: A Critical Race Analysis of Education Reforms in United States and England." *The Educational Forum* 78 (1): 26–41.

Giridharadas, A. 2018. *Winners Take All: The Elite Charade of Changing the World.* New York: Vintage Books.

Gringlas, S. (23 Feb 2022). Atlanta Rolls Out Pilot Basic Income Program Inspired by MLK Jr. *National Public Radio.* https://www.npr.org/2022/02/23/1082622845/atlanta-rolls-out-pilot-basic-income-program-inspired-by-mlk-jr

Hahn, R. (12 May 2020). These Moms Fought for a Home—And Started a Movement. *Vogue.* https://www.vogue.com/article/moms-4-housing

Hallett, R. E., and L. Skrla. 2016. *Serving Students Who are Homeless: A Resource Guide for Schools, Districts, and Educational Leaders.* New York, NY: Teachers College Press.

Hayes, C., and B.G. Juarez. 2009. "You Showed Your Whiteness: You Don't Get a 'Good' White People's Medal." *International Journal of Qualitative Studies in Education* 22 (6): 729–744. doi:10.1080/09518390903333921.

Hirsch, A. R. 1998. *Making the Second Ghetto: Race and Housing in Chicago 1940-1960.* Chicago: University of Chicago Press.

Jargowsky, P.A. 2018. "The Persistence of Segregation in the 21st Century." *Minnesota Journal of Law and Inequality* 36 (2): 207–230.

Johnson, A. (26 April 2022). Bloomberg Donating Millions to NYC Public Charter Schools. *The Root.* https://www.theroot.com/bloomberg-donating-millions-to-nyc-public-charter-schoo-1848842155

Johns, J., L. Robinson, and N. Chavez. 2021. A Black Couple Had a White Friend Show Their Home and Its Appraisal Rose by Nearly Half a Million Dollars. https://www.cnn.com/2021/12/09/business/black-homeowners-appraisal-discrimination-lawsuit/index.html

Kohli, R., M. Pizarro, and A. Nevárez. 2017. "The "New Racism" of K–12 Schools: Centering Critical Research on Racism." *Review of Research in Education* 41 (1): 182–202. doi:10.3102/0091732X16686949.

Kozol, J. 1988. *Rachel and Her Children: Homeless Families in America.*

Krogstad, J.M., and L. Noe-Bustamante (9 Sept. 2021). Key Facts About U.S. Latinos for National Hispanic Heritage Month. *Pew Research Center.* https://www.pewresearch.org/fact-tank/2021/09/09/key-facts-about-u-s-latinos-for-national-hispanic-heritage-month/

Little, S.J., and R. O. Welsh. 2019. "Rac(e)ing to Punishment? Applying Theory to Racial Disparities in Disciplinary Outcomes." *Race, Ethnicity & Education* 25 (4): 564–584. doi:10.1080/13613324.2019.1599344.

Love, B. 2019. *We Want to Do More Than Survive: Abolitionist Teaching and the Pursuit of Educational Freedom.* Boston: Beacon Press.

Martin, L.L., and K.J. Varner. 2017. "Race, Residential Segregation, and the Death of Democracy: Education and Myth of Postracialism." *Democracy & Education* 25 (1): 1–10.

Massy, D.S., and J. Tannen. 2016. "Segregation, Race and the Social Worlds of Rich and Poor." In *The Dynamics of Opportunity in America: Evidence and Perspectives*, edited by H. Braun and I. Kirsch, 13–33. Cham: Springer.

Matias, C. E. 2014. ""And Our Feelings, Just Don't Feel It anymore": Re-Feeling Whiteness, Resistance, and Emotionality." *Understanding and Dismantling Privilege* 4 (2): 134–153.

Matias, C.E. 2016a. *Feeling White: Whiteness, Emotionality and Education*. Boston: Sense Publishers.

Matias, C. E. 2016b. "White Skin, Black Friend: A Fanonian Application to Theorize Racial Fetish in Teacher Education." *Educational Philosophy and Theory* 48 (3): 221–236.

Matias, C.E., and M. Zembylas. 2014. "'When Saying You Care is Not Really caring': Emotions of Disgust, Whiteness Ideology, and Teacher Education." *Critical Studies in Education* 55 (3): 319–337. doi:10.1080/17508487.2014.922489.

McKinney–Vento Homeless Assistance Act of 1987, Pub. L. 100-628, 101 Stat. 482, 42 USC §§114301.

McKinney-Vento Homeless Assistance Act. 2015. Title IX, Part a of the Every Student Succeeds Act. 42 US Code § 11431–11435.

Mills, C. 1997. *The Racial Contract*. Ithaca and London: Cornell University Press.

Mills, C. 2003. *From Class to Race: Essays in White Marxism and Black Radicalism*. New York and Oxford: Rowman & Littlefield Publishers.

Milner, H.R. 2013. "Analyzing Poverty, Teaching and Learning Through a Critical Race Theory Lens." *Review of Research in Education* 37 (1): 1–53.

Moms 4 Housing. (n.d.). https://moms4housing.org/

Moore, N.Y. 2019. *The South Side: A Portrait of Chicago and American Segregation*. Picador Paper.

Morton, M.H., A. Dworsky, and G.M. Samuels. 2017. *Missed Opportunities: Youth Homelessness in America. National Estimates*. Chicago, IL: Chapin Hall at the University of Chicago.

Moser Jones, M. 2016. "Does Race Matter in Addressing Homelessness: A Literature Review." *World Medical & Health Policy* 8 (2): 139–156. doi:10.1002/wmh3.189.

Murphy, J. 2011. "Homeless Children and Youth at Risk: The Educational Impact of Displacement." *Journal of Education for Students Placed at Risk (JESPAR)* 16 (1): 38–55. doi:10.1080/10824669.2011.554143.

National Alliance to End Homelessness (NAEH). 2020. Racial Inequalities in Homelessness, by the Numbers. Data and Graphics. https://endhomelessness.org/resource/racial-inequalities-homelessness-numbers/

National Center for Homeless Education (NCHE) (20 August 2021). Student Homelessness in America: School Years 2017-2018 to 2018-2019. https://nche.ed.gov/wpcontent/uploads/2021/12/Student-Homelessness-in-America-2021.pdf

National Low-Income Housing Coalition (NLIHC). 2021. Out of Reach 2021. https://reports.nlihc.org/oor/about

Nellis, A. 2021. *The Color of Justice: Racial and Ethnic Disparity in State Prisons*. Washington, D.C: The Sentencing Project. October.

No Child Left Behind Act of 2001, Pub. L. 107-110, Title X, Part C, McKinney-Vento Homeless Education Improvements Act of 2001 § 20 U.S.C. 6301, 115 Stat. 1989 (2002).

Olivet, J., M. Dones, M. Richard, C. Wilkey, S. Yampolskaya, M. Beit-Arie, and L. Joseph. 2018. *Supporting Partnerships for Anti-Racist Communities (SPARC). Phase One Study Findings*. Center for Social Innovation.

Owens, A. 2020. "Unequal Opportunity: School and Neighborhood Segregation in the USA." *Race and Social Problems* 12 (1): 29–41. doi:10.1007/s12552-019-09274-z.

Paris, D. 2012. "Culturally Sustaining Pedagogy: A Needed Change in Stance, Terminology and Practice." *Educational Researcher* 41 (3): 93–97. doi:10.3102/0013189X12441244.

Payne, Y. A. 2017. "Participatory Action Research (PAR)." In *The Wiley Blackwell Encyclopedia of Social Theory*, edited by S. T. Bryan. Hoboken, NJ, USA: John Wiley & Sons.

Payne, Y.A., and T. Brown. 2016. ""I'm Still Waiting on That Golden Ticket": Attitudes Toward and Experiences with Opportunity." *The Journal of Social Issues* 72 (4): 789–811. doi:10.1111/josi.12194.

Picower, B. 2009. "The Unexamined Whiteness of Teaching: How White Teachers Maintain and Enact Dominant Racial Ideologies." *Race Ethnicity and Education* 12 (2): 197–215. doi:10.1080/1361332902995475.

Rafferty, Y. 1999. "Legal Issues in Educating Homeless Children: Past Accomplishments and Future Challenges." *Journal for a Just and Caring Education* 5: 19–33.

Raventos, D., and J. Wark. 2018. *Against Charity*. California: Counterpunch.

Rolfe, S., L. Garnham, J. Godwin, I. Anderson, P. Seaman, and C. Donaldson. 2020. "Housing as a Social Determinant of Health and Wellbeing: Developing an Empirically-Informed Realist Theoretical Framework." *BioMed Central Public Health* 20 (1): 1–19. doi:10.1186/s12889-020-09224-0.

Ross, C. E., J. R. Reynolds, and K. J. Geis. 2000. "The Contingent Meaning of Neighborhood Stability for residents' Psychological Well-Being." *American Sociological Review* 64 (4): 581–597. doi:10.2307/2657384.

Rothstein, R. 2017. *The Color of Law: A Forgotten History of How Our Government Segregated America*. New York London: Liveright Publishing.

Sandwick, T., M. Fine, A. C. Greene, B. G. Stoudt, M. E. Torre, and L. Patel. 2018. "Promise and Provocation: Humble Reflections on Critical Participatory Action Research for Social Policy." *Urban Education* 53 (4): 473–502. doi:10.1177/0042085918763513.

Schaeffer, K. (10 Dec 2021). America's Public School Teachers are Far Less Racially and Ethnically Diverse Than Their Students. *Pew Research Center*. https://www.pewresearch.org/fact-tank/2021/12/10/americas-public-school-teachers-arefarlessraciallyandethnicallydiversethantheirstudents/#:~:text=About%20eight%2Din%2Dten%20U.S.,or%20Asian%20American%202%25.

Schwartz, H.L. 2012. "Housing Policy is School Policy: Economically Integrative Housing Promotes Academic Success in Montgomery County, Maryland." *The Century Foundation* 1–57.

Shapiro, T. 2017. *Toxic Inequality: How America's Wealth Gap Destroys Mobility, Deepens the Racial Divide, and Threatens Our Future*. New York: Basic Books.

Smith, J., and D. Stovall. 2008. "'Coming home' to New Homes and New Schools: Critical Race Theory and the New Politics of Containment." *Journal of Education Policy* 23 (2): 135–152. doi:10.1080/02680930701853062.

Soss, J., R.C. Fording, and S.F. Schram. 2011. *Disciplining the Poor: Neoliberal Paternalism and the Persistent Power of Race*. Chicago: University of Chicago Press.

Stovall, D. 2015. "Schools Suck, but They're Supposed To: Schooling, Incarceration and the Future of Education." *Journal of Curriculum and Pedagogy* 13 (1): 20–22. doi:10.1080/15505170.2016.1138252.

Stovall, D. 2018. "Are We Ready for School Abolition? Thoughts and Practices of a Radical Imaginary in Education." *Taboo: The Journal of Culture & Education* 17 (1): 51–61. doi:10.31390/taboo.17.1.06.

Swope, C. B., and D. Hernández. 2019. "Housing as a Determinant of Health Equity: A Conceptual Model." *Social Science & Medicine* 243: 1–13. doi:10.1016/j.socscimed.2019.112571.

Tamir, C., A. Budiman, L. Noe-Bustamante, and L. Mora (25 April 2021). Facts About the U.S. Black Population, Pew Research Center. https://www.pewresearch.org/social-trends/fact-sheet/facts-about-the-us-black-population/

Tuck, E. 2009. "Suspending Damage: A Letter to Communities." *Harvard Educational Review* 79 (3): 409–427. doi:10.17763/haer.79.3.n0016675661t3n15.

UNCF (Accessed 5 April 2022). K-12 Disparity Facts and Statistics. https://uncf.org/pages/k-12-disparity-facts-and-stats

Walsdorf, A.A., L.S. Jordan, C.R. McGeorge, and M.O. Caughy. 2020. "White Supremacy and the Web of Family Science: Implications of the Missing Spider." *Journal of Family Theory & Review* 12 (1): 64–79. doi:10.1111/jftr.12364.

White racial ignorance and refusing culpability: how the emotionalities of whiteness ignore race in teacher education

Michalinos Zembylas ⓘ and Cheryl E. Matias

ABSTRACT

This article builds on Charles W. Mills' foundational concept of white racial ignorance to expand his work by exploring the inner dynamics and practices of teacher education (its rationales, student teaching, practicums, pedagogies, curriculum) and explaining how the emotionalities of whiteness play a significant role in the ways that whiteness persists perniciously in teacher education. In order to hold whiteness accountable and culpable, it is argued that teacher education needs to stop emotionally deflecting anti-racist critiques by over pontificating their lackluster commitments to race, a practice which only ignores, and diverts attention away from the hegemonic presence of whiteness. It suggests that teacher educators need to help pre-service and in-service teachers be attentive to how racial politics are felt, acted upon, and reproduced, and how emotionalities of whiteness become 'ordinary' in everyday life in schools. The article concludes by outlining some implications for research and theory in critical whiteness studies.

Introduction

In recent decades, scholars in Critical Race Theory (Delgado, 1995; Delgado & Stefancic, 2001) and Critical Whiteness Studies (Bonilla-Silva, 2014; DiAngelo, 2011; Leonardo, 2009; Matias, 2016, 2022) have provided crucial insights into the ways in which race, as a social construct, is imbued with different privileges that reproduce white supremacy, racial inequality, and racism. In his seminal work, *The Racial Contract*, Charles Mills (1997) has shown that white supremacy is a racialized sociopolitical system of power that structures material life, governs bodies and guides symbolic identifications in ways that normalize privileges for Whites, while disadvantaging people of color. As Bonilla-Silva (2014) explains, whereas pre-Civil rights era racism was overtly visible in laws, public discourses, and everyday manifestations of racial violence, post-Civil Rights era racism operates through the framework of *colorblindness*—a racial ideology that is rooted in the Whites' refusal to 'see' how racialization operates in society. Mills' (1997, 2007) use of the notion of 'epistemology of ignorance' to describe Whites' habits of conscious ignorance as well as Sullivan's (2006) idea of unconscious habits of whiteness provide fruitful ways to consider how both racism and whiteness are reproduced across generations. This theoretical paper pays homage to Charles Mills' conceptualization of white racial ignorance by showing how it undergirds today's work on racialized emotions, particularly the emotionalities of whiteness in teacher education.

A growing strand of scholarship on race and racialization in recent years is drawing on *affect theory* to examine how processes of racialization, like whiteness, are affectively created, experienced and reproduced, as they operate within power relations and structures of inequality (Ahmed 2004a; Berg & Ramos-Zayas, 2015; Blickstein, 2019). Racialization, understood here 'as the naturalization of social differences along "racial" lines [...], is a phenomenon deeply embedded in affective logics, practices and histories', according to Blickstein (2019, 152). Whiteness, as a marker of privilege and racialization, is thus historically rooted in affect and emotion and accumulates value and significance over time (Ahmed 2004a). In this sense, affects and emotions are central to understanding whiteness, racism and racialization processes (Berg & Ramos-Zayas, 2015). We argue that an analytical focus on the affects of racialization and whiteness provides scholars in critical whiteness studies with two crucial insights: first, it helps explain how the *emotionalities of whiteness* are embedded in Whites' refusal to 'see' the ways that racialization operates in society; and second, it enables an understanding of how the emotionalities of whiteness become so self-indulgent that Whites ignore the affective, material and political impact of whiteness on people of color (Leonardo & Zembylas, 2013; Matias, 2016; Matias & Zembylas, 2014). Both insights extend and exemplify Mill's concept of epistemology of ignorance.

In particular, teacher education in many western societies (US, Canada, Europe, Australia), replete with its overwhelming presence of whiteness (Sleeter, 2001, 2016, 2017), continues to be overwhelmingly white, despite proclaimed commitments to social justice, anti-racist pedagogies, and culturally relevant teaching practices. And yet, in this time of mass extermination of Black people in the US (e.g. George Floyd, Breonna Taylor) and the disproportionate deaths of Black and Brown people due to COVID-19 health disparities, the demand for racial justice is at an all-time high; for such work is not simply about educating minds, but rather about saving people's lives. Yet, the question remains, 'why do these efforts fall flat?' Is not advocating for various forms of socially just pedagogies (e.g. culturally responsive teaching, culturally relevant teaching, culturally sustaining pedagogy, antiracist teaching, multicultural education, etc.) and engaging in #BLM enough to thwart the omnipresence of whiteness in teacher education?

This article builds on Charles W. Mills' foundational concept of white racial ignorance to expand his work by bringing it into conversation with theory on the affects of racialization and whiteness. In particular, this theoretical paper explores the inner dynamics and practices of teacher education (its rationales, student teaching, practicums, pedagogies, curriculum, mentalities) to explain how the emotionalities of whiteness play a significant role in the ways that whiteness maintains its presence in teacher education, while at the same time reproducing epistemologies of ignorance. In other words, by bringing attention to how emotionalities of whiteness function – that is, how Whites use particular emotional practices in their encounters with issues of race and racism e.g. to deny race and racism – we show that epistemologies of ignorance are entangled with these emotionalities, rendering teacher education efforts towards racially just education fruitless. Hence, we argue that in order to hold whiteness accountable and culpable, teacher education needs to stop emotionally deflecting critiques by over pontificating about their lackluster commitments to race which serve as a way to ignore, moreover, divert away from, the hegemonic presence of whiteness. Our analytic perspective also calls out weaponized white emotionalities. We, therefore, suggest that teacher educators need to help pre-service and in-service teachers be attentive to how racial politics are felt, acted upon, and reproduced, and how emotionalities of whiteness become 'ordinary' (Stewart, 2007) in everyday life in schools. Until this happens, teacher education, despite its public commitments to social justice, will fail to lead us down a better path for racially just teaching.

We begin the article with a discussion of two foundational concepts from recent affect theory – namely, 'affects of racialization' and 'racialized affects'—that guide us to support our arguments about locating affect and affective relations in racialization processes and their histories. Next, we draw particularly on the phenomenological strand of affect theory to map more explicitly how racialized affects operate in economic terms that present themselves in ways that normalize whiteness and privilege white emotionalities. In the third part of the article, we specifically focus on Mills' concept of white racial ignorance and theorize it as an affective economy in the context of teacher education. In particular, we share examples from our experiences in various teacher education settings to show how the emotionalities of whiteness may be interrogated. We conclude the article by briefly outlining some implications for research and theory in critical whiteness studies, as those emerge from our analysis of racialized affects in teacher education.

Before we begin presenting the theoretical concepts driving this article, we think it is important to briefly say where each of us is coming from and what brings us together in critical whiteness studies, and particularly how we draw inspiration from Charles W. Mills and his work.

Where are we coming from? a short note on standpoint

Michalinos: As a white male living in a postcolonial country (Cyprus) that suffered the dire consequences of British colonization, I recognize the ambivalence of my positionality. I continue to benefit from my status as a white person, while struggling to make sense of the coloniality manifested in the institutions, practices and everyday life of my country long after the end of British colonial era in 1960. I am consistently and completely appalled by the racial ignorance of my fellow citizens in public discourses surrounding migrants and refugees (from the Middle East, Asia and North Africa) who find themselves in Cyprus (a member of the European Union) on their perilous journey to find a better and safer life in Europe. Charles W. Mills' foundational concept of white racial ignorance has always helped me frame an understanding of how the denial of racism in my country promotes actual ignorance about the ways the world works. Hence, my critique of white supremacy operates in tandem with my complicity in it. As Ahmed (2004a) reminds us, white people are not outside of the systems and social structures that benefit us at the expense of non-white people. We must also remember, she explains, that to be against something is to be in intimate relation with that which one is against. Therefore, I recognize that there is something awkward about claiming to be engaged in critical whiteness studies, while benefiting from the privileges of whiteness. Nevertheless, I eschew resolving my awkward position by resorting to feelings that re-center my whiteness (e.g. shame, guilt); rather, I embrace the responsibility of using my privileged position to work towards dismantling racial injustice and white supremacy. My long time research on issues of decolonization and racism at various levels of education both in

Cyprus and other settings around the world (e.g. S. Africa, Australia), especially through the lens of affect theory, marks my commitment to constantly invent new ways of interrogating the emotionalities of whiteness. Mills' work has been inspirational to my theorization of racialized affects in education, because it has offered a solid foundation for understanding the myriad ways that white supremacy is central in society – affectivity being one of those ways, sometimes incredibly powerful. I have gradually come to realize that white racial ignorance is reproduced precisely because it constitutes a powerful affective regime that feeds itself through mundane everyday emotional activities such as feelings of fear when Blacks and Whites encounter each other. To fight against white racial ignorance, then, is to create new affective communities that are truly inclusive for nonwhites.

Cheryl: As a brown skinned, Pinay (Filipina), daughter of immigrants, and single motherscholar of three, living in the settler colonial country of the United States-one which refuses to acknowledge its systemic violence against Black, Indigenous, people of Color, whilst presenting itself to the world as the bastion of freedom – nothing is more apparent to me than how race, class, gender, language, and nationhood impact how individuals experience communities, nation-states and the ideological and material state apparatuses embedded in them (see Althusser, 2006). Living amidst this paradoxical quandary of benefiting from national privilege in a world dominating country yet subjected to its racial and gender discrimination, especially when the U.S. colonization of the Philippines goes unrecognized, provides me with an almost exilic perspective (see Said 2000). It wasn't until I read Charles[1] Racial Contract, whilst at my doctoral program at UCLA, that I started to connect my exilic experience to the white supremacist world I lived on. With his work I realized that interrogations of why my immigrant parents speak English well or why my grandparents speak English, Spanish, and Tagalog without knowing the colonial context of the Philippines for the past 400 years, forces me in a surreal state of existence. Because as I am forced to the margins with regard to my race, title, gender, single mother status, I uneasily inhabit the privileges of the ivory tower in my full professoriate, middle class status, and my access to institutions that have given me my degrees. So, as I embark in spaces typically giveth only to those in elite social echelons, I am still made to 1) feel foreign in a country I was born in, 2) be presumed incompetent by virtue of my racial and gender identity (see Gutierrez y Muh et al., 2012), and 3) regardless of degrees, professional accomplishments, or class, still be associated with stereotypes that plague single mothers of Color worldwide. Therefore, my unique positionality affords me a multiplicity that allows me to see systems of oppression like that of whiteness, especially as one of the few teacher educators of color in a field dominated by white women professors and whiteness ideology. Or, as Charles wrote 'Another virtue of the "Racial Contract" is that it simultaneously recognizes the reality of race ... and demystifies race' (Mills, 1997, p. 125) and, in doing so, produces within nonwhites (otherwise people of color) like myself, a double consciousness to borrow from DuBois (1903). For in the end, unlike many of my white colleagues in the field of teacher education, I never entered the field to help, save, or teach those Black and Brown students, but rather to stop the trauma, pain, and abuse white teachers enact on diverse students every single day. Or, as Mills puts it, since "the ultimate triumph of education is that it eventually becomes possibly to characterize the Racial Contract as 'consensual' and voluntaristic' even for nonwhites" (1997, p. 89) I, teach, to reject it.

Affects of racialization

Recent work in affect theory shows that affects and emotions are central to understanding the history and politics of racialization processes, as those have been shaped by white supremacy in contemporary societies. In this and the next section, we draw from Blickstein's (2019) recent theorization of 'affects of racialization' and Ahmed's (2004a, 2004b, 2006, 2007, 2010) analysis of 'white phenomenology', respectively, to present the theoretical framework that drives our analysis concerning affect and affective relations in the history and politics of racialization and whiteness in U.S. and Western European settings. In particular, this framework will enable us to interrogate the emotionalities of whiteness in teacher education in the latter half of the article.

To begin, a fundamental idea emerging from affect theory is that all affects are historically contingent and reproducible through structural, embodied and material mechanisms; processes of racialization are a prime example of this (Blickstein, 2019). At the same time, emphasizes Blickstein, like all affective processes, racialization also entails visceral, non-conscious and thus invisible components; this can make the detection of racialized affects very difficult, despite the fact that the logics and technologies of racism and racialization are manifested through overt discourses, practices and policies. What this demonstrates, as other affect theorists have also pointed out (e.g. Ahmed, 2004a; Ngai, 2005), is that racialization is not about an isolated emotion or feeling within an individual, but rather a relational process and practice of 'affecting and being affected' (Seigworth & Gregg, 2010) that is historically, spatially, materially and socially situated. Indeed, many historical studies in colonial and post-colonial settings show how racialized experiences transcend time and space as they are embedded in historical, cultural and political structures (e.g. see Khanna, 2020; Stoler, 1995, 2002, 2010). And, in such a rooting, one can then ask 'what are the social institutions that structure our emotions' (Matias, 2016, 5).

As a conceptual term, 'affects of racialization' foregrounds that the implicitly or explicitly racializing character of affective relations that produce 'racialized affects' are situated in hierarchies of race (Blickstein, 2019). This concept, then, can be used as 'a tool for understanding the structural mechanisms of white supremacist affect as it is for understanding the affective impact of racialization on populations marginalized within white supremacist societies' (ibid., p. 153). Along similar lines, Berg and Ramos-Zayas (2015) use the concept of 'racialized affect' 'as an analytical tool to examine the contradictions embedded in the study of race and affect, both separately and at their intersection' (p. 654). Theorizing the entanglement of race and affect in racialization processes offers a conceptual vocabulary that enables scholars to historicize affects of racialization as an invention of white supremacy (Blickstein, 2019), trace its shifts in various social domains (e.g. education), and consider interventions that could possibly interrogate and transform established trajectories of racialized biopolitics (Schuller, 2018).[2]

Whiteness as a racialization process is affective, thus affect, as a relational process that also operates in a context of power relations, is crucial to 'understanding the historical biopolitics of domination and dispossession that continue to generate affects of racialization today' (Blickstein 2019, 153). A more nuanced examination of racialization that foregrounds the racializing and unequal ways in which 'affective practices, emotive manifestations, and evaluations of personhood are experienced and lived' (Berg &

Ramos-Zayas, 2015, 654) is valuable in understanding the historical development of subject formation of white and non-white identities and how they have evolved in their present-day forms (Slaby & Mühlhoff, 2019). Stoler's (1995, 2002, 2010) work, for example, shows how race politics were thoroughly embedded in the everyday affective life of the colonies; by paying attention to these archives of colonial affect, it is shown how racialized power relations functioned in the colonies (see also, Hartman, 1997, 2007).

In particular, affects of racialization demonstrate what Guilmette (2019) refers to as the 'coloniality of the affects', that is, the regimes of racialized biopower produced by legitimating the affects of white people, while invalidating those of non-white populations. In this sense, argues Guilmette, the historical development of white identities was formed through constitutive exclusions of non-white populations, thus 'framing concepts not only of "being", "power", "truth", and "freedom", but also of *affect* and capacities for *feeling*' (ibid., p. 79, original emphasis). Agathangelou (2019) also points out that in this colonial matrix of power white emotionalities are given more significance, 'while the emotions of subordinated/colonized communities and subjects are routinely ignored or even do not register' (2019, p. 205).

Similarly, Schuller (2018) shows how sentimentalism functioned as a fundamental mechanism of surveillance in the 19th century US that sought to regulate the circulation of feeling throughout the population, ascribing different affective capacities to white and non-white populations. Whiteness was ascribed with a full capacity for feeling, while the racialized (especially Black populations) were regarded as affectively deficient, either exhibiting too much emotion or none at all. In particular, there was also a perception of subordinated/colonized (Black, brown and native) peoples' affects as 'excessive', 'inappropriate' or 'animated' to mark their dehumanization (Ngai, 2005; Palmer, 2017). This 'sentimental politics of life', as Schuller calls this sentimental mode of biopower, distinguished civilized (white) bodies as receptive and capable of disciplining their emotions from primitive (non-white) bodies that were impulsive and insensate, and thus incapable of evolutionary improvement. As Schuller argues, this kind of biopolitical work of feeling continues into the present, and the Black Lives Matter meme 'Black lives>white feelings' captures the ongoing tensions around the affective dynamics of racial formation.

Importantly, the archives of colonial affect also show something else, equally remarkable: the *refusal* of white populations to 'feel' the pain of subordinated/colonized communities and subjects (Weheliye, 2014). This refusal can be interpreted by Charles Mills' (2007) foundational work in *The Racial Contract*. In a frequently cited quote, Mills states:

> On matters related to race, the Racial Contract prescribes for its signatories an inverted epistemology, an epistemology of ignorance, a particular pattern of localized and global cognitive dysfunctions (which are psychologically and socially functional), producing the ironic outcome that whites will in general be unable to understand the world they themselves have made. (1997, 18)

Mills emphasizes that white ignorance is not only cognitive but also psychological and social, alluding to the idea that white ignorance is not accidental but rather motivated by political and affective practices that produce and perpetuate white privilege. Mills makes an important contribution, then, by showing that ignorance is actually based on a deeply seated epistemic resistance to know – a refusal to know the Other. Here we want to build on this idea by arguing that ignorance is also based on a deeply seated affective resistance to know about Black feelings and the consequences of racism.

In particular, the fundamental opacity of Black feeling in archival accounts has been enabled by white-centered understandings of affect that position white affects as universal, concrete and true (Garcia-Rojas, 2017; Palmer, 2017). The structure of white affects, writes Garcia-Rojas, 'was constituted through the enslavement and genocide of Black and native indigenous populations, in addition to colonial practices of violence and terror' (2017, 259). White histories of affect, then, are prioritized and are informed by Eurocentric forms of knowledge, while Black feelings are dismissed and rendered insignificant. This inattentiveness to the value of Black affects, points out Palmer (2017), is indicative of how racialization has been used as a tool to dominate and dispossess Black, Brown and native populations. It is important to note, then, Palmer's argument that Blackness cannot be subsumed under a generalizable category of affective racialization – especially one that is rooted in white affects and Eurocentric thinking – because the Black body is marked by histories of 'absolute fungibility'.

This framing of Black affect as unsubstantiated, insignificant, and thus unworthy sets the basis for white emotional backlash, otherwise whitelash. Yet, unlike other emotional backlash that simply stings when enacted, whitelash, with its entanglement with hegemonic whiteness and white supremacy, inflicts tangible emotional trauma and violence onto people of Color. Take for example, Anderson's (2016) historical analysis of white rage in U.S. history. Analyzing the gains of African Americans in U.S. history, Anderson writes how that in and of itself was enough to cultivate white rage, which then enacted onto people of Color in tangibly hurtful ways. She explains:

> Trump supporters, therefore, saw their candidate as 'America's last chance' to recreate a nation that reminded them of the good ol' days. The country's growing diversity, Obama's very existence in the White House, and the ever-increasing visibility of African Americans in colleges and corporations had fueled a sense that these gains were; 'likely to reduce the influence of white Americans in society'. Trump's win exposed in frightening ways the 'ethnonationalist rage centered around a black president' and the fear that all of the resources and wealth accumulated through centuries of public policy would be subject to 'redistribution from older, white America to its younger, more diverse' population. (p. 170)

In acknowledging that white emotionality holds racial power, this ethnonationalist rage against growth in diversity was enough to emotionally substantiate many of the reversals of U.S. voting rights of the last decade such as the Supreme Court's *Shelby v. Holder* decision which eviscerated the Voting Rights Act and enabled and encouraged massive suppression of voting by Black, Indigenous, people of Color populations.

In their theoretical account of the co-constitutive relationship of racialization and affects, Berg and Ramos-Zayas (2015) make an important distinction between two kinds of affects: the first is 'liable affect', that is, 'the affective practices that serve to racialize, contain, and sustain conditions of vulnerability' (p. 662) for marginalized communities and subjects (as those are structured by the whiteness project such as the example of white rage discussed above); the second is 'empowering affect', namely, 'the affect associated with privilege and always-already perceived as complex, nuanced, and beyond essentialism' (ibid.). As Berg and Ramos-Zayas explain, a conception of 'liable affect' results in a simplified and essentialized account of an 'inner world' that undermines the complexity of populations racialized as Other, whereas a conception of 'empowering affect' reproduces the privileged and nuanced subjectivity reserved for Whites. Berg and Ramos-Zayas further characterize the 'empowering affect' of whiteness as self-protective, that is, in need for regular fortification in the face of racial formations that undermine its dominance:

> although "empowering affect" perpetuates privilege, such privilege has to be continuously reinvented and even developed in terms of "knowing" and recreating its racialized Other. This continuous attentiveness to changing racialization processes is, in fact, required for "empowering affect" to continue to effectively exert its disciplining power. An example of this would be the "racial paranoia" proposed by John Jackson (2008), which underscores forms of "political correctness" that require that privilege be maintained, not through overt forms of domination but by learning to manage white social anxiety. By becoming proficient in changing racial language and social expectations, fundamental power structures can still remain largely unaltered. (2015, p. 663)

In citing Jackson's work on 'racial paranoia', Berg and Ramos-Zayas call attention to how white emotionalities find ways to maneuver in order to maintain white privilege, while justifying these efforts in the name of security (securitization) and white vulnerability. This insight resonates with Bonilla-Silva's (2019) point that the racialized emotions of whiteness are used to protect white people's affective interests in ways that maintain white privilege.

All in all, the theorization of affects of racialization draws attention to two important perspectives for future research and theorizing in critical whiteness studies. First, there is need for new methodological designs and theoretical frames that account for the relational, materialist and historically situated affects of racialization in various social domains such as teacher education; for example, white supremacy needs to be understood in these domains not only as an overt ideological project but also one that is manifested in affective relations that might not always be visible (Blickstein, 2019). Second, it is important to decenter white affects and pay attention to Black affects, as those are generated in racialization processes—e.g. in teaching and teacher education (see Matias, 2022; Matias & Boucher, 2021); researching how white affects are reproduced needs to be complemented by how Black affects emerge in the affective histories of racialized colonial domination (Zembylas, 2022). Black affects enable the survival of people despite deadly forces arrayed against them, but they are also of great value to all people because they contain grammars, vocabularies, epistemologies, and ontologies that speak of 'we' instead of 'me' and that recognize the harms perpetuated by elevating things and money over people.

Phenomenology of whiteness

As shown so far, the historical biopolitics of race and racialization processes play a significant role in shaping our felt, embodied experiences as well as our (dis)identification and (dis)affiliations with (non)white subjectivities. Ahmed's (2004a, 2004b, 2006, 2007, 2010) landmark work on 'affective economies' and the 'phenomenology of whiteness' draws on feminist cultural studies of emotion and affect and what Schaefer (2015, 2019) has called the 'phenomenological strain' of affect theory to theorize how this (dis) identification happens and what consequences it has. In this section, we draw on Ahmed's work to extend our earlier analysis of racialized affects by focusing on how whiteness is racialized at the level of affect, namely, how white affects are mobilized and maintained to ignore race and Black affects.[3]

Phenomenology, as an approach, emphasizes how subjects experience the world (Schaefer, 2015). Schaefer explains that the experiencing body serves as the focal concern for both phenomenology and affect theory. At the forefront of the conversation linking phenomenology to affect theory, according to Schaefer (2019), is Sara Ahmed. Analyzing whiteness through a phenomenological lens, argues Ahmed (2007), 'helps us to show how whiteness is an effect of racialization, which in turn shapes what it is that bodies "can do"' (p. 150). In other words, bodies are enabled to move freely or are restricted to move, as a result of racialization processes. For example, the higher rate of incarceration among Black and Brown bodies or their disproportionate share in getting stopped by police in the US show that we live in a world that is 'white' (Ahmed, 2004b). These restrictions in bodily movement prevent Black and Brown people from moving forward in life (Ahmed, 2007). In this way, the phenomenology of whiteness functions as a certain type of ontology that shapes how certain bodies are made (in)visible.

Racial knowledge, then, is not detached from the body and the visceral; rather embodied experiences are bound up together in what Ahmed (2004a) has termed 'affective economies'. This term conceptualizes the way in which affects and emotions shape discourses and the materiality of bodies (e.g. creating sensations that are felt on the skin e.g. the fear of Black body), and how these affects/emotions create discourses that are attached to certain bodies (but not to others). In this sense, affects/emotions shape communities, producing social relationships that influence certain discourses and bodies (Ahmed, 2006). A historical analysis of the affective economies of whiteness shows how these economies – and whiteness with them – are reproduced. To go back to the previous example, the phenomenology of fear is rooted in affects about the violent Black man conspiring to harm the white man (Ahmed, 2007). Affect (fear, in this case) moves between bodies, shaping the discourses and politics of race, gender and sexuality (Ahmed 2004a). In an economic sense, then, affect circulates and creates value; the more an affect circulates, the more its value grows, according to Ahmed.

Similarly, Sullivan (2006) points at the onto-psychological dimensions of economy to explain white habits of ownership:

> The economic reasons for white habits of ownership cannot be understood apart from the onto-psychological [. . .]. Whiteness as possession describes not just the act of owning, but also the obsessive psychosomatic state of white owners. Commodifying non-white peoples and cultures, unconscious habits of white privilege tend to transform them into objects for white appropriation and use. The benefits accrued to white people through this process include not merely economic gain, but also increased ontological security and satisfaction of unconscious desires. (p. 122)

Here Sullivan is extending Ahmed's theorizing of affective economies by focusing on the psycho-ontological aspects of ownership (see also Moreton-Robinson 2015). In this sense, economic gain, commodification and ownership are entangled with the affective and onto-psychological processes of whiteness. In other words, the affective processes of whiteness are essentially material processes of commodification, possession and mobility, while simultaneously being processes of dispossession and immobility for Black bodies.

We want to further expand this discussion by focusing more explicitly on the affective economy of colorblindness – a racial ideology that is very much widespread among white teachers in teacher education (Bonilla-Silva, 2019; Matias, 2016). As Bonilla-Silva (2014) argues, an affective economy of colorblindness – which is created and sustained by the affective investments and attachments that frame white people's felt, embodied knowledge about race – is rooted in white 'common sense'. In other words, whiteness becomes an affectively powerful common sense, namely, a set of beliefs and practices about what is taken-for-granted in a society—e.g. how societies' white orientation views non-white bodies (Ahmed, 2006, 2007). Colorblind common sense, explains Hartzell (2020) who draws on both Ahmed and Bonilla-Silva, is

> constructed by and works to shape white perspectives on the (in)significance of race and racism ('if I don't see/experience racism, it must not be happening'), which are framed as objective, thereby universalizing whiteness, deracializing white perspectives, and strengthening white folks' presumptions of race neutrality. In turn, the perceptions and experiences of people of color are particularized and racialized, positioning them in opposition to normative common sense and rendering them unreasonable and biased. (p. 134)

Hence, we agree with Hartzell that white 'common sense' is affective. For example, a colorblind common sense functions to provide a comfortable space for Whites; 'because they do not have felt experiences with the negative realities of racism, colorblindness *makes sense* to them in ways that *feel* right' (Hartzell, 2020, p. 135, original emphasis). As DiAngelo (2011) shows, when white people are confronted with the realities of racial inequality and racism, and especially white privilege, they feel uncomfortable; this discomfort is manifested as a form of 'white fragility'—such as feelings of denial, avoidance, anger, guilt and shame. Yet, what is problematic about white fragility and white ignorance of race and racism is that the focus remains on white affects and how to restore white people's comfort rather than paying attention to Black suffering and pain as a result of racism and racial inequality: a process like how 'white scholarship that either morally justified this oppression or denied its existence' (p. 131) through the upholding of the Racial Contract. Clearly, affect becomes a function that upholds the Racial Contract.

All in all, moving white people out of their racial unconsciousness and toward racial consciousness and the recognition of Black affects is fundamentally an affective process (Hartzell 2020). Needless to say, engaging white people in this 'difficult' and 'discomforting' affective process neither guarantees any emotional transformation nor does it change the structures of racial inequalities. However, what it *can* do is to start interrogating how white identity historically consists of a naturalized racial superiority – either practicing blatant racism or claiming colorblindness. The importance of dismantling 'white fantasies' of racial superiority is to challenge white affective investments that function as 'common sense' and are passed on from generation to generation in order to disrupt white racial ignorance. This process entails more than just convincing white people to accept certain beliefs (e.g. racial equality); it requires them to care deeply about those they turn away from (Hartzell, 2020). Of particular interest to this article are the ways that white racial ignorance refuses to care about Black affects and mobilizes affects to maintain white common sense, while strategically negotiating white emotionalities to avoid discomfort. To illustrate this process in teacher education, we turn now to our own experiences from teacher education settings that show the multiple ways through which white racial ignorance operates as an affective economy, and particularly how emotionalities of whiteness may be interrogated in these settings.

White racial ignorance, affect, and teacher education

The idea of connecting love and teaching has been around a long time. Take for example, Darder (1998) who relates Freirian principles to teaching, claiming that teaching as an act of love must come from 'A love that could be lively, forceful, and inspiring, while at the same time, critical, challenging, and insistent' (2). Corroborating Darder's pairing of love and teaching, Nieto (2003) argues that teaching as love means recognizing that the entire profession is nothing but a 'vocation based on love' (p. 37). To Nieto (2003) 'Love, then, is not simply a sentimental conferring of emotions; it is a blend of confidence, faith, and admiration for the students and the strength they bring with them' (pp. 37–38). Thus, the idea of teaching and love are as inseparable as peanut butter and jelly; for parceling one out would render it an entirely new concept. However, in as much as love and teaching are quite simply a thing, there still exists lovelessness in teaching that is violent to students of Color. Love (2019), for instance, argues that teachers, many of whom are White in the U.S., lack love for Black students simply because they cannot love those they do not know. That is to say, it is not only ignorant for white teachers to deny the racism Black students face daily, but also dangerous. And, in presenting this danger to Black students they simply cannot be loving to them. Simply put, this is the enactment of the affective Racial Contract par excellence.

Johnson et al. (2019) echo this sentiment proving the disconnect of teachers who proclaim they love their Black students, yet, in the end, still do not show them love. Instead, as Johnson et al. suggest, teachers need to have a revolutionary love that acknowledges African Diasporic literacy, histories, and identities. Matias (2016) extends this argument claiming that beyond the idea of love, teachers who refuse to interrogate their own whiteness are actually abusive, and within this abuse, create the condition by which students of Color can learn to hate themselves. As Matias shows through her empirical work, the love so often professed by teachers is not *felt* by students. This is dangerous because if love is solely defined by those who claim its expression, then we negate the testimony of how that expressed and conceived love is felt by others. The definition of love relies solely on teachers who claim to be loving regardless of how that love is felt or received by students. In doing so, the voices of students, many of whom are of Color, are silenced. Within this emotional manipulation is violence. In fact, there is a latent violence that manifests in the field of teacher education that, if not explored, will remain; a process that ultimately harms students of Color. And, in refusing to voyeuristically observe this violence like mass society has done for so many other brutalities, teacher education needs to 1) learn how to bear witness to said violence, and 2) intervene to interrogate and stop this violence. For those who sit idle whilst violence occurs are as culpable in the crime as those who perpetrate it. As such, we present how Mills' concept of white racial ignorance explains the basis for these violent white emotionalities to exist and be enacted in teacher education settings. To do so, we discuss a few examples from our experiences in teacher education, highlighting how the emotionalities of whiteness ignore race and Black affect, while individualizing and psychologizing the problem of racism. Although these examples focus on our own experiences, we believe that they will resonate with the experiences of teacher educators in other western societies.

The all lives matter rhetoric in social justice efforts

With the heightened visibility of police brutality disproportionately targeting Black and Brown people in the United States, global society responded in 2020 with mass support for #BlackLivesMatter. Millions took to the streets during the COVID-19 global shutdown to air their dissent against anti-Black policing practices specifically after the racially motivated murders of George Floyd, Breonna Taylor, and Ahmaud Arbery. Founded by Black and AfroLatina women, the Black Lives matter organization works 'inside and outside of the system to heal the past, re-imagine the present, and invest in the future of Black lives through policy change, investment in our communities, and a commitment to arts and culture' (https://blacklivesmatter.com/transparency/#mission). Much like the Ten point Plan from the 1960s U.S. Black Panther Movement, fighting to have justice in their communities, healthy food for their children, and a loving curriculum that honors their being, #BlackLivesMatter sought to uplift, honor, and strengthen Black love. Essentially, as Love (2019) so offers, instead of promoting anti-Blackness in the daily operations of whiteness and white supremacy in the U.S., #BlackLivesMatter promotes Black joy, which is essential in that it 'makes the quest for justice sustainable' (p. 120). Despite this altruistic and humanistic approach to society that literally honors Black affect, white emotionality ensues in ways that once again performs white racial ignorance as a way to enact an affective economy, whereby white emotionalities again control, as Mills (1997) proffers, the racial contract. To exemplify this a growing opposition to #BlackLivesMatter is #AllLivesMatter; a strategic countermovement specifically employed to counter promotions that affirm, acknowledge, or honor Black affect. To be noted is that beyond the hashtags, twitter feeds, and social media presence #AllLivesMatter in and of itself has no solid foundation, purpose, mission, or vision other than to once again silence Black affect.

Sadly, this same rhetorical maneuver enacts within teacher education in ways that disguise racial disgust (see Matias & Zembylas, 2014) for performative social justice. Take, for example, how certain U.S. teacher education programs responded to the racial unrest by issuing racial justice statements, some even embedded racial justice in their mission statements. Yet, even in the face of this seemingly lofty approach, more often than not initiated by the few racially just professors or professors of Color at the institution, whitelash grew and couched itself within the rhetoric of white racial ignorance. Meaning, instead of explicitly engaging in racial justice, they chose to apply a common rhetorical maneuver (e.g. what about class?) that diverts attention from anything that supports Black affect. In fact, Allen (2009) provides an overarching analysis of how this rhetorical maneuver (e.g. what about poor white folks) masks the powerful affective economy of whiteness by redirecting the white gaze, per Yancy (2008), on anything but race.

Worse yet, some of the rationales behind whitelash reappropriate justice-oriented concepts and terminologies as a ruse to further white supremacist ideals. Clearly, when witnessing individuals like Kimberly Jean Davis, a straight white woman, who, as a public county clerk, refused to issue a marriage certificate to a gay couple, and then was likened to U.S. civil rights leader, Dr. Martin Luther King, claiming she was fighting for religious rights (see Cornish 2015), this becomes an era 'characterized by the perverse re-appropriation of civil rights and socially just terminologies and concepts – once used to support the rights of People of Color – to instead strengthen White Nationalism' (Matias & Newlove, 2017, p. 921). To illustrate this, Cheryl, a teacher educator in several states for many years, has had white faculty members push back on the incorporation of culturally responsive approaches claiming that just as white teachers need to be culturally responsive to their students of Color, professors of education (many of whom are white) need to be culturally responsive to teacher candidates, many of whom are white again. In this sense the good 'ole #AllLivesMatter rhetoric is yet again taken up pretending that if we are to acknowledge specificities that honors Black affect, like culturally responsive teaching, we then must do the same for whites; as if curricula, pedagogies, and instructional practices have not catered systematically to whiteness for years (see Arday, 2018).

Furthermore, recently, when bringing up the need for racial and social justice in a teacher education program by specifically including instruction on English Language Learning instruction, racial trauma-based pedagogy, and foundations in whiteness, one white woman faculty member responded with 'Ya, but we need to focus on assessments because assessments is all about social justice'. This rhetorical maneuver diverts attention away from topics that inform, affirm, and listen to Black affect. Instead, she re-appropriates social justice in ways that again silence Black affect, thus reiterating the affective economy of white emotionality. In other words, this trope not only silences Black affect, it portrays social justice as assimilation and deracination, as changing nonwhite students to meet 'standards' designed to reward whites. That is to say, instead of focusing directly on instruction that supports Black and Brown communities in the U.S., this faculty member opts to re-situate assessment practices – which, according to Gillborn (2010) are an expression of whiteness – as socially just. This perversion obscures the underlying intent of social justice. That is, social and racial justice is to dismantle social hierarchies that operationally privileges one group at the expense of another. And, if assessments, which have been historically employed to engage in eugenic racism along the lines perversely presented in Charles Murray's racist book *The Bell Curve* (see Newby and Newby 1995), are likened to social justice, it then perverts the entire intent behind justice and perpetuates a process that effectively maintains the affective economy of whiteness in teacher education.

Interestingly, the All Lives Matter rhetoric of white teachers and the affective economies of whiteness in teacher education are not unique to the US, per Cheryl's experiences, but are also present in Western European settings. For example, in Michalinos's context (Cyprus) in which he has taught for years in various pre-service and in-service teacher education programs, a widespread strategy that is often used by some white teachers involves claiming that Cypriots will be replaced by migrants (mostly Muslims from Africa and the Middle East) who, in these teachers' words, 'flood' or 'invade' Cyprus. This position is often accompanied by an affective stance of white fragility that trivializes the widespread exclusion of other peoples (often people of Color or people of non-Christian religions) from a predominantly white public life that ignores Black and other marginalized populations' affects. As a (white) Greek-Cypriot female teacher responded in the context of a teacher education workshop on diversity and racism, 'When the ethnic survival of our race [Greeks] is at stake, with all this flooding of migrants, then we are entitled to be racist. You have to understand that we have to do what we have to do to save our race, otherwise in a few years we are going to be replaced by them. Is it wrong to teach our children our own ethnic and racial ideals?' (which seems to boil down to hating people who are not like us!). The rhetoric of white victimhood and white fragility woven through this statement mobilizes rhetorical and affective appeals to rights and ethnoracial identity, while imagining white people as having been harmed by mainstream approaches to diversity and multiculturalism and endangered by the presence of other communities – i.e. migrants and refugees fleeing to Cyprus to save their lives from war, conflict and dire economic conditions. This sort of rhetoric – which erases racism and appropriates the affective experiences of racialized others – preserves and promotes an affective economy of whiteness that prioritizes the affective positioning of whiteness, while undermining racism and the affects of refugees, exiles and migrants.

Weaponizing white emotions as emotional abuse

Undoubtedly, emotional manipulation and abuse do occur and are serious problems. Worldwide almost 80% of the global population experiences emotional abuse (Karakurt & Silver, 2013) which is alarming because 'Emotionally abused women can be more lonely and despairing than physically abused women (Loring, 1994)' and can contribute to the 'severity of illnesses such as chronic fatigue syndrome and fibromyalgia' (Karakurt & Silver, 2013, n.p). Regarding white emotionality and its hegemonic power to enact an affective economy where it subjects all other emotions as subordinate, just as emotional abuse is oftentimes more damaging than physical abuse, so too is white emotional manipulation, coercion, and racial ignorance.

Van Dijk (2006), for instance, explicates how racist discourse is a form of manipulation and that 'Manipulation not only involves power, but specifically *abuse* of power, that is, *domination*' (original emphasis, p. 360). When applied to considering how an affective economy operates to again reinforce Mills' (1997) racial contract, emotional manipulation embedded in maintaining white emotionality is nonetheless racial abuse and domination. For manipulation implies 'a form of illegitimate influence by means of [emotional] discourse: manipulators make others believe or do things that are in the interest of the manipulator, and against the best interests of the manipulated' (Van Dijk, 2006, 360). That is, as Mills (2007) states, white racial ignorance is an active stance, which as Matias (2016) argues, is embraced strategically to relinquish culpability for racial manipulative behaviors that racially oppress people of Color. In doing so, Black affect is rendered insignificant, or more precisely, emotionally minimized, which is nonetheless a manipulative process. For when racialized emotional minimization happens it 1) obscures the harm, trauma, and attack away from the real victims, 2) recenters white emotionality and 3) because of this *crazymaking*, qua distortions, accountability is never recognized.

Suffice it to say, racialized emotional manipulation, otherwise racialized emotional abuse, enacted through tactics like gaslighting/crazymaking is just another form of psychological manipulation, where an abuser abuses her power to engage in tactics that denigrate, confuse, and disorient the abused (Matias, 2020)[4]. Frustrating as it is to enable a process that obscures reality, so too is it dangerous.

Because as this abuse remains unchecked, the victim (abused) will forever be manipulated in ways to believe they are the problem instead of holding the abuser accountable for said abuse (see also Leonardo, 2009).

To better illustrate this emotional phenomenon, Cheryl shares an incident in her early career as a teacher education professor – the only tenure-lined faculty of Color specifically hired into the core urban teacher education program. During one meeting the director of the urban teacher education program (a white woman, non-tenured line staff member) instructed each professor in the program (tenure track or not) to share their research with other stakeholders within the program. These stakeholders included corroborating K-12 classroom teachers who serve as master teachers for teacher candidates/college students who want to be teachers, K-12 administrators, and university supervisors who are typically retired K-12 classroom teachers. Knowing most of these stakeholders were white and had no training in race, racism, let alone whiteness in education (which is why Cheryl was hired in the first place) Cheryl knew that such a space maintained a white affective economy; one which is structured to never emotionally upset white emotionality. So, to push back on white affective economy which only caters to white emotionalities and denies Black affect, Cheryl interjected concerns, especially since her research was directly about studying white emotionalities in teacher education that do harm to students of Color and that she herself was the only person of Color being requested to do this task.

In her concerns, Cheryl specifically discussed Black, or in this case Brown, affect such as safety, fear, emotional isolation and even verbal assault which has, in the past, even occurred amongst this very faculty at the same university faculty meeting. Essentially, instead of simply kowtowing to white emotionality, Cheryl asserted Brown affect. Yet instead of honoring, listening, or affirming it, the white faculty refused to acknowledge it. In fact, they emotionally manipulated Cheryl trying to get her to believe she has no reason to worry; that such concerns of emotional retaliation were just figments of her imagination. One white male faculty member who did not have a doctorate whereas every single other white woman did earn doctorates, started shouting, 'What is it now, Cheryl?' rolling his eyes as if her concerns were nothing. These emotionally manipulative maneuvers to minimize real fear not only attempted to gaslight Cheryl but were also employed to reify the white affective economy where people of Color are not given any credence about their racialized concerns. In the end, Cheryl's concerns were real. Because as she was forced to sit at a large table ready to discuss her research in a two-hour slot, none of the approximately 70 white K12 teachers, administrators, or university supervisors chose to sit at her table, even when people were expected to rotate freely on topics of their own interests. Of course these individuals would not be interested in learning about the dangers of white emotionalities because at the end of the day white affective economy enforces white emotional maintenance. This maintenance includes never having to feel upset, conflicted, or even realize its excessive need for coddling: all of which Cheryl initially expected. Clearly, white emotionalities can be weaponized in ways that hegemonically enforce and reify white affective economies. In doing so, Black, or in this case, Brown affect are minimized by tactics like gaslighting, distortions, delusions, and active manipulation; all of which contribute to the emotional abuse of people of Color and maintain the falsity of white racial ignorance.

Resiliency and white racial ignorance

An often used trope in education, especially with respect to diverse students, is the commonplace and uncritical concept of resiliency. When applied to students and academic success, the concept merely focuses on a student's need to develop grit, qua resiliency, in order to excel academically. Yet, the social conditions of diverse students are so complex that merely ignoring oppressive social conditions that plague specific communities which then, according to resiliency theory, allows them to academically succeed is not sufficient. It is not just that theory on student resiliency does not account for larger social conditions; it is also that the onus of correction never gets appropriately directed to those who contribute to the social conditions. Simply put, should Black and Brown students in the US be taught simply to ignore oppressive mechanisms like racism and white supremacy in schools, developing unhealthy callousness to academically 'excel'? And if so, at what cost must Black and Brown students incur to excel? Essentially, student resiliency theory does exactly what the Racial Contract states, 'by not holding people responsible of what they cannot help' (Mills, 1997, 126). That is, if social conditions are not to be addressed as a culprit in the academic success of diverse students, then those who uphold those same social conditions relinquish their culpability for actually doing something to change the oppressive social condition.

Or, in the global context, should nonwhite students in predominantly white societies be expected to develop an uncritical sense of resiliency regardless of the grave educational disparities that exist in these societies? To be clear, the idea of resilience amidst white supremacy "fail[s] to account for socio-political contexts of oppression and structural inequalities (Zembylas 2021a, 1967), which, in the end maintains a white affective economy. As resilience theory flourishes in many western societies, it forces these societies to overlook the oppressive behaviors, actions, and even emotions of whiteness and, by doing so, also forces a state of psychological manipulation whereby the psychologization of resilience is enforced. This 'psychologization of social problems not only pathologizes social problems as individual psychological deficiencies or traits, but also obscures the recognition of serious structural inequalities and ideological commitments that perpetuate social injustices in higher education' (ibid., p. 1971). In this sense, vulnerable populations, like Black and Brown students in the U.S. context or nonwhite students in other western societies, are emotionally blamed for their lack of educational attainment, disregarding how schools may function in ways that strategically leave behind Black and Brown children (Leonardo, 2009).

Examining more deeply, this psychologization of resilience is a dangerous affective weapon used to subjugate Black affect while elevating white emotionalities above all. In a sense, this emotional maneuver is enforcing a state of forever gaslighting whereby the victims of racial oppression are made to internalize societal racial oppression. Consider, for instance, how faculty of Color in teacher education programs are gaslit to feel as if they are the problem when issues of race come about in higher education (Choudhury, 2017). The academy, despite its pontificated commitment to diversity, often fails truly to achieve its said goal, and this delusion steeped in narcissistic grandeur, then makes it 'easy to gaslight minorities into doubting their experiences of exclusion and unfair treatment' (470). For faculty of Color this racial gaslighting, otherwise racelighting per Wood and Harris (2021), 'lead[s] BIPOC [faculty] to doubt themselves and their abilities'

(12), as if they are forced to internalize racialized presumptions of incompetence (see Gutierrez y Muh et al., 2012). And, in raising doubt the white affective economy is maintained because instead of realizing the real issues of race, racism, whiteness, and white supremacy, this process allows for systems to then pass off their accountability for upholding systemic racism. As Mills (2007) argues, this becomes another emotional maneuver employed to strategically feign white racial ignorance. Whilst this happens, systemic racism is individualized towards the victim; a process that then turns around and blames Black and Brown faculty for their experiences of racial oppression. Clearly, Black affect is rendered useless in a system that continues to promulgate white emotional homeostasis and cater to white emotions. And, when this happens the racial contract, per Mills (1997), is not only maintained. Indeed, it is also psychologized in ways where white emotionalities are the standard for emotional homeostasis.

Implications and conclusion

This article has explored how the emotionalities of whiteness play a significant role in the ways that white racial ignorance is reproduced in teacher education settings. In particular, we have suggested that the affectivity of whiteness is a key site in which to examine white racial ignorance in teacher education. Extending Mills (2007) seminal work on white supremacy as a racialized sociopolitical system of power and bringing it in conversation with affect theory (its phenomenological branch), we have particularly emphasized how this system produces racialized affects that have crucial implications for teacher education. Researching the social, political and affective dimensions of the emotionalities of whiteness in teacher education is significant, because these affects constantly reproduce white racial ignorance throughout western societies. Specifically, paying attention to how white emotionalities evolve and reproduce themselves in teacher education settings illuminates how whiteness maneuvers through various strategies (e.g. All Lives Matter; weaponizing white tears). Our theorization here, then, builds on previous work about how emotionality has perpetuated Whiteness in teacher education by turning attention to the importance of recognizing Black affects in struggles to disrupt white racial ignorance. Researching racialized affects enables the recognition of Black affects and the struggles of racialized minorities to challenge the emotional imperialism of white supremacy.

To that end, systematic empirical research is needed to examine the various formations of racialized affects in various teacher education settings, and particularly ways of intervening that interrogate white affective economies. A focus on racialized affects adds complexity to existing theories of critical whiteness studies in education (see Matias, 2022; Matias & Boucher, 2021) while also identifying how to move white teachers from racial ignorance toward racial consciousness – a deeply affective process that requires affective disinvestment to racial ideology. However, asking how to compel white teachers or teacher educators to care deeply about people of Color and racial injustice is deeply challenging (cf. Hartzell, 2020), because white feelings have long been centered in mainstream discourse on race and racism. Hence, the point is not to dismiss the tendency of white emotionalities to maintain white comfort, but rather to also highlight that Black affects are recognized, shedding light to new solidarities that could emerge from the experiences of racialized populations. Scholars of critical whiteness studies, then, must grapple with the messy relationship among whiteness, affect and (anti-) racism (Hartzell, 2020), not only to identify productive possibilities emerging from attending to white emotionalities in teacher education, but also to honor Black affects and discover ways of challenging the emotional hegemony of white supremacy.

Our theoretical analysis has two important implications for future research and theory in teacher education. First, our analysis suggests the usefulness of a theoretical framework that explicitly examines the affective mechanisms of racialization in teacher education, especially in relation to white supremacy. After Maiese (2022), white supremacy has to be understood as an affective milieu, that is, an affective and embodied phenomenon that shapes how racist habits are formed over the course of learning and ongoing affective engagement in the context of various social settings, including teacher education settings. The affects of racialization, then, need to be a central focus of empirical research, hence the phenomenology of whiteness and affectivity can be a useful frame to name and begin to understand the process of white teachers' emotionalities as well as the affective complexities that characterize intersubjective connections with racialized populations. This means also that new methodological designs must be developed that account for the relational, material, phenomenological, and historically situated character of racialized affects (Blickstein, 2019).

Second, affective analyses of racialization in teacher education can challenge scholars in critical whiteness studies to develop a more intersectional understanding of how white emotionalities and Black affects are intertwined – a reality that is ignored when white emotionalities are foregrounded, while Black affects are backgrounded. Conceptualizing the intertwinement of Black and white affectivity helps shed light on how persistent affective habits in teacher education generate and sustain white racial ignorance patterns and in turn how to break those habits (Zembylas, 2021b). As Mills (2007) has shown, racialized habits are deeply engrained affective habits that often obscure the workings of oppression and white privilege, making it difficult to dismantle them. And yet, unless educators, activists, and other stakeholders find ways of intervention that can begin to truly challenge those affective habits, even if the cracks are small, it will be impossible to break the hegemony of the affective economy of whiteness in various social domains, including teacher education. Many small cracks will eventually become bigger, threatening the emotional imperialism of white supremacy.

Notes

1. Charles Mills was a professional mentor who became a good friend of mine. I, along with many others, am still mourning his death and still cry writing this. Therefore, I mean no disrespect in calling him by his first name. It is how I remember him.
2. Foucault (2003, 2008) explains that biopolitics is concerned with how individual bodies and populations are subjected to self-discipline through technologies of power like reporting, surveillance and other techniques that aim at submission and docility.
3. We wish to clarify that our goal here is not to provide any phenomenological data from any empirical study, but rather to introduce the phenomenological approach in affect theory as the conceptual framework that guides our theoretical analysis.
4. Gaslighting is a form of emotional and psychological manipulation that attempts to engage in crazymaking, whereby the victim begins to doubt their own reality.

Special note

To Charles, you are missed.

Disclosure statement

No potential conflict of interest was reported by the authors.

ORCID

Michalinos Zembylas ⓘ http://orcid.org/0000-0001-6896-7347

References

Agathangelou, A. 2019. "Sexual Affective Empires: Racialized Speculations and Wagers in the Affective IR Turn." In *Methodology and Emotion in International Relations*, edited by E. V. Rythoven, 205–220. New York: Routledge.

Ahmed, S. 2004a. *The Cultural Politics of Emotion*. Edinburgh: University of Edinburgh Press.

Ahmed, S. 2004b. "Declarations of Whiteness: The Non-Performativity of Anti-Racism." *Borderlands E-Journal* 3 (2).

Ahmed, S. 2006. *Queer Phenomenology: Orientations, Objects, Others*. Durham, NC: Duke University Press.

Ahmed, S. 2007. "A Phenomenology of Whiteness." *Feminist Theory* 8 (2): 149–168. doi:10.1177/1464700107078139.

Ahmed, S. 2010. *The Promise of Happiness*. Durham, NC: Duke University Press.

Allen, R. L. 2009. "What About Poor White People?" In *Handbook of Social Justice in Education*, edited by W. Ayers, T. Quinn, and D. Stovall, 209–230. Abingdon: Routledge.

Althusser, L. 2006. "Ideology and the Ideological State Apparatuses (Notes Towards an Investigation)." In *The Anthropology of the State: A Reader*, edited by A. Sharma and A. Gupta, 86–111. Malden, MA: Blackwell Publishing. Original work published 1971.

Anderson, C. 2016. *White Rage: The Unspoken Truth of Our Racial Divide*. New York: Bloomsbury.

Arday, J. 2018. "Dismantling Power and Privilege Through Reflexivity: Negotiating Normative Whiteness, the Eurocentric Curriculum and Racial Micro-Aggressions Within the Academy." *Whiteness and Education* 3 (2): 141–161. doi:10.1080/23793406.2019.1574211.

Berg, U., and A. Ramos-Zayas. 2015. "Racializing Affect: A Theoretical Proposition." *Current Anthropology* 56 (5): 654–677. doi:10.1086/683053.

Blickstein, T. 2019. "Affects of Racialization." In *Affective Societies: Key Concepts*, edited by J. Slaby and C. Scheve, 152–165. London: Routledge.

Bonilla-Silva, E. 2014. *Racism Without Racists: Color-Blind Racism and the Persistence of Racial Inequality in America*. 4th ed. Lanham, MD: Rowman & Littlefield Publishers.

Bonilla-Silva, E. 2019. "Feeling Race: Theorizing the Racial Economy of Emotions." *American Sociological Review* 84 (1): 1–25. doi:10.1177/0003122418816958.

Choudhury, C. A. 2017. "In the Shadow of Gaslight: Reflections on Identity, Diversity, and the Distribution of Power in the Academy." *CUNY Law Review* 20 (2): 467–480.

Cornish, S. 2015. Kentucky County Clerk Kim Davis is No Martin Luther King Jr. AFRO News. September, 16. https://afro.com/kentucky-county-clerk-kim-davis-is-no-martin-luther-king-jr/

Darder, A. 1998. Teaching as an Act of Love: Reflections on Paulo Freire and His Contributions to Our Lives and Our Work. Paper presented at the American Educational Research Association, San Diego, CA.

Delgado, R., Ed. 1995. *Critical Race Theory: The Cutting Edge*. Philadelphia: Temple University Press.

Delgado, R., and J. Stefancic. 2001. *Critical Race Theory*. New York: New York University Press.

DiAngelo, R. 2011. "White Fragility." *International Journal of Critical Pedagogy* 3 (3): 54–70.

Foucault, M. 2003. *Society Must Be Defended: Lectures at the Collège de France, 1975-1976*. New York: Picador.

Foucault, M. 2008. *The Birth of Biopolitics: Lectures at the Collège de France, 1978-1979*. New York: Picador.

Garcia-Rojas, C. 2017. "(Un)disciplined Futures: Women of Color Feminism as a Disruptive to White Affect Studies." *Journal of Lesbian Studies* 21 (3): 254–271. doi:10.1080/10894160.2016. 1159072.

Gillborn, D. 2010. "Reform, Racism and the Centrality of Whiteness: Assessment, Ability and the 'New eugenics'." *Irish Educational Studies* 29 (3): 231–252. doi:10.1080/03323315.2010.498280.

Guilmette, L. 2019. "Unsettling the Coloniality of the Affects: Transcontinental Reverberations Between Teresa Brennan and Sylvia Wynter." *philoSophia* 9 (1): 73–91. doi:10.1353/phi.2019. 0014.

Hartman, S. 1997. *Scenes of Subjection: Terror, Slavery, and Self-Making in Nineteenth-Century America*. New York: Oxford University Press.

Hartman, S. 2007. *Lose Your Mother: A Journey Along the Atlantic Slave Route*. New York: Farrar, Straus and Giroux.

Hartzell, S. 2020. ""Whiteness Feels Good here": Interrogating White Nationalist Rhetoric on Stormfront." *Communication and Critical/Cultural Studies* 17 (2): 129–148. doi:10.1080/ 14791420.2020.1745858.

Jackson, J. L., Jr. 2008. *Racial Paranoia: The Unintended Consequences of Political Correctness*. New York: Basic Books.

Johnson, L. L., N. Bryan, and G. Boutte. 2019. "Show Us the Love: Revolutionary Teaching in (Un) critical Times." *The Urban Review* 51 (1): 46–64. doi:10.1007/s11256-018-0488-3.

Karakurt, G., and K. E. Silver. 2013. "Emotional Abuse in Intimate Relationships: The Role of Gender and Age." *Violence and Victims* 28 (5): 804–821. doi:10.1891/0886-6708.VV-D-12-00041.

Khanna, N. 2020. *The Visceral Logics of Decolonization*. Durham, NC: Duke University Press.

Leonardo, Z. 2009. *Race, Whiteness, and Education*. New York: Routledge.

Leonardo, Z., and M. Zembylas. 2013. "Whiteness as Technology of Affect: Implications for Educational Theory and Praxis." *Equity & Excellence in Education* 46 (1): 150–165. doi:10. 1080/10665684.2013.750539.

Maiese, M. 2022. "White Supremacy as an Affective Milieu." *Topoi* 41 (5): 905–915. doi:10.1007/ s11245-022-09805-1.

Matias, C. 2016. *Feeling White: Whiteness, Emotionality and Education*. Rotterdam, The Netherlands: Sense Publishers.

Matias, C. 2022. "Towards a Black Whiteness Studies: A Response to the Growing Field." *International Journal of Qualitative Studies in Education* 1–11. doi:https://doi.org/10.1080/ 09518398.2022.2025482.

Matias, C. E. 2020. "Ripping Our Hearts: Three Counterstories on Terror, Threat, and Betrayal in US Universities." *International Journal of Qualitative Studies in Education* 33 (2): 250–262.

Matias, C., and C. Boucher. 2021. "From Critical Whiteness Studies to a Critical Study of Whiteness: Restoring Criticality in Critical Whiteness Studies." *Whiteness and Education* 8 (1): 64–81. doi:10.1080/23793406.2021.1993751.

Matias, C. E., and P. M. Newlove. 2017. "Better the Devil You See, Than the One You don't: Bearing Witness to Emboldened En-Whitening Epistemology in the Trump Era." *International Journal of Qualitative Studies in Education* 30 (10): 920–928.

Matias, C., and M. Zembylas. 2014. ""When Saying You Care is Not Really caring": Emotions of Disgust, Whiteness Ideology and Teacher Education." *Critical Studies in Education* 55 (3): 319–337. doi:10.1080/17508487.2014.922489.

Mills, C. 1997. *The Racial Contract*. Ithaca, NY: Cornell University Press.

Mills, C. 2007. "White Ignorance." In *Race and Epistemologies of Ignorance*, edited by S. Sullivan and N. Tuana, 11–38. New York: State University of New York Press.

Moreton-Robinson, A. 2015. *The White Possessive: Property, Power, and Indigenous Sovereignty.* Minneapolis, MN: University of Minnesota Press.

Newby, R. G., and D. E. Newby. 1995. "The Bell Curve: Another Chapter in the Continuing Political Economy of Racism." *The American Behavioral Scientist* 39 (1): 12–24. doi:10.1177/0002764295039001003.

Ngai, S. 2005. *Ugly Feelings.* Boston, MA: Harvard University Press.

Nieto, S. 2003. *What Keeps Teachers Going?.* New York: Teachers College Press.

Palmer, T. 2017. ""What Feels More Than feeling?" Theorizing the Unthinkability of Black Affect." *Critical Ethnic Studies* 3 (2): 31–56. doi:10.5749/jcritethnstud.3.2.0031.

Said, E. 2000. *Reflections on Exile and Other Essays.* Boston, MA: Harvard University Press.

Schaefer, D. 2015. *Religious Affects: Animality, Evolution, and Power.* Durham, NC: Duke University Press.

Schaefer, D. 2019. *The Evolution of Affect Theory: The Humanities, the Sciences, and the Study of Power.* Cambridge, UK: Cambridge University Press.

Schuller, K. 2018. *The Biopolitics of Feeling: Race, Sex, and Science in the Nineteenth Century.* Durham, NC: Duke University Press.

Seigworth, G. J., and M. Gregg. 2010. "An Inventory of Shimmers." In *The Affect Theory Reader*, edited by M. Gregg and G. J. Seigworth, 2–25. Durham, NC: Duke University Press.

Slaby, J., and R. Mühlhoff. 2019. "Affect." In *Affective Societies: Key Concepts*, edited by J. Slaby and C. von Scheve, 27–41. London: Routledge.

Sleeter, C. 2016. "Wrestling with Problematics of Whiteness in Teacher Education." *International Journal of Qualitative Studies in Education* 29 (8): 1065–1068. doi:10.1080/09518398.2016.1174904.

Sleeter, C. E. 2001. "Preparing Teachers for Culturally Diverse Schools: Research and the Overwhelming Presence of Whiteness." *Journal of Teacher Education* 52 (2): 94–106. doi:10.1177/0022487101052002002.

Sleeter, C. E. 2017. "Critical Race Theory and the Whiteness of Teacher Education." *Urban Education* 52 (2): 155–169. doi:10.1177/0042085916668957.

Stewart, K. 2007. *Ordinary Affects.* Durham, NC: Duke University Press.

Stoler, A. L. 1995. *Race and the Education of Desire: Foucault's History of Sexuality and the Colonial Order of Things.* Durham, NC: Duke University Press.

Stoler, A. L. 2002. *Carnal Knowledge and Imperial Power: Race and the Intimate in Colonial Rule.* Berkeley, CA: University of California Press.

Stoler, A. L. 2010. *Along the Archival Grain: Epistemic Anxieties and Colonial Common Sense.* Princeton: Princeton University Press.

Sullivan, S. 2006. *Revealing Whiteness: The Unconscious Habits of Racial Privilege.* Bloomington, IN: Indiana University Press.

Van Dijk, T. A. 2006. "Discourse and Manipulation." *Discourse & Society* 17 (3): 359–383. doi:10.1177/0957926506060250.

Weheliye, A. 2014. *Habeas Viscus: Racializing Assemblages, Biopolitics, and Black Feminist Theories of the Human.* Durham, NC: Duke University Press.

Wood, L., and F. Harris. 2021. Racelighting in the Normal Realities of Black, Indigenous, and People of Color: A Scholarly Brief. http://bmmcoalition.com/wp-content/uploads/2021/03/Racelighting-BRIEF-2021-3.pdf

Y Muhs, G. G., Y. F. Niemann, C. G. González, and A. P. Harris, Eds. 2012. *Presumed Incompetent: The Intersections of Race and Class for Women in Academia.* Boulder, CO: University Press of Colorado.

Zembylas, M. 2021a. "Against the Psychologization of Resilience: Towards an Onto-Political Theorization of the Concept and Its Implications for Higher Education." *Studies in Higher Education* 46 (9): 1966–1977. doi:10.1080/03075079.2019.1711048.

Zembylas, M. 2021b. "Transforming Habits of Inattention to Structural Racial Injustice in Educational Settings: A Pedagogical Framework That Pays Attention to the Affective Politics of Habit." *Emotion, Space and Society* 40: 100817. doi:10.1016/j.emospa.2021.100817.

Zembylas, M. 2022. "Sylvia Wynter, Racialized Affects, and Minor Feelings: Unsettling the Coloniality of the Affects in Curriculum and Pedagogy." *Journal of Curriculum Studies* 54 (3): 336–350. doi:10.1080/00220272.2021.1946718.

Expectations as property of white supremacy: the coloniality of ascriptive expectations within the Racial Contract

Daniel D. Liou ⓘ

ABSTRACT

To celebrate and honor Charles Mills' intellectual legacy in social science and political philosophy, this paper utilizes the racial contract as an analytical lens to both extend his work and reenvision the field of the sociology of expectations. In doing so, this paper draws on Mills' idea of the epistemological contract to theorize the term expectations as a form of epistemological violence associated with coloniality. The contractarian perspective suggests that the appearances and realities of inclusion and exclusion in social institutions are co-constituted in defining the coloniality of being between the signatories and the subjugated and in forming the ascriptive expectational status quo. Through a historical and contemporary analysis of policies and practices in the United States, this paper calls for further inquiries and moral outrage concerning coloniality and the intersecting dimensions of structurally, relationally, and knowledgeably ascriptive expectations.

Introduction

An 'expectation' is commonly understood as a standard with a minimum of requirements that measures success or as an individualistic social practice of discerning one's interactions with others that may induce acts of discrimination and implicit bias (Rist 2000). For decades, expectancy research has greatly contributed to our understanding of the pernicious impact of educators' racialized expectations, which are one of the most direct and powerful influences in creating student outcomes (Brophy and Good 1970; Delpit 2012; Landsman 2004; Clark and Weinstein 2008; Milner 2021; Nieto 2004; Steele 2011; Weinstein 2009). This body of research has mainly focused on educators' thoughts, decisions, and behaviors and has yet to fully contextualize such expectations as a distinct property of white supremacy. To further expectancy research, I draw on Charles Mills (2014) seminal work, *The Racial Contract*, to reenvision the sociology of expectations in schools and society. Specifically, this paper generates insight into how expectations for one's intellectual superiority and inferiority are authored into the racial contract, functioning as a form of coloniality in regulating racial hierarchies within the global systems of white supremacy (Allen 2001). With the following question, I attempt to contextualize the work of expectations to deal more directly with white supremacy:

How does the racial contract weaponize the sociology of expectations in steering individuals into the ascriptive hierarchies of society?

Because whiteness is the assumed racial default for societal expectations, it is necessary to deploy a contractarian perspective to further expand the study of expectations as an epistemological force and social practice in the production of racial common sense (Omi and Winant 2018). As expectancy researchers, we often explore expectations without fundamentally exposing their logic and purpose. These prescriptive dimensions of expectations include what expectations are based on; who sets the terms and guidelines for acceptable knowledge and behaviors; the premise with which such expectations are superimposed through policies and incentive structures; and how the ethics of expectancies shape individuals' ways of thinking, knowing, and being. Exploring these important features of expectations can help us further understand the performative and contradictory aspects of expectations. Exploring these particularities of expectations can give us further insight on why whiteness continues to be a psychological and emotional default despite educators' good intentions to ameliorate racial injustices (Milner 2021).

Through this article, I look to broaden the scope of expectancy research by using the racial contract as a framework to question the embedded logic. First, I turn to the racial contract in setting the terms within which the sociology of expectations functions as an arbiter for social policies and engagement. As such, the racial contract activates expectations by assigning colonial values to discern personhood, giving conscious and unconscious preference to whiteness in the making of social institutions. Second, from this contractarian perspective, I reconceptualize expectations as not merely individualized thoughts and decisions in the forms of stereotypes or implicit bias. Rather, the behavioral analysis of low expectations masks the fact that these expectations are deeply entrenched and institutionalized (Liou, Leigh, Rotheram-Fuller, and Deits Cutler 2019). As such, expectations play a central role in determining the racial structure, race relations, and knowledge systems. I contend that expectations produce and perpetuate injustices as they serve as the eyes of coloniality, carrying out a course of actions bound by the racial contract.

Third, in the continual construction of a hierarchical white supremacist society, in this article I provide examples of public policies and laws that set expectations for subsequent courses of action. Concurrently, the racial contract structurally and epistemologically influences interpretations of and interactions with policies and laws. Embedded in the racial contract, this paper engages in fuller dialogue and recognize three important features of expectations that are hierarchical at their core: *structural, relational, and knowledge ascriptions*. In doing so, the aim of this article is to extend the racial contract theory as a framework to provide an analysis of the structural, relational, and epistemological ordering in expectancy effects in schools and society.

Using the racial contract as an expectancy framework

Before going into expectancy research, I forefront Mills (2014) racial contract theory to shed light on how his work can significantly influence the reconceptualization of expectations. To begin with, as an analytical lens, the racial contract exposes the policies, laws, and practices of dehumanization that have been central to the racial struggles against white supremacy. Mills (2014) existential claims of white supremacy further give meaning to the multidimensionality of race consciousness, wherein the human-subhuman dialectic brings structural and relational hierarchies into existence. His racial contract theory challenges classical accounts of the social contract by suggesting that the political philosophy of justice is deceitful when it does not account for the racialized history of society. Based on this premise, the normative social contract fraudulently suggests that all law-abiding citizens are treated individualistically and fairly, with the promise of the Protestant work ethic giving equal chances to obtain the American Dream. In truth, the race-neutral notions of the social contract mask the rights and privileges of whiteness as the gold standard for being fully human, a moral and patriotic citizen, and a high-potential student (Leonardo and Broderick 2011). As such, the political systems give inalienable rights to whiteness through discovery and conquest, and the naturalization of these unmarked political and material advantages is assumed and cannot be legally challenged (Allen and Liou 2019; López 2006).

Under the racial contract, people across intersectional markers of difference are born, assigned, and subjugated into a contract of domination via forms of white supremacy. Mills (2014) scholarship sheds light on the affordances of human rights, delineating between a whitestream social contract consensually agreed upon amongst Whites and a racial contract of exclusion and resistance imposed upon People of Color. According to Mills (2014), the racist violation of the social contract upholds the basis for the racial contract, wherein laws are perceived to be fair and just while insufficiently confronting racism as individual acts of discrimination. Such forms of racial divisions and subjugation include state-sanctioned genocide, slavery, indentured servitude, and restrictive covenants (Mills 2014).

In turn, people subjugated to the racial contract are subordinated through laws and policies that regulate them as subhuman. The nature of the racial contract is hierarchical and extractive (Mills 2014), meaning that People of Color are disproportionately confined to inferior schooling, employment opportunities, work conditions, housing, and other socioeconomic hierarchies to maintain the racialization of labor (Bonacich, Alimahomed, and Wilson 2008; Purifoy and Seamster 2021). The basis of such a contract, decenters the knowledge of People of Color by reproducing neoliberal knowledge systems that are exploitative and ascriptive at its core. For this reason, People of Color, especially those who are migrants and immigrants, are consistently economically exploited and politically scapegoated around the world (Koyama and Gonzalez-Doğan 2021).

Although there is no legitimate biological basis to the notions of race and intelligence (Omi and Winant 2018), the ideological and categorical concepts of race are central to the construction and evolution of the social contract. As such, Mills (2014) argues that the rationality of whiteness is concealed as an unmarked category and a commonly accepted value in adhering to humanism. In describing whiteness as property, Harris (1993) contends that whiteness functions as a valorization for expectations in institutional life. Harris (1993) explains the settled expectations that underlie racial hierarchy,

> In ways so embedded that it is rarely apparent, the set of assumptions, privileges, and benefits that accompany the status of being white have become a valuable asset that whites sought to protect and that those who passed sought to attain—by fraud if necessary. Whites have come to expect and rely on these benefits, and over time these expectations have been affirmed, legitimated, and protected by the law (p. 1713).

Under the racial contract, the advantages of whiteness delineate differences through an expectation of negation, facilitated by the simultaneities of disability, gender, immigration status, sexuality, social class, and religion (Collins 2018; Lorde 2012). Any distinction from the whitestream social contract functions as an appraisal of one's humanness, coalesced into the dichotomy between Whites and People of Color (Mills 2014).

The political construction of race is part of the structural ascription that socializes People of Color into the interlocking systems of domination through state-sanctioned knowledge (Collins 2018; Lorde 2012). Through whiteness, expectations are utilized as a moral compass to objectively interpret society, constructing a racial structure that naturalizes White people's pursuits of their own racial interests (Bonilla-Silva 2015). The functioning of the racial contract requires the deployment of racist expectations to diminish the basic human dignity of the racially subjugated, giving legitimacy to white supremacy (Fanon 2005).

Expectations as a property of white supremacy: a literature review

In the following, I draw on the fields of political philosophy, ethnic studies, social psychology, and critical multicultural education to theorize the term expectations. The intent underlying this approach is not to diminish the importance of school-centric expectations. Rather, I intentionally blur those lines because the racial contract is pervasive. It requires a society to constantly educate its peoples through law and social policies regarding the ways they are raced in direct comparison to the racialization of Others (Allen 2009). It is within these discussions that I contextualize expectations and its influence on schooling.

By building on Mills' work (Mills 2014), I am extending the scope and status of the racial contract theory to include the role of expectations in the ascriptive dimension of society. Since current notions of diversity have largely focused on the biological representation of non-whites without recognizing the centricity of whiteness in social institutions, the use of the term ascription becomes necessary to contextualize expectations and its racist manifestations. In applying these concepts to education, Leonardo (2013) illuminates how school-based inequities are predicated on two fundamentally different sets of standards, wherein White students are treated as fully capable while Students of Color are racially profiled in the opposite. Given that education is a form of racial contract (Leonardo 2015), the curricular expectations of the school system also sort and socialize students into the ascriptive hierarchies of society (Allen and Liou 2019; Leonardo 2013). By extending the notion from descriptive to ascriptive, I contend that the whitestream social contract, both real and imagined, cannot exist without the racial contract. As neither can be understood without the other, I build on Mills' legacy by exposing the contractual logic of expectations in generating social standings, and the making and remaking of the structural, relational, and knowledge ascriptions of race.

According to Campbell (1999), humans are constantly expectant, and these expectations are based on present knowledge, norms, and assumptions anchored by dominant ideologies. Moreover, an expectation can be described as the anticipatory sensor for operating within the existing society while also a process by which the status quo is reproduced. As a part of coloniality, settled expectations provide the psychic conditioning for developing racial algorithms of domination and resistance in the everyday politics of relative rights, power, and worthiness of individuals (Campbell 1999). Within the interlocking systems of oppression, settled expectations play a significant role in sustaining the normative dimension of society.

In the United States, ability to include and exclude others is based on the power of expectations, which can be institutionalized and made into law. The 1790 Nationality Act defines U.S. citizens as 'free White persons', which continues to serve as a lens for how one is publicly perceived and identified. The institutionalized perceptions of citizenship often work in tandem with white nationalism and nativist sentiments in shaping societal expectations regarding existence and membership within social institutions. In the United States, racial attitudes distinguishing White Americans from the foreign Others are evident in the historical and contemporary treatment of racial groups such as Asian Americans. The 1854 California Supreme Court decision on *People vs. Hall* effectively barred Chinese people, along with people of African and Indigenous descent, from testifying in court against White people (People v. Hall 1854). Later, the 1882 Chinese Exclusion Act effectively banned immigration from the majority of Asia while rendering the population ineligible for naturalization (Takaki 2012).

Takao Ozawa, who was born in Japan but grew up in the United States, challenged the racial contract for his rights to be naturalized as a citizen in the 1922 U.S. Supreme Court decision *Ozawa v. the United States* (López 2006; Matias 2016). The high court did not consider him to biologically meet the definition of a free White person, despite his English fluency, Christian beliefs, and high educational attainment. One year later, Bhagat Singh Thind, a Sikh American who served in the U.S. army, was denied citizenship in the 1923 U.S. Supreme Court case *United States v. Bhagat Singh Thind*, as it was determined that he failed to meet the cultural definition of a White American (López 2006; Matias 2016). The 1944 *Fred Korematsu v. The United States* U.S. Supreme Court case showed that, despite citizenship status, Japanese Americans were treated with suspicion during World War II (Korematsu 2020). As such, the legal definitions of being White naturalize social expectations that whiteness is to be upheld and defended as a status and a value system (López 2006). The historic anti-miscegenation laws in the U.S. were one of the ways whiteness was politically inflated and envisioned as a biological status to be kept Whites separate from others (López 2006). Despite individual pursuits of whiteness, these court cases also demonstrate that one's racially subordinated position cannot be altered precisely because of the racial contract (Allen 2009).

Even now, Asian Americans' experiences with the racial contract are largely overlooked through their permanent status either as immigrants or as post-racial model minorities, minimizing their political struggles and achievements within the dominant civil rights discourse (Covarrubias and Liou 2014). To this day, their physical and verbal expressions are largely exaggerated as exotic, and as a continual threat to U.S. national security (Korematsu 2020). At the same time, Asian Americans' model minority status conceptualizes them as capable of acquiring whiteness, even though the Ozawa and Singh decisions cast this population as perpetual outsiders (Matias 2016). For this reason, Asian Americans have been racially valorized while ostracized by the racial contract, obscuring their racial positioning while eliminating their ability to be politically self-reliant (Kim 1999).

The American judicial systems have clearly demonstrated that the rights and entitle-ments of People of Color are non-binding and that the racial contract can arbitrarily mutate and correct itself by using whiteness to recalibrate the terms of the contract. By defining the fit and unfit characteristics of a full human being, these social policies and laws have generated expectational parameters in outlining acceptable behaviors within the racial contract. Further, the legal and political constructions of People of Color as subhuman are an epistemological distortion that decenter their knowledge systems. Since such expectations are institutionalized and systemic, the reset button within the racial contract is designed to nullify antiracist and other anti-oppressive resistance, reaffirming white supremacy.

Harris (1993) emphasizes that the irrationality of whiteness is an epistemological distortion of ancestral knowledge and a systematic negation of subjugated knowledge. The historical ideals of white citizenship relegate People of Color to unrealistic expecta-tions to obtain whiteness as a precondition for gaining their freedom. In order to rationalize this part of the epistemological racial contract, school systems assume a normative function in animating curricular expectations to establish political and knowledge structures of society (Allen and Liou 2019; Liou and Deits Cutler 2020). These curricular expectations include the centering of Eurocentrism in the process of knowledge production (Wayne, Brown, and Calderón 2016), the implementation of disciplinary policies to insist students' behavioral compliance to facilitate the racial school-to-prison pipeline (Lomotey and Kendra 2015), and a disproportionate number of Students of Color assigned to vocational and special education (Artiles 2019). In the process of constructing the racial common sense, schools draw on race-evasive frame-works of social policies and the law in conditioning Whites and People of Color with settled expectations about the nature of society. Settled expectations are then deployed in the dual role of protecting the educational advantages of White populations and socializ-ing the racial Others with the educational racial contract (Leonardo 2013).

As the basis of the educational racial contract, school systems are required to comply with state-sanctioned knowledge in the organization of learning and teaching. The persistence of low educational expectations has significant consequences for Students of Color. Expectations have been well documented in the forms of pedagogy, capturing the subtle and explicit verbal and physical expressions manifested based on one's beliefs and values, shaping their relationships with racial and gendered others (Rist 2000). In this context, researchers have traditionally defined expectations at the micro-level study of classrooms consisting of the following dynamics between students and teachers: (1) one's individualistic biases and attitudes activated to influence social contingencies (Steele 2011); (2) a set of measurable psychological responses to meeting standards and yielded results, such as students' test scores (Clark and Weinstein 2008); (3) one's beliefs and prognosis of future happenings (Rubie-Davies et al. 2020); (4) emotions that influence one's decision-making into a range of predicted possibilities (Campbell 1999); (5) the stated and unstated rules of conduct within organizational environments (Liou and Rotheram-Fuller 2019); (6) policy priorities shaped by expectations which then set expectations to act toward expected outcomes (Garcia 2022); and (7) the knowledge structure of expecting (Campbell 1999). When expectations are operative in schools, teachers' racialized belief and disbelief in students' intellectual capacity are the leading cause of educational inequities (Holbrook 2006).

Educators and scholars alike have been attempting to foster equity-oriented approaches to expectancy practices as a strategy to reduce deficit mindsets and implicit bias. Starting with Edmonds (1979) effective school research, organizational practices of high expectations are considered an important correlate for the success of Students of Color. More recently, a growing body of research has shown high expectancy is related to the practice of cultural relevant pedagogy (Aronson and Laughter 2016; Ladson-Billings 2021), warm demanders (Bondy et al. 2013), sympathetic touch (Terry et al. 2014), academic press (Lee and Smith 1999), and academic optimism (Hoy, John Tarter, and Woolfolk Hoy 2006).

While this body of research has greatly repudiated biological and cultural explanations of school failure, expectancy research has remained stagnant in exploring the binaries of 'high' versus 'low' expectations (Rojas and Liou 2023). Instead of exposing how racist expectations are rooted in white supremacy, it is preoccupied with a comparative analysis of success and ways to increase academic achievement under Eurocentric models of education. Such expectations often are fixated on the problem of the expectational gap among the races by using the education of White students as the benchmark for high expectations, which infers the inferiority status of Students of Color. At the same time, this tendency presumes that Students of Color must bear the burden to defy White educators' low expectations in order to exonerate themselves from racist stereotypes. Under meritocracy, the widespread acceptance of the expectational status quo automatically casts Students of Color in a subordinate epistemological position. Such 'achievement' under Eurocentric models of education is to give appearance of a rearrangement of schooling and not a complete transformation towards decoloniality.

Without broadening the scope of expectancy research, falling through the cracks are questions concerning the epistemological origins of these expectations and the role of coloniality in regulating educational practice. Consequently, research that solely draws on normative claims of expectations may have missed the mark in problematizing meritocracy and the colonial purposes of education. These claims have also failed to fully account for the reliance on neoliberal knowledge in teaching technical ways of ameliorating the most perplexing moral, economic, and political problems.

Coloniality of ascriptive expectations: expansion for the racial contract

In the subsequent section, I introduce the concept of the *coloniality of ascriptive expectations* through a contractarian perspective for the purposes of interrogating three distinctive features of education: Structural, relational, and knowledge. Specifically, both Leonardo (2013) and Mills (2014) point to the contractual linkages between race and education and, by extension, an epistemological contract through the racialized expectational status quo that naturalizes racial domination through white epistemological ignorance (Mills 2007, 2015). From an expectational standpoint, the moral dimension of the racial contract implicitly shapes deficit ideologies when looking at a world operating outside of white entitlement (Matias and Boucher 2021). In doing so, it also strengthens the superior status of whiteness as moral (Matias 2016; Matias and Boucher 2021), thus justifying ascriptive expectations using whiteness as the standard for moral deliberations and paternalistic actions (Fanon 2005).

Within the school system, white morality often serves as a source for racial learning and racial conditioning (Matias 2016; Matias and Boucher 2021). For the past decade, my research has focused on White school leaders and their leadership approaches with their own children who are struggling in school. Overwhelmingly, their responses focused on providing support beyond the school day, including tutors for more structured learning time and resources to accelerate learning, all the while expecting that college was still within the realm of possibility. When I asked about support for Students of Color who are experiencing similar difficulties at school, their responses focused on slower instruction, easier assignments, grade retention, and merely expecting such students to graduate high school. While noting these differences in expectations, many school leaders still made moral arguments about the need to 'empathize' with students' experiences outside of school, based on overgeneralized information – such as having parents in jail, experiencing poverty, and cultural disinterest in education – as justifications for their actions and complacency.

In my previous research, some White school leaders considered such practices a part of their social justice work, focusing on alleviating hardships while minimizing students' learning opportunities (Liou and Rotheram-Fuller 2019). Such epistemological ignorance demonstrates a clear disconnect in White educators' distorted sense of antiracist morality and their paternalistic actions to advance their own political interests. Their expectations are more concerned with the work of humanitarianism, the idea of rescuing Students of Color from their racial sufferings, than engaging in the liberatory work of abolitionism (McNeill et al. 2021). Although such moral judgments can serve as stabilizing forces to assume the appropriate actions in life situations, I gradually noticed educators' well-intended expectations can also be misguided by the racial contract.

Coloniality is the hegemonic control over the ways of knowing, being, and social institutions (Quijano 2000). Maldonado-Torres (2007) further explains that coloniality of knowledge is related to the impact of colonization on different areas of knowledge production. Therefore, an essential political project of coloniality is to exert control over the sociology of expectations as a method of sustaining racial order. In this enduring coloniality of race and education, ascriptive expectations is projected upon the racially subjugated, manifesting in three distinctive ways. First, people are born into a world of social injustice consumed by a widely accepted whitestream social contract (Quijano 2000). Second, the political construction of race socializes individuals via schooling associated with the ascriptive social contract, sorting races hierarchically through forced assimilation, gender and economic exploitation, epistemicide, and the distorted Western knowledge systems (Mignolo and Walsh 2018). Third, through the intersubjective dimensions of expectations, racial domination is justified and maintained, resulting in structural and relational systems of ascriptive inequities (Maldonado-Torres 2007). The coloniality of ascriptive expectations constitutes meritocracy with the whitestream social contract to give legitimacy to its ideals. Such mental conditioning keeps people subordinated and forces them to accept the existing hierarchy, based on skin color, as factual and static (Fanon 2005).

Sue et al. (2009) characterize the ascriptions of intelligence as 'White people attribute a degree of intelligence to Students of Color' (p. 186). Bringing this concept into expectancy research, ascription is a form of expectations in assigning social status based on the terms of the racial contract. My usage of 'ascription' is intended to be understood in two fundamental ways: (1) To problematize racist projects and the essentialist frameworks that reduce ascriptive outcomes to those of biology and culture, and (2) To underscore a structural view of ascription in the expectancy practice of white supremacy along with other intersecting and interpersonal forms of domination. That is, ascriptive expectation often activates race and other politically constructed differences as expectational defaults in influencing social practice within the global systems of white supremacy. My discussion of the coloniality of ascriptive expectations is intended to deconstruct this dimension of relational and systematic negation as a part of the racial contract. Such usage of ascription contends that expectations are not power-neutral, wherein individuals are born into a hierarchical world and expected to confront the mechanisms that stratify their racial and other intersectional forms of advantages and disadvantages. This structural conception of ascription does not suggest people are passive participants of coloniality. Rather, it is both a prescribed context and a condition that makes expectations a site for epistemological injustice.

Structural ascription

Bonilla-Silva (2015) defines racial structure as 'a network of social relations at social, political, economic, and ideological levels that shapes the life chances of the various races' (p. 1360). Similarly, *structural ascription* refers to expectations assigning one's material status within the racial contract through ideologies, policies, economic systems, mass media, and social practices. Mills (2014) asserts that the racial contract is a condition of structural relations whereby an expectation serves as the logic for hierarchy and domination. I contend that racist expectations mediate structural ascriptions, which then naturalize Jim Crow-like expectations to perpetuate injustice.

For example, the 1954 U.S. Supreme Court landmark decision *Brown v. The Board of Education of Topeka* attempted to repudiate Jim Crow laws and racially integrate the public school system. During this time, White segregationists actively defied such expectations with racial violence and vigilante actions (Lipsitz 2006). Additionally, Whites leveraged their authorship to rearticulate the terms of the racial contract in the following ways: (1) Establish racial ordinances to exclude People of Color from homeownership in white neighborhoods, (2) Rely on restrictive covenants to legally subjugate People of Color to housing discrimination and keep property in Whites' possessions, (3) Build white enclaves through governmental and private partnerships in creating suburban communities, and (4) Effectively challenge desegregation efforts in the court system and uphold the constitutional rights of White people with the free market, school choice, and local control arguments (Lipsitz 2006; Orfield and Eaton 1996; Reardon and Owens 2014). By leveraging their institutional control over segregation and homeownership, Whites were able to circumvent the *Brown* decision and the 1968 Fair Housing Act. Further, the ways that properties are assessed often are determined by the racial status of the resident instead of its actual value, resulting in Black homes being appraised less and taxed more (Kahrl 2016). The combination of these efforts have also led to the accumulation of intergenerational wealth, which furthered Whites' economic advantages in relations to the racially subjugated (Oliver and Shapiro 2013).

White opposition to racial integration sets the course for racial conflict, especially since strategies and timelines for desegregation were left in the hands of White segregationists. Given that education is only a fundamental right while individual rights are constitutionally guaranteed (Lipsitz 2006), local control became a playbook for Whites to defend their racial advantages. For example, the Supreme Court 1973 decisions on *San Antonio ISD v. Rodriguez* determined that education is not a constitutional right. Therefore, funding inequities created by local property taxes as supplemental revenue between districts and neighborhoods were deemed as lawful and not a form of discrimination. Such structural ascriptions are not protected under the Equal Protection Clause of the Fourteenth Amendment to the United States Constitution, and thus school funding does not require absolute or precise educational equality. In *Milliken v. Bradley* (1974), the Supreme Court once again found that de facto segregation was not a violation of the *Brown* decision (Green and Gooden 2016). Thus, the court deferred their authority over systematically desegregation to the rights of local control and individual's freedom, which abandons its earlier decision to subject districts of strict scrutiny under *Swann v. Charlotte-Mecklenburg Board of Education (1971)*. Specifically, the court decided that racial balance in schools should not be imposed with rigid guidelines or race-conscious policymaking (Green and Gooden 2016). Typically, federal laws supersede state laws. The court's race-neutral stance on desegregation remedies activates structural ascription to ensure that the *Brown* decision does not supplant the racial contract.

The lack of constitutional protections for equitable education further maintains racial segregation by a stratifying housing market, effectively put the burden on communities of color to secure educational justice by themselves. These efforts legally and systematically prohibited Black families and other families of color from home ownership (Rothstein 2017). Through the federal housing policies, whiteness became a basis for social entitlements through the privatization of Indigenous lands for Whites' homeownership, inequitably defining freedom and economic security. Despite the 1968 Fair Housing Act, these restrictive covenants were conceived as a racial project in ensuring whiteness as the prerequisite to owning property, while the government played its part to help suburban Whites privatize homes through low interest mortgages to protect the property values of these neighborhoods and build intergenerational wealth (Rothstein 2017). Lipsitz (2006) describes such public and private partnership as a possessive investment in whiteness, perpetuating structural ascription.

This history of public-private alliance to defeat racial desegregation has maintained Whites as the most segregated group while communities of color are politically and systematically excluded from making key decisions on their students' education (Orfield, Frankenberg, and Lee 2003). The expectations to racially desegregate schools were constantly reverting to White racial interests, while the opportunities to learn for Students of Color must be litigated, further slowing down efforts to making school just and equitable (Orfield, Frankenberg, and Lee 2003). Undoubtedly, I posit structural ascription is one dynamic where the racial contract activates racist expectations in steering individuals into the ascriptive hierarchies of society.

Relational ascription

Inspired by Steele's (2011) concept of the stereotype threat, *relational ascription* refers to social contingencies wherein expectations assign hierarchical values and memberships for individuals, networks, or groups in ways that perpetuate the racial contract. As such, relational ascription shapes the interactions between individuals in constituting racial hierarchy, setting the terms for engagement and appraises one's social status in connection to the Black-White intersubjectivity. Thus, relational ascription functions as a form of expectations in association with: (1) racial selfing and racial othering (Allen 2009) and (2) the emotionality of whiteness (Matias 2016). I argue that an unjust political system, these two interconnected concepts elicit ideologies of superiority and inferiority in driving a sequence of expectations, decision-making, and relationships with others.

Through the continuing legacy of the aforementioned legal decisions and exclusionary residential policies, whiteness functions as the expectational status quo in bringing racial meaning to both the beneficiaries and those who are subordinated to the racial contract. Through structural ascription, the way we see others often constitutes who we think we are and what we can expect of ourselves and of others (Allen 2009). As such, our expectations are externally influenced by systems of racial domination and internally negotiated in discerning our courses of action. Our ability to care for, relate to, love, connect with, and build solidarity with others rests on our level of acceptance with people and how they are related to a range of social issues that are of concern to us. In a normative sense, it is how a social contract in society comes to materialize.

These social arrangements help us understand who we are in relation to Whites and the racial Other, fostering relational ascription based on white supremacist policies and the materiality of race. According to Allen (2009), such dynamic is also known as *racial selfing as racial othering*, defined as the hierarchical construction of the white racial status in direct contrast to the negative construction of the racial Other. That is, if Whites define themselves as normal, moral, and fully human, then People of Color are externally constructed through the images of deficiency and abnormality (Liou and Deits Cutler 2020). Mills (2014) provides the historical context for such relational ascription,

> Whereas slavery was practiced, as in the United States and the Americas, so that a sustained relation between races obtained, whiteness and blackness evolved in a forced intimacy of loathing in which they determine each other by negation and self-recognition in part through the eyes of the other (p. 58).

Through the Black-White dialectic of white supremacy, Whites are perceived as worthy of home loans and home ownership and have the ability to live in exclusive parts of town and attend the most prestigious schools and colleges. Comparatively, People of Color are deemed uncredible, undeserving, and unqualified. Whereas the segregated residential patterns among Whites are attributed to their freedom of choice to move to safer neighborhoods and better schools, the concentration of People of Color in certain communities is negatively perceived as self-segregation and a threat to public safety. While People of Color are profiled as perpetual immigrants and non-English speakers, Whites are seen as legal and English-speaking All-Americans (Kim et al., 2023).

In schools in the United States, the occurrences of racial selfing as racial othering are commonly manifested between students and teachers. As such, school's Title 1 designation, school ranking, and community demographics all serve as racialized cues for educators' sense of responsibilities and classroom expectations. These racialized expectations often influence teachers' beliefs about students' capacities to learn, which elicit emotional and pedagogical interactions based on these white moral judgements (Levin 2014). In turn, the racial othering of students in casting them as less capable also solidifies the teachers' positions as the authorities, creating a cycle of belief and disbelief in perpetuating white supremacist logics of student-teacher relationships (Holbrook 2006; Rist 2000). Although some teachers and school leaders may be committed to anti-deficit and antiracist practices, ultimately, they are still expected to conform to the mechanisms affirming the educational racial contract: test-based standards, punitive disciplinary policies, Eurocentric curriculum, and White parental expectations (Noguera 2003). Even in racially integrated school systems, differences in teachers' expectations continue to be salient in subjugating students to within-school segregation through tracking and ability grouping (Noguera and Wing 2008). The appearance of racial progress is still arranged within the existing system, where relational ascription creates a two-tiered system that treats Students of Color as disposable (Royster 2003).

Expectations are an emotional-eliciting condition (Campbell 1999; Liou and Alvara 2021). The materiality of race can shape and elicit emotions in steering expectations to define the racial self in relation to the racial Other. These emotions are regulated by how people see one another and their behaviors in association with systems of reward and punishment. White emotionality is another form of relational ascription that contributes to the expectational negation of People of Color. According to Matias (2016), white emotionality includes verbal, physical, and other forms of expressions associated with deflections, denials, anger, frustrations, and distress, which are politically constructed to counteract discussions and questionings of the power and privileges connected to whiteness. The images of White Americans lashing out in urging local school boards around the country to ban race-conscious curriculum, White males who carried tiki torches in Charlottesville shouting 'White lives matter', and White males who stormed and attacked the U.S. Capitol on 6 January 2021, to defy presidential election results are all a part of the white emotionality apparatus translating into social practice. In summarizing these events before the House Armed Services Committee, Army General Mark Milley, the Chairman of the Joint Chiefs of Staff, referred to such reactionary resistance as 'white rage'.

Undoubtedly, Milley's congressional testimony is a public recognition of the reality of white rage, which destabilizes the dominant narrative of white victimhood and white innocence that shapes the contemporary anti-Critical Race Theory (CRT) political climate (López et al., 2021; Pollock and Matschiner 2022). Anderson (2016) further elaborates that such emotionality is more than a form of terrorizing violence or white extremism. Rather, it is a subtle and corrosive force embedded within the law and social institutions. For Anderson, white rage is operational not merely in the presence of Black Americans but is conceived as a racial project to deter the advancement of Black populations as their success is considered a direct threat to White people's superior racial status. Beyond its individualistic or relational dimensions, Anderson (2016) expands the definition of white rage by illuminating how such emotionality permeates social institutions in ways that manifest federal, state, and local policies aimed to deter the racial progress of Black Americans.

White rage facilitates racial selfing as racial othering as it triggers emotional responses associated with white nativist and nationalistic moral thinking against antiracist and anti-oppressive efforts. That is, white rage takes the form of white repression of antiracist resistance and is externally co-constituted in reaction to social contingencies where whiteness is challenged (Matias and Allen 2013). Because the racial contract insists whiteness represents all that is good and positive, the occurrence of white rage can never become a persistent stereotype for all White people. However, the same standard does not apply to People of Color as the notions of anger is deeply racialized as a part of the racial contract. White rage forces People of Color to readjust their expectations for antiracism as they must navigate white emotionality and normative expectations of society. For Whites, it is a defensive move through settled expectations to protect the racial contract and how they have come to envision themselves, 'their' schools, 'their' country, and the world. The continual demographic transformation in the United States, diversification of traditionally white spaces and communities, multilingualism and multiculturalism, and social movements such as Black Lives Matter are seen as violations of the racial contract. In its sustainment of America as a white country, white rage has been activated locally and legislatively to ban all forms of race- and gender-conscious teachings while institutionalizing nationalistic views of White racial selfing through racist policymaking (Pollock and Matschiner 2022). In effect, I maintain that ascriptive hierarchies of society are predicated on a racial contract in establishing ascriptive divisions for social relations bounded by race and other intersectional markers of difference.

Knowledge ascription

According to Campbell (1999), settled expectations play a foundational role in structuring the self and 'the relations of expectations to self-stability and racist perceptions' (p. 224). While Eurocentric knowledge of the self and others are written into the racial contract, *knowledge ascription* functions as a form of expectations in constructing the hierarchies of knowledge, especially for the racially and linguistically subjugated. In this case, White people are considered as key holders of knowledge while People of Color are profiled as subknowers (Leonardo 2013). As stated earlier, knowledge of the self induces methods of social engagement in making meaning of the world. To disrupt knowledge ascription, I assert that school curriculum must understand its contractual obligation to the racial contract and reject such terms of engagement through the production of race and anti-oppressive consciousness.

The anti-critical race theory (CRT) organizers' strategies to sustain coloniality are a way of repudiating antiracist expectations in schools and society (Liou and Alvara 2021). By activating the hierarchical arrangements of emotionality, school leaders are expected to account for a few White parents' dependencies on structural advantages and discomfort with race- and gender-conscious curricula. While U.S. society has been consumed by political rhetoric of the anti-CRT agendas, many schools continue to commit epistemological violence through settled expectations (Bang et al. 2012) and distort the experiential knowledge of People of Color (Bell 2019).

As an act of knowledge ascription, anti-CRT organizers have exercised their institutional power to take control of the knowledge produced in schools and libraries, assigning criminality to the teaching of race and gender in the classroom (Liou and Deits Cutler 2023). In the United States, the emotions and knowledge of People of Color are seen as illogical and a detriment to their progress in becoming fully civilized. As a part of knowledge ascription, the emotionality of whiteness is valued as a source of reason that one can weaponize, resulting in significant oversight to control knowledge. In contrast to the emotions of People of Color, White families' discomfort with exposing their children to anti-oppressive curricula, multilingualism in schools, and ethnic studies (Cabrera et al. 2013) is treated as a representative voice for all, legitimating their emotions as factual and undisputable knowledge. Even though many school districts have repudiated accusations of the teaching of CRT, the racial contract's political control over knowledge legitimizes white rage as an unavoidable contingency for school leaders, shifting the context of educators' racial justice work.

For Mills (2014), textbook knowledge are forms of miseducation about the world and indicative of methods of maintaining the racial contract. Under this knowledge industrial complex, People of Color are not considered intellectual equals with Whites (Leonardo 2013). In education, the school systems are still grounded in Eurocentric knowledge, including the ways that race- and gender-conscious texts are interpreted to reinforce ascriptive expectations of People of Color (Author). The epistemological racial contract ensures that Students of Color are compliant with a race-evasive curriculum under the guise of academic standards, orienting them toward Eurocentrism while they learn to racialize others as a method of racializing themselves (Carbado 2002). Within such a system of structural relations, racial othering as racial selfing is an expectancy dynamic within which whites interpret and construct the self and their racial knowledge through Eurocentric curriculum. At the same time, the political processes of constructing racialized others are perpetuated through negative images and narratives in textbooks that legitimize their subordination (Liou and Detis Cutler 2020).

For People of Color, the meritocratic system regulates and undermines the ancestral and experiential knowledge of the racially subjugated, manifesting expectations upholding the conditions of coloniality. Further, the coloniality of ascriptive expectations gives legitimacy to deficit thinking, as its perceptual framework naturalizes the White epistemological contract as universally beneficial, objective, and without bias. In school curriculum, questions regarding the ideologies underlying what students are expected to know, how their racialized history and experiential knowledge with structural and relational ascription are represented in the curriculum, and how the images and narratives within textbooks are interrogated with criticality to construct new social justice knowledge are seldom a part of schools' curriculum audit (Liou and Deits Cutler, 2020). When students do not see themselves reflected with historical accuracy, curricular expectations are consciously and unconsciously utilized as a tool for knowledge ascription and racial subordination (Carbado 2002; Wayne, Brown, and Calderón 2016). In summation, I consider knowledge ascription to uphold the racial contract by hierarchical expectations, sorting society between knowers and subknowers.

Conclusion

Expectations matter. I have seen first-hand how educators define situations influences their practice. If the racial contract sets the term for one's perceptual framework of the world, by consequence, the sociological manifestations of expectations are ascriptive at their core. From my perspective, Mills' work could further inform the existing body of expectancy research and break new ground to more thoughtfully foster corrective epistemological justice. This is a necessary strategy to theoretically and empirically expose the salience of the racial contract in the organization of classrooms, schools, and society. By problematizing expectations as the basis for understanding the inner workings of the racial contract, educators and activists alike can commit to delinking colonial knowledge from education to transform the interconnecting and intersecting points of ascription (Wiggan, Teasdell, and Parsons 2022). There is a pressing need for a critical mass of social justice educators and communities across differences to build coalitions, engage in a reflexive dialogue of moral outrage, and actively work toward the restructuring of the self and ultimately the decoloniality of ascriptive expectations. I believe collective actions are necessary to reject the racial contract, destabilizing the hegemonic dominance of white supremacy.

Disclosure statement

No potential conflict of interest was reported by the author.

ORCID

Daniel D. Liou ⓘ http://orcid.org/0000-0001-5911-0181

References

Alejandro, Covarrubias, and Daniel D. Liou. 2014. "Asian American Education and Income Attainment in the Era of Post-Racial America." *Teachers College Record* 116 (6): 1–38.

Allen, Ricky Lee. 2001. "The Globalization of White Supremacy: Toward a Critical Discourse on the Racialization of the World." *Educational Theory* 51 (4): 467–485. doi:10.1111/j.1741-5446. 2001.00467.x.

Allen, Ricky Lee. 2009. "What About Poor White People?." In *Handbook of Social Justice in Education*, edited byW. Ayers, T. Quinn, and D. Stovall, 227–248. New York: Routledge.

Allen, Ricky Lee, and Daniel D. Liou. 2019. "Managing Whiteness: The Call for Educational Leadership to Breach the Contractual Expectations of White Supremacy." *Urban Education* 54 (5): 677–705. doi:10.1177/0042085918783819.

Anderson, Carol. 2016. *White Rage: The Unspoken Truth of Our Racial Divide*. New York: Bloomsbury.

Aronson, Brittany, and Judson Laughter. 2016. "The Theory and Practice of Culturally Relevant Education: A Synthesis of Research Across Content Areas." *Review of Educational Research* 86 (1): 163–206. doi:10.3102/0034654315582066.

Artiles, Alfredo J. 2019. "Fourteenth Annual Brown Lecture in Education Research: Reenvisioning Equity Research: Disability Identification Disparities as a Case in Point." *Educational Researcher* 48 (6): 325–335. doi:10.3102/0013189X19871949.

Bang, Megan, Beth Warren, Ann Rosebery, and Doug L. Medin. 2012. "Desettling Expectations in Science Education." *Human Development* 55 (5–6): 302–318. doi:10.1159/000345322.

Bell, Sana. 2019. "Critical Race Theory in Education: Analyzing African American Students' Experience with Epistemological Racism and Eurocentric Curriculum." Thesis, DePaul University.

Bonacich, Edna, Sabrina Alimahomed, and Jake B. Wilson. 2008. "The Racialization of Global Labor." *The American Behavioral Scientist* 52 (3): 342–355. doi:10.1177/0002764208323510.

Bondy, Elizabeth, Dorene D. Ross, Elyse Hambacher, and Melanie Acosta. 2013. "Becoming Warm Demanders: Perspectives and Practices of First Year Teachers." *Urban Education* 48 (3): 420–450. doi:10.1177/0042085912456846.

Bonilla-Silva, Eduardo. 2015. "The Structure of Racism in Color-Blind,"post-racial" America." *The American Behavioral Scientist* 59 (11): 1358–1376. doi:10.1177/0002764215586826.

Brophy, Jere E., and Thomas L. Good. 1970. "Teachers' Communication of Differential Expectations for Children's Classroom Performance: Some Behavioral Data." *Journal of Educational Psychology* 61 (5): 365. doi:10.1037/h0029908.

Cabrera, Nolan L., Elisa L. Meza, Andrea J. Romero, and Roberto Cintli Rodríguez. 2013. "'If There is No Struggle, There is No Progress': Transformative Youth Activism and the School of Ethnic Studies." *The Urban Review* 45 (1): 7–22. doi:10.1007/s11256-012-0220-7.

Campbell, Sue. 1999. "Dominant Identities and Settled Expectations." In *Racism and Philosophy*, edited by S. E. Babbitt and S. Campbell, 216–234. Ithaca: Cornell University Press.

Carbado, Devon W. 2002. "Afterword: (E)racing Education." *Equity & Excellence in Education* 35 (2): 181–194. doi:10.1080/10715760100300731.

Clark, McKown, and Rhona S. Weinstein. 2008. "Teacher Expectations, Classroom Context, and the Achievement Gap." *Journal of School Psychology* 46 (3): 235–261. doi:10.1016/j.jsp.2007.05.001.

Collins, Patricia H. 2018. "Black Feminist Thought in the Matrix of Domination." In *Social Theory: The Multicualtural and Classic Readings,* edited byC. Lemert, 413–420. New York: Routledge.

Delpit, Lisa D. 2012. *"Multiplication is for white people": Raising expectations for other people's children.* the new press

Edmonds, Ronald. 1979. "Effective Schools for the Urban Poor." *Educational Leadership* 37 (1): 15–24.

Fanon, Frantz. 2005. *The Wretched of the Earth.* New York: Grove/Atlantic, Inc.

Garcia, David R. 2022. *Teach Truth to Power: How to Engage in Education Policy.* Cambridge: MIT Press.

Green, Terrance L., and Mark A. Gooden. 2016. "The Shaping of Policy: Exploring the Context, Contradictions, and Contours of Privilege in Milliken V. Bradley, Over 40 Years Later." *Teachers College Record* 118 (3): 1–30. doi:10.1177/016146811611800306.

Harris, Cheryl I. 1993. "Whiteness as Property." *Harvard Law Review* 106 (8): 1707–1791. doi:10.2307/1341787.

Holbrook, Carolyn L. 2006. "Low Expectations are the Worst Form of Racism." In *White Teachers, Diverse Classrooms: A guide to building inclusive schools,* edited byJ. Landsman, and C. W. Lewis, 110–121. Sterling, Virginia: Stylus Publishing, LLC.

Hoy, Wayne K., C. John Tarter, and Anita Woolfolk Hoy. 2006. "Academic Optimism of Schools: A Force for Student Achievement." *American Educational Research Journal* 43 (3): 425–446. doi:10.3102/00028312043003425.

Kahrl, Andrew W. 2016. "The Power to Destroy: Discriminatory Property Assessments and the Struggle for Tax Justice in Mississippi." *The Journal of Southern History* 82 (3): 579–616. doi:10.1353/soh.2016.0165.

Kim, Claire Jean. 1999. "The Racial Triangulation of Asian Americans." *Politics & Society* 27 (1): 105–138. doi:10.1177/0032329299027001005.

Kim, Taeyeon, Soo Bin Jang, Jin Kyeong Jung, Minhye Son, and Sun Young Lee. 2023. "Negotiating Asian American Identities: Collaborative Self-Study of Korean Immigrant scholars' Reading Group on AsianCrit." *Journal of Diversity in Higher Education.* Advance online publication. doi:10.1037/dhe0000481.

Korematsu, Karen. 2020. "Carrying on 'Korematsu': Reflections on My Father's Legacy." *Women & Law* 95–108.

Koyama, Jill, and Shyla Gonzalez-Doğan. 2021. "Displacement, Replacement, and Fragmentation in Order Making: Enacting Sovereignty in a US-Mexican Border State." *Ethnography* 22 (1): 70–87. doi:10.1177/1466138119845395.

Ladson-Billings, Gloria. 2021. *Culturally Relevant Pedagogy: Asking a Different Question.* New York, NY: Teachers College Press.

Landsman, Julie. 2004. "Confronting the Racism of Low Expectations." *Educational Leadership* 62: 28–33.

Lee, Valerie E., and Julia B. Smith. 1999. "Social Support and Achievement for Young Adolescents in Chicago: The Role of School Academic Press." *American Educational Research Journal* 36 (4): 907–945. doi:10.3102/00028312036004907.

Leonardo, Zeus. 2013. "The Story of Schooling: Critical Race Theory and the Educational Racial Contract." *Discourse: Studies in the Cultural Politics of Education* 34 (4): 599–610. doi:10.1080/01596306.2013.822624.

Leonardo, Zeus. 2015. "Contracting Race: Writing, Racism, and Education." *Critical Studies in Education* 56 (1): 86–98. doi:10.1080/17508487.2015.981197.

Leonardo, Zeus, and Alicia A. Broderick. 2011. "Smartness as Property: A Critical Exploration of Intersections Between Whiteness and Disability Studies." *Teachers College Record* 113 (10): 2206–2232. doi:10.1177/016146811111301008.

Leticia, Rojas, and Daniel D. Liou. 2023. "The Role of Mestiza Consciousness in Three Dimensions of Educational Expectations: A Self-Narrative of Borderland Pedagogy." *Journal of Latinos and Education* 22 (2): 793–803. doi:10.1080/15348431.2020.1825961.

Levin, Barbara B. 2014. "The Development of teachers' Beliefs." In *International Handbook of Research on teachers' Beliefs*, edited byH. Fives and M. G. Gill, 60–77. New York: Routledge.

Liou, Daniel D., and Raquel Alvara. 2021. "Anti-Critical Race Theory Movement in Postsecondary Education: Faculty Expectations Confronting Emotionalities of Whiteness." *Journal of Higher Education Policy and Leadership Studies* 2 (4): 77–98. doi:10.52547/johepal.2.4.77.

Liou, Daniel D., and Kelly Deits Cutler. 2023. "A Framework for Resisting Book Bans." *Eeducational Leadership* 80 (5): 48–53.

Liou, Daniel D., and Kelly Deits Cutler. 2020. "Disrupting the Educational Racial Contract of Islamophobia: Racialized Curricular Expectations of Muslims in Children's Literature." *Race Ethnicity and Education* 24 (3): 410–430. doi:10.1080/13613324.2020.1753680.

Liou, Daniel D., Patricia Randolph Leigh, Erin Rotheram-Fuller, and Kelly Deits Cutler. 2019. "The Influence of teachers' Colorblind Expectations on the Political, Normative, and Technical Dimensions of Educational Reform." *International Journal of Educational Reform* 28 (1): 122–148. doi:10.1177/1056787918824207.

Liou, Daniel D., and Erin Rotheram-Fuller. 2019. "Where is the Real Reform? African American Students and Their School's Expectations for Academic Performance." *Urban Education* 54 (3): 397–429. doi:10.1177/0042085915623340.

Lipsitz, George. 2006. *The Possessive Investment in Whiteness: How White People Profit from Identity Politics*. Philadelphia: Temple University Press.

Lomotey, Kofi, and Lowery. Kendra. 2015. "Urban Schools, Black Principals, and Black Students Culturally Responsive Education and the Ethno-Humanist Role Identity." In *Handbook of Urban Educational Leadership*, edited by M. A. Khalifa, N. W. Arnold, A. F. Osanloo, and C. M. Grant, 118–134. Lanham: Rowman & Littlefield.

López, Ian Haney. 2006. *White by Law (10th Anniversary ed.)*. New York: New York University Press.

López, Francesca, Alex Molnar, Royel Johnson, Ashley Patterson, LaWanda Ward, and Kevin Kumashiro. 2021. *Understanding the Attacks on Critical Race Theory*. National Education Policy Center.

Lorde, Audre. 2012. *Sister Outsider: Essays and Speeches*. Berkeley: Crossing Press.

Maldonado-Torres, Nelson. 2007. "On the Coloniality of Being: Contributions to the Development of a Concept." *Cultural Studies* 21 (2–3): 240–270. doi:10.1080/09502380601162548.

Matias, Cheryl E. 2016. *Feeling White: Whiteness, Emotionality, and Education*. Leiden: Brill.

Matias, Cheryl E., and Colleen Boucher. 2021. "From Critical Whiteness Studies to a Critical Study of Whiteness: Restoring Criticality in Critical Whiteness Studies." *Whiteness and Education* 8 (1): 1–18. doi:10.1080/23793406.2021.1993751.

Matias, Cheryl E., and Ricky Lee Allen. 2013. "Loving Whiteness to Death: Sadomasochism, Emotionality, and the Possibility of Humanizing Love." *Berkeley Review of Education* 4 (2): 285–309. doi:10.5070/B84110066.

McNeill, Olivia, Bettina L. Love, Leigh Patel, and David Omotoso Stovall. 2021. ""No Trifling Matter": A Kitchen-Table Talk on Abolition and Fugitivity." *Equity & Excellence in Education* 54 (2): 112–120.

Mignolo, Walter D., and Catherine E. Walsh. 2018. *On Decoloniality: Concepts, Analytics, Praxis.* Durham: Duke University Press.

Mills, Charles W. 2007. "White Ignorance." In *Race and Epistemologies of Ignorance*, edited by S. Sullivan and N. Tuana, 11–38. Albany: State University of New York Press.

Mills, Charles W. 2014. *The Racial Contract.* Ithaca: Cornell University Press.

Mills, Charles W. 2015. "Global White Ignorance." In *Routledge International Handbook of Ignorance Studies*, edited by M. Gross and L. McGoey, 217–227. New York: Routledge.

Milner, H. Richard. 2021. *Start Where You Are, but Don't Stay There: Understanding Diversity, Opportunity Gaps, and Teaching in Today's Classrooms.* Cambridge: Harvard Education Press.

Nieto, Sonia. 2004. "Racism, Discrimination, and Expectations of Students' Achievement." In *Educational Foundations: An Anthology of Critical Readings*, edited by A. S. Canestrari and B. A. Marlowe, 44–63. Los Angeles: Sage.

Noguera, Pedro. 2003. *City Schools and the American Dream: Reclaiming the Promise of Public Education.* Vol. 17. New York: Teachers College Press.

Noguera, Pedro A., and Jean Yonemura Wing, eds. 2008. *Unfinished Business: Closing the Racial Achievement Gap in Our Schools.* Hoboken: John Wiley & Sons.

Oliver, Melvin, and Thomas Shapiro. 2013. *Black Wealth/White Wealth: A New Perspective on Racial Inequality.* New York: Routledge.

Omi, Michael, and Howard Winant. 2018. "Racial Formation in the United States." In *Social Stratification*, edited by D. B. Grusky and K. R. Weisshaar, 682–686. New York: Routledge.

Orfield, Gary, and Susan E. Eaton. 1996. *Dismantling Desegregation. The Quiet Reversal of Brown V. Board of Education.* The New Press, 500. New York, NY 10110: Fifth Avenue.

Orfield, Gary, Erica D. Frankenberg, and Chungmei Lee. 2003. "The Resurgence of SchoolSegregation." *Educational Leadership* 60 (4): 16–20.

People v. Hall. 1854. 4 Cal. 399

Pollock, Mica, and Andrew Matschiner. 2022. "'Well, What's Wrong with the Whites?': A Conversation Starter on Raising Expectations for Inservice Professional Development on Race with White Teachers." *Urban Education.* doi:10.1177/00420859221119109.

Purifoy, Danielle M., and Louise Seamster. 2021. "Creative Extraction: Black Towns in White Space." *Environment and Planning D, Society & Space* 39 (1): 47–66. doi:10.1177/02637758209685.

Quijano, Aníbal. 2000. "Coloniality of Power and Eurocentrism in Latin America." *International Sociology* 15 (2): 215–232. doi:10.1177/0268580900015002005.

Reardon, Sean F., and Ann Owens. 2014. "60 Years After Brown: Trends and Consequences of School Segregation." *Annual Review of Sociology* 40 (1): 199–218. doi:10.1146/annurev-soc -071913-043152.

Rist, Ray C. 2000. "HER Classic Reprint – Student Social Class and Teacher Expectations: The Self-Fulfilling Prophecy in Ghetto Education." *Harvard Educational Review* 70 (3): 257–302. doi:10. 17763/haer.70.3.1k0624l6102u2725.

Rothstein, Richard. 2017. *The Color of Law: A Forgotten History of How Our Government Segregated America.* New York: Liveright Publishing.

Royster, Deirdre. 2003. *Race and the Invisible Hand: How White Networks Exclude Black Men from Blue-Collar Jobs.* Berkeley: Univ of California Press.

Rubie-Davies, Christine, Kane Meissel, Mohamed Alansari, Penelope Watson, Annaline Flint, and Lyn McDonald. 2020. "Achievement and Beliefs Outcomes of Students with High and Low Expectation Teachers." *Social Psychology of Education* 23 (5): 1173–1201. doi:10.1007/s11218-020-09574-y.

Steele, Claude M. 2011. *Whistling Vivaldi: How Stereotypes Affect Us and What We Can Do.* New York: WW Norton & Company.

Sue, Derald Wing, Annie I. Lin, Gina C. Torino, Christina M. Capodilupo, and David P. Rivera. 2009. "Racial Microaggressions and Difficult Dialogues on Race in the Classroom." *Cultural Diversity & Ethnic Minority Psychology* 15 (2): 183. doi:10.1037/a0014191.

Takaki, Ronald. 2012. *Strangers from a Different Shore: A History of Asian Americans. Updated and Revised Edition* ed. Boston: Back Bay Books.

Terry, Sr., L. Clarence, K. Flennaugh Terry, and M. Blackmon Samarah. 2014. "Does the "Negro" Still Need Separate Schools? Single-Sex Educational Settings as Critical Race Counterspaces." *Urban Education* 49 (6): 666–697. doi:10.1177/0042085913496798.

Wayne, Au, Anthony L. Brown, and Dolores Calderón. 2016. *Reclaiming the Multicultural Roots of US Curriculum: Communities of Color and Official Knowledge in Education.* New York: Teachers College Press.

Weinstein, Rhona S. 2009. *Reaching Higher: The Power of Expectations in Schooling.* Cambridge: Harvard University Press.

Wiggan, Greg, Annette Teasdell, and Tierra Parsons. 2022. "Critical Race Structuralism and Charles Mills' Racial Contract: Pedagogical Practices for Twenty-First-Century Educators." *Sociology of Race and Ethnicity* 8 (4): 456–463. doi:10.1177/23326492221119893.

Naming the unnamed: a Millsian analysis of the American educational contract

Wyatt Driskell

ABSTRACT

This article uses Charles W. Mills' Racial Contract to interrogate the political, historical, and philosophical roots of the conservative campaign against critical race theory (CRT) in schools. Prescribing that political power will be used to maintain a white supremacist racial hierarchy, the Racial Contract connects itself to American schools through what I have termed the American Educational Contract (AEC). To investigate these connections, I rely upon critical race hermeneutics (CRH) to better understand how American educational history and philosophy have been interpreted in ways that legitimate and normalize the whiteness inherent in the AEC. Finally, I demonstrate how the American Right resurrected time-tested tactics of the white polity – fiscal oppression, epistemological tampering, and emotional responses – to leverage the unique power of schools and reify Mill's Racial Contract.

Introduction

In the opening of his esteemed work, *The Racial Contract* (Mills 1997), Charles W. Mills is unequivocal: 'White supremacy is the unnamed political system that has made the world what it is today' (9). In the wake widespread protests for racial justice in 2020, there were hopes that mainstream America finally recognized white supremacy as a violent and pervasive blight on the realization of a just American society.[1] For the first time, phrases like 'structural racism', 'individual biases', 'anti-Black racism', entered the public discourse (Nguyen et al. 2021). Media outlets like National Public Radio even went so far as to brand the events of the summer as a long overdue 'racial reckoning' (Chang, Martin, and Marrapodi 2020).

However, if one lesson from American history is to be heeded, it is that white supremacy never goes quietly. As captured by historian Anderson (2016), this white response is inexorable: 'The trigger for white rage, inevitably, is black advancement' (3). In this cycle of progress and backlash, schools are positioned as central to Black advancement and, conversely, also become focal points for white anger (Anderson 2016; Love 2019). Beginning with antebellum crackdowns on literacy education, more than a century of white fiscal oppression, epistemological tampering, and emotional responses has weaponized educational policy against Black Americans. Mere months after a so-called racial reckoning, these tactics are seen again with the multi-level political movement to proscribe and chill the teaching of what is purported to be critical race theory (CRT) in public schools. In this pivotal moment of educational history, how can Mills' (1997) Racial Contract be used to understand the political, historical, and philosophical context surrounding the current controversy over CRT?

To this end, I employ the Racial Contract to demonstrate how educational policy ensures that the American social contract continues to favor the 'white polity' (Mills 1997, 20). From this vantage, the current controversy over CRT is an unmistakable attempt by conservative political actors to use educational policy to conserve[2] an obfuscated but ever-present white supremacist status quo. Inspired by Mills, my concept of the American Educational Contract[3] insists that white efforts to shape and control schools are a cornerstone of the larger American social contract and its ever-present Racial Contract. Bounded by this paper's focus on formal and informal educational policy-making as a tool in the racial reproduction of whiteness, I first review Mills' critique of contractarianism and the 'epistemology of ignorance' that undergirds white supremacy. From these philosophical foundations, epistemology – the theoretical study of the development and dissemination of knowledge – must be connected with research on whiteness in schools. Using Allen's (2021) 'critical race hermeneutics', I demonstrate how American educational history, including the current anti-CRT movement, ought to be interpreted through the frame of Mills' Racial Contract. Finally, in my conclusion, I reflect on Mills' prescience and how Millsian philosophy can be used in educational spaces to 'call out' white supremacy.

Conceptual framework: Mills and whiteness

Millsian contractarianism

Mills begins The Racial Contract by admonishing Western philosophy for its centuries-long preoccupation with dissecting, designing, and disseminating the rules that undergird political and social life. Centered in Mills' sights is 'contractarianism'; a philosophical school of thought that explores the idea that 'the legitimate authority of government must derive from the consent of the governed, where the form and content of this consent derives from the idea of contract or mutual agreement' (Cudd and Eftekhtari 2000, para. 1). Contractarianism would not be so offensive if the treatises of classical philosophers paid any attention to the inconsistencies presented to their own theories by slavery, colonialism, or white supremacy. Mills was forthright in naming John Rawls as a contemporary white political philosopher who continued this tradition by 'writ[ing] a book on justice … in which not a single reference to American slavery and its legacy can be found' (58). Moreover, Rawls (1971) insists that justice is 'the first virtue of social institutions' while skirting any meaningful discussion of how justice is denied to communities of Color by these institutions (3).

The need for Western political philosophy to move beyond 'discussions of justice and rights in the abstract' was evident to nonwhite philosophers whose political realities were often shaped by encounters with white violence and aggression (Mills 1997, 10). By operating from an 'inverted epistemology, an epistemology of ignorance' (19), the Racial Contract is not only a sociopolitical exercising of power – hegemony, even – but also a self-sustaining method of creating knowledge. In such a system, knowledge that does not affirm whites' place atop the global hierarchy is discarded. From this, Europe's self-proclaimed reverence of logic and objectivity has been retrofitted to support the irrationality of white supremacy. On an individual basis, Mills bluntly notes that white thinkers are so attuned to the norms of white domination, or vice versa, that this process of knowledge creation is rendered largely invisible to them: 'One could say then, as a general rule, that white misunderstanding, misrepresentation, evasion, and self-deception on matters related to race are among the most pervasive mental phenomena of the past few hundred years' (20).

Mills (1997) further demonstrates that white supremacy and coloniality was integral to development of foundational and celebrated philosophical arguments. There is an implicit presumption in much of contractarianism that the development of the social contract is an undertaking reserved for groups of individuals who, previously living bound only by the rules of nature, have now banded together to form a *society*. This concept of a society ruled by a government, bound by social and cultural norms, and engaged in political and economic processes has long been juxtaposed against the Rousseauian or Hobbesian idea of the ungoverned and primal influence that rules the *state of nature* (d'Agostino, Gaus, and Thrasher 1996). Just beneath the surface of this philosophical model was the implicit notion that the label *society* was reserved for the communities of the Western white world: 'The establishment of society thus implies the denial that a society already existed; the creation of society *requires* the intervention of white men, who are thereby positioned as *already* sociopolitical beings' (Mills 1997, 16, emphases in original). The working assumption for many classical philosophers was that colonized territories operated without the civilizing influence of the social contract and, therefore, depended upon colonizers for the introduction of social order. Tellingly, even after introducing the supposed rationality of social order, the colonizer's hierarchy-one that situated white above nonwhite – remained immutable.

The need to further delineate between nature and society inspired the great European thinkers of the 18th century. One of these thinkers, Immanuel Kant, was possessed to devise a racial classification that, as Mills (1997) writes, 'demarcates and theorizes a color-coded racial hierarchy' (54). As translated by Emmanuel Eze (1997), Kant insisted that 'The Negroes of Africa have by nature, no feeling that rises above the trifling .... So fundamental is the difference between these two races of man [Black and white], and it appears to be as great in regard to mental capacity as in color' (55). These classifications were influential in legitimizing early European racial pseudoscience (Bernasconi and Lott 2002; Sandford 2018). Further, Kant's position as a professor meant that his lectures on racist pseudoscience inculcated his students in a worldview that justified the evils of the slave trade, colonialism, and scientific racism (Mills 1997, 53–54). Though part of a philosophical tradition that was intimately informed by white supremacy, Kant's legacy as a luminary of Western moral philosophy illustrates the Racial Contract's power in determining the knowledge still lauded by modern society (Mills 1997, 2014, 2017).[4]

Beyond epistemology, because white supremacy undergirds much of the deliberation on Western political thought it has subsequently infiltrated its political processes. Rather than the tendency of Western philosophy to pontificate on 'normative' inquiry – what *ought* to be included in modern conceptions of justice, law, or rights – there is a need to also enter into a 'descriptive' analysis that is able to plainly diagnose what is occurring in the social world (Mills 1997, 10). For instance, according to Mills, it should be no surprise that the American court system is inherently unneutral in its decision-making and application of law. Further, whether examining courts or other arbiters of justice, the appearance of neutrality and rationality is maintained by outwardly invoking the normative nature of the ideals associated with Western liberality while inwardly assuring that whiteness will be protected in any judicial deliberations (11). Thus, rather than offering legitimate redress to people of Color, 'justice continue[s] to be restricted to "just us" [whites]' (93). Even more simply, Mills is explicit about the Racial Contract's power to distort reality (the descriptive) to continue favoring a collection of Eurocentric fables (the normative).

Finally, the refusal to reckon with white supremacy's 'epistemology of ignorance' takes the Racial Contract and adds a predictive quality to it. Consistent with Anderson's (2016) assertion that 'white rage' always follows Black advancement, if, at any point, white supremacy is 'called out', then there will be a corrective effort to ensure that conditions of the Racial Contract remain favorable to white domination. To accomplish this aim, white supremacy must escape the epistemological and metastasize to infect social institutions. In addition to legal and political institutions, racial power is exercised by the white polity to ensure that schools, the institutions responsible for transmitting knowledge to new generations, continue to privilege whiteness.

Whiteness in educational spaces

A central theme of Mills's (1997) work is that white supremacy works to obfuscate its impact by socializing white and nonwhite individuals to its legitimacy. As Matias (2016) writes, whiteness serves as the socially constructed ideology that reproduces the racialized social hierarchy of white supremacy (5). The effects of this hierarchy and socialization are dependent upon whether an individual's racial identity permits them to be admitted as a member of the dominant racial group – a process of categorization that is an obsessive pursuit of white Western society (Bonilla-Silva 1997; Mills 1997; Matias 2016; Omi and Winant 1994). In describing this differential effect, Matias notes that "the racial processes that purport whiteness to an elevated social echelon render Whites' behaviors, emotionalities, discourse, and ideologies as supreme, while socially denigrating the emotionalities of people of Color" (5). This central tenet of whiteness describes the more intimate, psychosocial processes through which white supremacy has become normalized in Western society. For instance, the survival of people of Color in a social system that inherently delegitimizes one's perspectives and experiences may require hiding one's genuine self and engaging in a certain performativity – what Fanon (2008) might call donning the 'white mask' (Matias 2016, 83).

The omnipresent influence of white supremacy also informs these more psychosocial dimensions of whiteness to affect the identity development, cognition, and behavior of white individuals. Whiteness as an ideology manifests itself through overt and covert elicitations of emotionality (Matias 2016). Consequently, while white supremacy operates systemically within social institutions, the insidious nature by which white ways of knowing and doing are privileged makes the advantages conferred to white individuals seem natural (Matias 2016, 86). Once steeped in this ideology-one that insists that opportunities have been awarded based on intelligence, hard work, or merit; not ill-gotten, hoarded advantages – white reactions are often emotion-laden refutations of whiteness. As Matias (2016) continues, 'When challenged with the realities of the social order that are plain for others to see, the neurotic oppressor group member will respond with defensiveness, anger, denial, absurdities, false or distorted facts, and other forms of deflection' (52). As a historical example, Matias points to white fears of interracial marriage and the resultant passage of miscegenation laws to illustrate the codification of white anxieties and emotionalities (185–186). Underscoring this point, Myrdal (1944) claimed that white sexual anxiety was 'the principle around which the whole structure of segregation . . . is organized' (587).

As much of the initial socialization to society's norms, laws, and structures occurs in schools, white supremacy has been infused throughout educational spaces; insulating white students from discomfiture and subjecting students of Color to various forms of violence (Johnson, Bryan, and Boutte 2019). Historical evidence for this phenomenon is seen in the campaign of educational erasure levied against newly freed enslaved persons in the American South: '[T]he denial of a past, of history, of achievement . . . [was done] so that as far as possible they would accept their prescribed roles of servant and menial laborer' (Mills 1997, 65). Moreover, because it was central to a larger worldview predicated on defending the boundaries of whiteness – what Mills (1997) names the 'transnational white polity' (27)—the erasure of history and the promulgation of white supremacist curricula was not isolated to the United States. In the Caribbean, Fanon (2008) found that schools indoctrinated Black children to conform with whiteness:

> Little by little, one can observe in the young [Black] Antillean the formation and crystal-lization of an attitude and a way of thinking and seeing that are essentially white. When in school he has to read stories of savages told by white men, he always thinks of the Senegalese. . . .It will have already been noticed that I should like nothing more nor less than. . . the publication of history texts especially for them [Black students], at least through the grammar-school grades. For, until there is evidence to the contrary, I believe that if there is a traumatism it occurs during those years (148).

Whether through Mills' 'transnational white polity' or Allen's (2001) 'globalization of white supremacy', students across the world are exposed to an educational context – textbooks, school structures, educational policies, and other facets of the 'education industrial complex'[5]—that, through the ideology of whiteness, legitimate and perpetuate white supremacy.

Perhaps the most comprehensive attempt to 'name' the areas where white supremacy has infiltrated American schools, Lewis and Manno (2011) reveal that nearly every facet of the current educational enterprise is undergirded by an intertwined and historically-informed system of racial inequality: '[R]ace shapes educational opportunities and experiences, including where children go to school, what kinds of expectations staff have for students, how children are disciplined, which courses they enroll in, and how educational resources get divvied up' (108). The continuance of this influence of white supremacy in schools has also been a product of educational policy mechanisms enacted from the top down. Leonardo (2009) makes explicit the connections between the landmark suite of federal legislation represented in the No Child Left Behind (NCLB) Act of 2002 and its unadvertised purpose as an 'instantiation of whiteness' (128). More specifically, the celebration of NCLB as a bipartisan policy remedy when it exacerbated educational inequality by snatching away resources from already under-resourced schools in urban communities of Color was farcical (Leonardo 2009, 130). Even more maddening was NCLB's 'refus[al] to acknowledge the causal link between academic achievement and the racial organization of society' (132). Like Fanon's demonstration of the commonalities between the white supremacy exercised in the Caribbean and the white supremacy exercised in the United States, Gillborn (2005) examines the ways in which educational policy in the United Kingdom (UK) operates from an assumption of whiteness and Eurocentricity – a baseline that alienates the growing diversity of school-children in the UK and further entrenches an established racial hierarchy.

I am not the only voice that uses Mills' work to insist there is change afoot in the American sociopolitical discourse regarding whiteness and white supremacy. As Matias and Newlove (2017) explore, the election of Donald Trump indicated that American society had moved beyond the 'colorblind epistemological moment' and into the uncharted territory of an 'emboldened en/whitening epistemology' (921). Particularly apt is the authors' prescient description of this 'emboldening' occurring through 'the perverse re-appropriation of civil rights and socially just terminologies and concepts. . .to instead strengthen white nationalism' (921)—an inescapable characteristic of anti-CRT legislation. This co-opting of the terms coined during movements for racial justice has been a consistently employed tactic of the post-Civil Rights Movement colorblind brand of white supremacy (Anderson 2016; Bonilla-Silva 2014; Kendi 2016; Leonardo 2009). Alarmingly, in the years since the publishing of Matias and Newlove's piece, educational policy has become a pivotal tool in this emboldening. Even more menacing is that when acknowledging the power of schools to shape future society the end goal of the white polity comes into clearer view.

Because '[w]hiteness is not really a color at all, but a set of power relations' (Mills 1997, 90), the hegemony of systemic and institutionalized white supremacy ensures that any-where power is exercised, whiteness will be privileged. This power is so normalized that it often goes unnoticed or unchallenged. Further, as work by Matias (2016) explores, whiteness invades individuals' psyches to affect behaviors, emotions, interpersonal inter-actions, and thought processes. Connecting the psychosocial to the political, Leonardo and Zembylas (2013) argue that whiteness is a 'technological affect' in which emotions can be 'instrumentalized' to achieve the political aims of the white polity (151). Further, Leonardo (2016) connects these expressions to the political nature of the Racial Contract by remarking that just as the "'the personal is political", we may argue that "the emotional is political"' (xiv). Agreed upon by the white polity, the Racial Contract depends upon a multilevel political effort to police the norms of whiteness when they may be threa-tened. Thus, in addition to upholding the American racial hierarchy through federal, state, and local policymaking, expressions of emotionality during school board politics, school decision-making, or teacher-student interactions are used to preserve the white-ness at the center of the AEC.

Methods

Predicated on philosophical and historical analysis, the methodological inspiration for this paper comes from Allen's (2021) 'critical race hermeneutics' (CRH). At its base, hermeneutics is concerned with the interpretation of messages and enriching these interpretations by looking beyond the text to consider 'the experience, motivations, and context of the speaker/author' (Tracy 2019, 51). These processes constitute an important element of everyday educational experiences: 'Teachers act in ways to guide, or even control, how students learn not only to interpret texts but also what counts as "proper" meanings and "correct" interpretive approaches' (Allen 2021, 16).[6] And because white supremacy is structural, it has embedded itself throughout our educational and social context (Allen 2021). CRH's melding of critical hermeneutics and critical race theory[7] provides a frame for centering white supremacy and racial injustice in the interpretation of this context (Allen 2021). For instance, CRH prompts us to reexamine historical events, literature, public discourse, or current events so that these sources can be more thoroughly interrogated for connections to the white supremacist status quo. Finally, akin to Mills' (1997) efforts to name the unnamed influence of white supremacy, CRH aims to interpret this context in ways that 'reveal the distorted lens of white supremacy' (Allen 2021, 22).

Methodologically, 'a CRH study will emphasize making meaning of racial texts through the context of structural white supremacy' (Allen 2021, 23). As suggested by Allen, this piece assumes the form of Schubert's (1991) speculative essay that encourages scholars to 'tailor, adapt, and combine extant knowledge to fit the problem under inquiry' (69). Thus, inspired by the extant knowledge of Mills' (1997) explication of white supremacy as 'an unnamed global political structure' (88), CRH is applied to better understand the historical, political, and racial context that informs the problem at hand: the anti-CRT movement. Focusing on the interpretation of the contextual and inspired by this Millsian foundation, this piece reexamines American educational history for moments in which the white polity exerted various kinds of political control over schools in order to maintain racial dominance.

Historical analysis: excavating the racial contract within the AEC

The roots of contractarianism in American education

Much of the attention of contractarianism has been dedicated to determining the ideal composition of the 'social arrangements' charged with maintaining the 'fundamental social rules, laws, institutions, and/or principles of that society' (d'Agostino, Gaus, and Thrasher 1996, 1). The centrality of public education to the modern American social arrangement may now be taken for granted—'improving education' was named by Americans as the fourth most important issue facing the country in 2022 (Schaeffer 2022). Despite its current place atop polls, this collective concern about public education is relatively recent. For instance, the terms of the nineteenth-century social contract were more concerned with the governmental distribution of parcels of land for settlement. But, as the American frontier became increasingly occupied, education assumed a greater and greater importance as the mechanism for providing access to opportunity (Carnevale, Schmidt, and Strohl 2020).

But because there was not yet a communal preoccupation with schooling does not mean that there were not those who were captivated by the connection between educa-tion and the sociopolitical organization of the nascent country. Throughout his life, Thomas Jefferson recorded various proposals that advocated for publicly funded educational systems. In a letter to Virginia official Charles Yancey, Jefferson makes plain the connection between an informed citizenry and the survival of liberal democracy: 'If a nation expects to be ignorant and free, in a state of civilization, it expects what never was and never will be....Where the press is free, and every man able to read, all is safe' (Jefferson 1899, 4). From this letter, a critical component of the American social contract comes into view: An informed citizenry needs access to knowledge to be able to negotiate favorable conditions with their government. A century later, this line of thinking was resurrected by Dewey (1916): 'Since a democratic society repudiates the principle of external authority, it must find a substitute in voluntary disposition and interest; these can be created only by education' (101). Education, taken broadly, has long been considered an essential input of democracy that affects the ability of the governed to petition and shape their government.

The linkages between education and the social contract are also multidirectional.

Schools and other educational institutions have been tasked with the transmission of culture and knowledge – what Dewey (1916) might call 'the great collective institutional products of humanity' (69). Importantly, these 'products' form the foundation of the knowledge that is expected to be imparted to students and citizens and stand to affect how future social contracts are negotiated and formed. Further, epistemic differences in perspectives due to a diversity of cultural backgrounds may affect these fonts of knowledge and, when introduced to one another, these differences are presented as obstacles to the formation of a cohesive society (Muldoon 2009, 4). But, as Muldoon continues, there is no reason to believe that 'different perspectives [do not] have epistemic advantages in different kinds of situations .... [W]e can take advantage...of our diversity of perspectives to better assess our moral beliefs to help create the initial foundation of agreement in a social contract'. (4). From Muldoon's assertion, we can see that epistemology constitutes an important, foundational piece of the social contract. Corroborating Mills's (1997) argument, contractarianism has long worked from an assumption that the more homogenous a society's collection of perspectives, the easier it is to develop a cohesive social contract (d'Agostino, Gaus, and Thrasher 1996; Muldoon 2009).

As advanced by Mills (1997), it is important that investigations of the context surrounding education and the social contract adopt a more critical tone. For instance, any discussion of the Jeffersonian foundations of public education is incomplete without acknowledging that access to educational opportunity was limited to white men and boys who occupied the upper echelons of social standing. Indeed, just 15 years after Jefferson waxed about the potential of public education, educational access in his home state became a racialized privilege. In 1831, Virginia lawmakers amended their slave codes after the Southampton Rebellion[8] by adding a provision that made illegal the literary education of Black Virginians, enslaved and free:

> Sec. 4: Be it further enacted, That all meeting of free negroes or mulattoes, at any schoolhouse, church, meeting house or other place for teaching them reading or writing, either in day or night, under whatsoever pretext, shall be considered as an unlawful assembly (Virginia General Assembly 1831).

It is apparent that even two centuries ago, racialized decision-making about education – even as simple as who was to be educated and who was not – constituted a critical part of the American social contract and helped transform it into a Racial Contract. The reactions of white Virginians in the wake a bloody slave rebellion demonstrate that, throughout American history, redrafting the social contract is driven by white anxieties about retaining their position atop the social hierarchy. And, increasingly, access to knowledge for Black Americans became a scrutinized piece of this social contract to be codified and enforced through white political power. In this way, the American Educational Contract (AEC) came to constitute an important part of the larger Racial Contract.

Reconstruction of the racial contract

Historian Foner (2014) introduces his work on Reconstruction by noting the postbellum potential for unprecedented political, social, and racial reorganization in South: '[E]nfranchising the freedmen constituted . . . a radical experiment in interracial democracy' (xix). Indeed, in the context of the Racial Contract, the temporary displacement of existing social hierarchies – those headed by ostracized and politically exiled ex-Confederates – afforded newly freed enslaved persons with some measure of political autonomy. The creation of the Freedmen's Bureau and the intervening influence of federal troops superseded the previously established social contract of the region. Newfound political agency finally imbued Black southerners with the ability to establish schools and other educational institutions (Anderson 1988; Foner 2014). From Foner, the immediate reaction of freed enslaved persons was to create educational opportunities that were long denied under the South's slavocracy: '[T]he most striking illustration of the freedmen's quest for self-improvement was their seemingly unquenchable thirst for education' (42). In short time, as Anderson (1988) writes, southern Blacks reconfigured the region's attitudes towards public education and succeeded in 'la[ying] the first foundation for universal public education in the South' (4). However, because white supremacy dictates that the Racial Contract must be reasserted when challenged, this influence and agency were fleeting.

The downfall of the more relaxed postbellum Racial Contract for Black southerners stemmed from decisions made by those occupying the highest political offices in the country. Informing President Andrew Johnson's vision for reorganizing the southern political and social order was a racialized plan to ensure that 'white men alone must manage the South' (Foner 2014, 84). Further, Johnson's decision to exercise leniency upon ex-Confederates was a calculated and self-serving bid to maintain his presidential power: 'Johnson came to view cooperation with the planters as indispensable to two goals – white supremacy and his own reelection' (89). Johnson's subsequent desertion of Black southerners provides a prime example of how the political structures undergirding the Racial Contract intersect with an individual's efforts to appease whiteness so that personal advantages can be maintained.

This Johnsonian precedent trickled down to state governments where newly installed state officials leaned upon the influence of ex-Confederates to form their governments. With this, the Racial Contract was allowed to be redrawn and as Anderson (1988) writes, 'blacks were ruthlessly disenfranchised; their civil and political subordination was fixed in southern law' (2). As a result, Black southerners were denied access to the system of educational opportunities they themselves had developed. Importantly, though intending to eliminate challenges to the South's system of white supremacy, there was a prolonged campaign of resistance by Black southerners (Anderson 1988). Despite this resistance, most southern policymakers had devised a new tactic for ensuring that their states' social contracts limited educational opportunities for Black students: financial destitution. In 1916, expenditures for Black students were a fraction of those for white students. Typical of the 'Deep South', Alabama allocated $9.41 for white students and $1.78 for Black students. Louisiana was even more egregious—$13.73 was spent per white student while only $1.31 was spent on Black students (Bureau of Education 1916). Thus, the South's postbellum social contract was also a Racial Contract predicated on viciously maintaining the racial hierarchy of Jim Crow. As evidenced by state educational spending, this Racial Contract also began to use schools as a tool for furthering this vision of white supremacy.

The epistemology of the AEC

The Racial Contract extended beyond the South to exert its influence over the curriculum used to teach students throughout the United States (Yacovone 2022). That overt white supremacy was taught in 20th century schools from Boston to New Orleans demonstrates Mills's (1997) 'epistemology of ignorance'. The Western world's white supremacist vision infiltrated all levels of education and became transmitted by educational narratives and texts. The starkest demonstration of this phenomena can be found in the conclusion of W.E.B. Du Bois's *Black Reconstruction* (Du Bois 1935). Aptly entitled 'The Propaganda of History', the final chapter included a study of history textbooks. Du Bois identified three themes from the texts' discussion of Reconstruction: 'All Negroes were ignorant', 'All Negroes were lazy, dishonest and extravagant', and 'Negroes were responsible for bad government during Reconstruction' (699). To American schoolchildren, Reconstruction was not a white regime's violent takeover, but rather, the only course of action left to reasonable white citizens looking to save the region from corruption and mismanagement. Like the insistence of white Europeans that colonization was an introduction of social order, white authors of these history textbooks sanitized the South's system of white domination so that it appeared to be a necessary and justified piece of the region's social contract.

Even more consistent with the Millsian Racial Contract, history textbooks that diminished the importance of Black contributions to the American fabric were not the product of some provincial publishing operation run amok. Instead, they were distilled from the histories written by professors and students at America's most prestigious universities (McRae 2018; Smith and Vincent Lowery 2013). A postbellum network of historians now known as the 'Dunning School' was intent upon proffering white supremacist propaganda as sound historical analysis. William A. Dunning, the namesake of the group, was a professor of history at Columbia University and had an assemblage of students that were united in basing their histories on propagandized and racist perspectives. For instance, a member of the Dunning School studied the Florida Ku Klux Klan (KKK) and 'interviewed only white Floridians' because 'the experience of Klan victims was not worth investigating' (Smith and Vincent Lowery 2013, x-xi). In fact, the historical narratives taught in schools – the ones that Du Bois (1935) found justified white oppression and fabricated Black mismanagement – were offshoots of Dunning School histories (Smith and Vincent Lowery 2013, 35–36).

The adoption of Dunning School histories by schools and broader society validates Mills' (1997) 'epistemology of ignorance' on two fronts. Firstly, it validates Mills' arguments that the Racial Contract is entrenched not only through political processes but also by overseeing the knowledge produced and privileged in society. For those acclimatized to such norms, this process appeared natural and even empirical. The historical narratives peddled by the Dunning School, were, after all, endorsed by voices situated atop American education's ivory towers. Consistent with the emergence of European philosophical traditions and their spread via colonialism, the Western system of evaluating and creating knowledge have long been thoroughly rigged to only value dominant perspectives (Mills 1997, 45–46).

Secondly, the survival of this epistemological system mandates that new knowledge conform to its established paradigm. Any contradictory findings that ran against the norms of the Racial Contract must be dismissed. And Du Bois's (1935) central thesis, that Black Americans meaningfully contributed to the social and political fabric of the country, certainly ran counter to the prevailing notions of the time. Notably, one reviewer charged in his review of *Black Reconstruction* that Du Bois was guilty of 'distorting facts and reviewing abolition propaganda in the name of history' (Craven 1936, 536). In the view of many white academics, Du Bois's arguments merely confirmed that there was an inescapable bias to be expected when a Black researcher examined topics pertaining to Black history. From Mills (2007), Du Bois and other Black scholars needed to remain 'epistemologically ghettoized by the Jim Crow intellectual practices of the white academy' so that there would be no risk of throwing the legitimacy of the American racial hierarchy into doubt (33). In the early decades of the 20th century, linkages between American educational institutions revealed the ways in which 'ideological conditioning' (61) at prestigious universities perpetuated an epistemology of ignorance that came to inform history classrooms across the country. This multi-level complicity with white supremacy laid a foundation of knowledge that was not disrupted until American society was confronted with visible white brutality during the Civil Rights Movement (Anderson 2016; Delmont 2016; McWhorter 2001).

Mitigating the promise of *Brown*

In the years preceding the *Brown* ruling, the South's de facto social contract stipulated that white residents could not, and would not, be compelled to pay taxes for Black schools (Irons 2004, 7). In Prince Edward County, Virginia, this meant that white voters were sure to strike down a 1950 tax measure to fund an expansion of the county's only Black high school. Because there was not sufficient funding to expand Moton High School's facilities, Black parents, with help from the NAACP, banded together to file suit against the county (Irons 2004). The resultant court case, *Davis v. Prince Edward County* (1951) was later subsumed under *Brown v. Board of Education of Topeka* (1954). In addition to financial divestiture, Jim Crow regimes and groups like the United Daughters of the Confederacy were committed to curricula that epistemologically affirmed white supremacy (McRae 2018; Yacovone 2022). McRae (2018) details the decades-long effort to ensure that white southern students avoided histories that "minimized states' rights, put forth slavery as the cause of the Civil War, rejected the right of secession, glorified Lincoln, and focused on the cruelty and injustice of slaveholders" (41). Most brazenly, the curricular instantiation of white supremacy converged with political domination when financially deprived Black schools could not buy their own books and had to put secondhand whitewashed textbooks in the hands of Black students (McRae 2018, 56).

Accompanying this multi-level curricular, economic, and political oppression, a new component of the AEC emerged after *Brown*: white emotionality. As demonstrated by Mills (1997), the political nature of the Racial Contract means that it is not beholden to what is most moral or most just. Rather, the Racial Contract is shaped by arguments that are found by the polity to be the most persuasive. This reliance upon white anxiety and emotionality did not appear from thin air, of course – white sexual and economic anxieties about the oppressive racial order they had erected were an animating element of white southern life since the introduction of colonial slavery (Blassingame 1972; Wood 1974). In the antebellum period and beyond, anxieties about acts of resistance from enslaved persons were manifested through horrific and disproportionate acts of violence against people of Color (Aptheker 1936; Mills 1997; Wood 1974). Even McRae (2018, 46) describes the deep fear Southern educational activists had over losing their influence over textbooks. However, in the wake of *Brown's* shock to the segregationist status quo, white political leaders validated and incited emotional responses as a political tactic in order to resist changes to the Racial Contract via the AEC, and vice versa.

Returning to Prince Edward County, the post-*Brown* era in Virginia was marked by a concerted effort to undermine the Supreme Court's ruling. Branded as a state-wide strategy of 'massive resistance' by Senator Harry F. Byrd, white governmental officials ordered that schools were to be closed rather than be desegregated. Invoking the language of contractarianism by referring to the negotiated norms of Virginian society, Byrd railed that *Brown* was 'the most serious blow that has yet been struck against the rights of the states in a matter vitally affecting their authority and welfare' (Irons 2004, 172). Reasserting some control over the state's social contract, the Virginia legislature held hostage the purse strings of any schools that heeded *Brown's* ruling. In a vile example of political rhetoric, Governor J. Lindsay Almond (1959) pandered to the age-old sexual anxieties of southern whites:

> To those who defend or close their eyes to the livid stench of Satanism, sex, immorality, and juvenile pregnancy infesting the mixed schools of the District of Columbia and elsewhere . . . let me make it abundantly clear for the record now and here after as governor of this state; I will not yield to that which I know will be wrong and will destroy every rational semblance of public education for thousands of the children of Virginia (J. Lindsay Almond 1959, 1).

Employed by white officials in other states, linking desegregation to putting children at risk represented a shift in rhetoric and tactic. No longer were segregationist politicians and parents to be considered backwards opponents of racial equality. Now they could insist that they were concerned about the welfare of children made vulnerable by, as they rationalized it, the unwarranted interference of the federal government. Later during busing protests of the 1970s, white fury about interracial relationships was renewed (K'Meyer 2009; McRae 2018). This time, white sexual anxieties were combined with unfounded concerns about white students being exposed to drugs and violence. Importantly, white emotionality began to be coated with a veneer of colorblind language that became endemic during the 1970s and 80s

(Anderson 2016; Bonilla-Silva 2014; Kendi 2016; Leonardo 2009). Together with fiscal oppression and epistemological tampering, these expressions of emotionality completed a formidable tripartite responsible for instantiating the Racial Contract in American schools.

The next episode: the movement to ban CRT

At the time of writing, more than 100 pieces of anti-CRT legislation have been introduced in 42 statehouses and 17 measures have become law (Schwartz 2021). Most of the bills did not explicitly name CRT but employed vague and euphemistic proscriptions against classroom discussions of 'divisive concepts' or 'controversial issues'. Schools deemed in violation of these laws are at risk of losing funding. This political preoccupation with CRT has trickled from statehouses to inform the grassroots efforts of parents and local educational activism groups. In local elections across the country, concerns about CRT in educational curricula have contributed to the largest effort to recall hundreds of local school board members the country has ever seen (Nierenberg 2021).

Today, the policy mechanisms of anti-CRT bills work to qualify which curricular conversations are worthy of public funding. Once again, the white polity is exercising political control over curricula to deny access to educational opportunities that are affirming of the historical realities and lived experiences of students of Color. And like Andrew Johnson's use of presidential power to backpedal from racial justice in the postbellum period, the precedent for the anti-CRT movement came from on high. Equating its aims with the vision for racial justice advanced by Martin Luther King Jr., President Trump signed a 2020 executive order[9] 'to combat offensive and anti-American race and sex stereotyping and scapegoating' by making certain projects ineligible for federal grant funding (Exec. Order 2020, 1). In addition to state attempts to pull funding for schools, conservative groups like the Heritage Foundation encouraged parents concerned about CRT to leave public schools altogether (Pollock et al. 2022)—a revival of the white polity's time-worn strategy of educational and fiscal protest (Irons 2004; McRae 2018). In essence, the AEC is once again moving to relegate important conversations about race to a kind of second-class educational status.

Beyond the willingness to provide public funding for certain educational conversations and cut funding for others, the epistemological elements of the Racial Contract point to a need to interrogate *what* is being taught. Further, political factions have recognized, perhaps implicitly, that an epistemological debate is being waged in statehouses. Just as there was a decades-long concerted effort to maintain control over education through textbooks that privileged white southern interpretations of history (Du Bois 1935; McRae 2018; FitzGerald 1979; Yacovone 2022), today's anti-CRT movement seeks to exert similar control. Derided as being too vague to be enforced, the legislative language employed covers a range of topics related to Black history, social justice, slavery, and oppression. Because these concepts are improperly assembled beneath the umbrella of CRT, educators have reported exercising caution when talking about salient current events or important issues in a democratic society (Cineas 2021; Florido 2021; Lopez 2021; Meckler and Natanson 2022; Pendharakar 2022). As an indication that the American Right's targeting of critical, diverse histories is a resurrection of past debates, a recent piece by conservative columnist Andrews

(2021) employed many of the same criticisms of Du Bois's *Black Reconstruction* as those that appeared when the work was first published more than 80 years ago (Jones 2022).

From the work of Matias (2016), the most recent piece of the AEC to emerge was the political strategy of stoking white emotionality. Aiming to reassert white control over schools, supporters of CRT bans have dubiously claimed that exposing white students to more critical, diverse curricula creates the potential for psychological trauma. Tennessee Senator Marsha Blackburn insists that because of CRT, 'mental and emotional trauma will worm its way into every classroom in America' (Blackburn 2021, para.1). In a multi-layered demonstration of the white polity's power, Mills' (1997) Racial Contract serves to (1) insulate the ability of white legislators to make this claim, (2) have white parents agree to this line of thinking, and (3) present anti-CRT bills to white society as needed warranted policymaking. Further validating Mills' insistence that justice is for whites only, work by Johnson, Bryan, and Boutte (2019) shows the long history of students of Color being exposed to traumatic school experiences – a component of the AEC that has long gone unaddressed without the intervention of state legislators.

Finally, in his later writing on an 'epistemology of ignorance', Mills (2007) leaves room for the existence of both 'racist cognizer[s]' and 'nonracist cognizer[s] who may form mistaken beliefs...because of the social suppression of the pertinent knowledge' (21). The anti-CRT movement makes clear that there is a concerted, organized effort headed by 'racist cognizers' who are intent upon reaffirming the Racial Contract by protecting the dominant white mythical history from being supplanted. Further, there is an implicit assumption in this dichotomy that, if racist cognizers successfully install 'feel-good histories' in schools, they can shape social epistemology and gather the support of nonracist cognizers (Mills 2007). In previous iterations of the AEC, this 'ideological conditioning' was accomplished through overt appeals to white supremacy and white nationalism (Mills 1997, 61). Crucially, analysis aided by the Millsian framework of the Racial Contract reveals that the organizing and motivating factor of this moment in educational history is what it has always been, the affirmation of white supremacy via the unique power of educational institutions.

Conclusion

The brilliance of *The Racial Contract* (Mills 1997) is Mills' forthright diagnosis of white supremacy. For white readers like myself, Mills is intent upon providing a straightforward heuristic for revealing what has long been known to communities of Color. In this way, the white polity's efforts to distort the social world can be unscrambled and the tenets of the Racial Contract are laid bare before the reader. When applied to the anti-CRT movement, the illumination provided by the Racial Contract is a resounding (and troubling) validation of Mills' lifelong work to understand the linkages between whiteness, knowledge, and political power. Since the Right turned its attention to CRT, I have spent a great deal of time trying to understand how we arrived at this moment in educational history. Aided by Mills' work, the roots of this controversy reveal itself: The white polity is easily whipped into a frenzy when there is a perceived threat to the Racial Contract and the AEC. Indeed, after reading *The Racial Contract*, the utter unoriginality of conservative politicians becomes evident.

Ewing (2021) describes critical race theory as the 'one school of thought that gives us [people of Color] language for saying the things my grandma told me count. That those things are real' (25). As such, CRT's potential for educational affirmation is a departure from the Racial Contract's previous use of educational policy to ensure 'the denial of a past, history, of achievement' for communities of Color (Mills 1997, 65). The 'epistemology of ignorance'—white supremacy's in-house, self-sustaining brand of knowledge – means that schools are crucial sites for the entrenchment of the Racial Contract. Conversely though, the system's reliance upon controlling the production of knowledge means it is left vulnerable to outside perspectives beyond its sphere of influence. In this way, curricula critical of whiteness stands to chip away at the shared knowledge at the foundation of the Racial Contract.

It is no mistake that the American Right has propped up CRT and used their political power to, as Jamelle Bouie puts it, excise 'an accurate history of racism in the United States' from schools (2022, para. 2). This epistemological threat to white supremacy is now expressed in existential terms. Black history, needing to be rebranded into something dangerous by the Right, became CRT. To this end, political actors have resurrected the AEC's most dependable tactics – white fiscal oppression, epistemological tampering, and elicitations of emotionality – to re-exert control over schools. Most of all, the anti-CRT movement's pulling out of all the stops betrays its own fear that the 'epistemology of ignorance' will crumble when challenged (Bouie 2022).

In addition to 'calling out' white supremacy, Mills (1997) provides key points for accelerating its collapse. The Racial Contract is first and foremost a political agreement. And if the anti-CRT movement has demonstrated anything, it is that the AEC is also undeniably shaped by white political power. In addition to being issues of racial justice, subversions of democracy like voter suppression, gerrymandering, and disinformation are also educational issues. Relatedly, at all levels of society, whiteness is afforded refuge in the leeway granted by abstractions, unexplored context, and vague language. A hallmark of anti-CRT legislation, this imprecise language is used to target, among other things, 'revisionist histories'. As the Racial Contract and the epistemology of ignorance prescribe, this condemnation comes without the necessary context that historical revision was made necessary because of the blatantly white-washed histories of the Dunning School. The racial power inherent in this vagueness is also manifested in curricula. Even through my undergrad, I was assured that courts and laws were just, schools were meritorious, and racism was confined to dwindling groups like the KKK. It is no coincidence that the scholarship responsible for unscrambling my own 'ideological conditioning' (61) are now slandered by conservative politicians as divisive. This should serve as a clarion call for educators at all levels – especially those involved in teacher education – to redouble their attention upon teaching pieces that expose the 'uncomfortable realities' of the Racial Contract (92).

Finally, despite his forthrightness, Mills (1997) is dismayed that white supremacy is still allowed to hide in plain sight. Skillfully, Mills' arguments assume a form that is revelatory but also recognizable. For instance, if we reduced his thesis to its core, we find that something resembling the 'epistemology of ignorance' is implicitly accepted by society. We learn that because 'history is written by the victors', interpretations of the past can be propagandized; because 'knowledge is power', information can be used to liberate or oppress. As it introduces 'the necessary theoretical focus for these issues to be honestly addressed', the first step towards justice requires '[n]aming this reality' (Mills 1997, 93). In the next thought, Mills makes sure that those who now recognize the Racial Contract and have been given the words to name the previously unnamed influence of white supremacy share in the responsibility to resist it. Ignorance is a product of ignoring, after all.

Notes

1. Notably, in this process of increasingly acknowledging white supremacy, the language employed for decades by critical race theorists like Derrick Bell, Kimberle Crenshaw, Mari Matsuda, and others has been vital.
2. Laats (2015) details the development of conservative political efforts to shape schools and remarks that 'Educational conservatism has been the tradition of defending tradition itself' (13). A major argument of this piece is that white supremacy and racism constitute a central component of the American educational tradition.
3. I am certainly not the first to use the tenets of Mills' Racial Contract in an educational context. See Leonardo (2013) for an example of his concept of the 'educational racial contract' that uses CRT to investigate educative processes occurring in American schools. Implicit in my concept of the American Educational Contract is that the development of American education and the wider American social contract has been inextricably tied to a history of white supremacy and racial oppression. Therefore, it would be redundant to refer to this as the American Educational Racial Contract.
4. In a later piece, Mills (2014) lambasts the backwardness of assuming that Kant's racism was somehow superfluous to his larger body of philosophical work (126).
5. A concept first coined by Anthony Picciano (1994) but, as employed by Aronson and Boveda (2017) notes the role that policy, bureaucracy, and educational commodification play in affirming the white supremacist status quo.
6. Of course, one must look no further than the present controversy over CRT in schools to find a current example of how interpretations of curricula can become sites for contestation and be shaped by a larger political context.
7. As I am referring to the actual academic theory, I leave critical race theory unabbreviated so that it is differentiated from the distorted concept of CRT decried by conservative political actors.
8. Also referred to as Nat Turner's Rebellion, historian Vanessa Holden (2021) offers a persuasive argument for renaming this instance of slave resistance to, as she writes, capture that the episode 'was far bigger than one man's inspired bid for freedom' (7).
9. Executive Order 13,950 was revoked on January 20, 2021—the day that President Joseph Biden took office.

Disclosure statement

No potential conflict of interest was reported by the author.

References

An Act to Amend the Act Concerning Slaves, Free Negroes and Mulattoes, Vir. 39 § 4 1831, https://encyclopediavirginia.org/wp-content/uploads/2020/11/11750_e6e9bd51565c130-scaled.jpg

Allen, Ricky Lee. 2001. "The Globalization of White Supremacy: Toward a Critical Discourse on the Racialization of the World." *Educational Theory* 51 (4): 467. doi:10.1111/j.1741-5446.2001.00467.x.

Allen, Ricky Lee. 2021. "Critical Race Hermeneutics: A Theoretical Method for Researching the Unconscious of White Supremacy in Education." In *The Handbook of Critical Theoretical Research Methods in Education*, edited by C. E. Matias, 15–30. Abingdon: Routledge.

Almond, J. L. . 1959. "School Integration Speech, 1959 Transcription." *Library of Virginia*. https://edu.lva.virginia.gov/dbva/files/original/b254a6c256c78dc44b0cbc8cc1685a94.pdf.

Anderson, Carol. 2016. *White Rage: The Unspoken Truth of Our Racial Divide*. New York: Bloomsbury Publishing USA.

Anderson, James D. 1988. *The Education of Blacks in the South, 1860-1935*. Chapel Hill: University of North Carolina Press.

Andrews, Helen. 2021. "Reconstruction Revisionism." *The American Conservative*, December 7. https://www.theamericanconservative.com/reconstruction-revisionism/

Aptheker, Herbert. 1936. *American Negro Slave Revolts*. New York: Columbia University Press.

Aronson, Brittany A., and Mildred Boveda. 2017. "The Intersection of White Supremacy and the Education Industrial Complex: An Analysis of #blacklivesmatter and the Criminalization of People with Disabilities." *Journal of Educational Controversy* 12 (1): 1–20.

Bernasconi, Robert, and Tommy Lee Lott, eds. 2002. *The Idea of Race*. Indianapolis: Hackett Publishing.

Blackburn, Marsha. 2021. "Why is Critical Race Theory Dangerous for Our Kids?" *Marsha Blackburn U.S. Senator for Tennessee*, July 12. https://www.blackburn.senate.gov/2021/7/why-is-critical-race-theory-dangerous-for-our-kids

Blassingame, John W. 1972. *The Slave Community*. New York: Oxford University Press.

Bonilla Silva, Eduardo. 1997. "Rethinking Racism: Toward a Structural Interpretation." *American Sociological Review* 62 (3): 465–480. doi:10.2307/2657316.

Bonilla Silva, Eduardo. 2014. *Racism Without Racists: Color-Blind Racism and the Persistence of Racial Inequality in America*. New York: Rowman & Littlefield.

Bouie, Jamelle. 2022. "The Backlash Against C.R.T. Shows That Republicans are Losing Ground. *New York Times*, February 4. https://www.nytimes.com/2022/02/04/opinion/crt-backlash-du-bois.html

Bureau of Education. 1916. *A Study of the Private and Higher Schools for Colored People in the United States*. Washington DC: Department of the Interior, Bureau of Education.

Carnevale, Anthony P., Peter Schmidt, and Jeff Strohl. 2020. *The Merit Myth: How Our Colleges Favor the Rich and Divide America*. New York: The New Press.

Chang, Ailsa., Rachel Martin, and Eric Marrapodi. 2020. "Summer of Racial Reckoning." *National Public Radio*, August 16. https://www.npr.org/2020/08/16/902179773/summer-of-racial-reckoning-the-match-lit

Cineas, Fabiola. 2021. "Critical Race Theory Bans are Making Teaching Much Harder." *Vox*, September 3. https://www.vox.com/22644220/critical-race-theory-bans-antiracism-curriculum-in-schools

Craven, Avery. 1936. "Review of *Black Reconstruction: An Essay Toward a History of the Part Which Black Folk Played in the Attempt to Reconstruct Democracy in America, 1860-1880*, by W. E.B. Du Bois." *The American Journal of Sociology* 41 (4): 535–536. doi:10.1086/217207.

Cudd, Ann, and Seena Eftekhari. 2000. "Contractarianism." *Stanford Encyclopedia of Philosophy*. https://plato.stanford.edu/entries/contractarianism/

d'Agostino, Fred, Gerald Gaus, and John Thrasher. 1996. "Contemporary Approaches to the Social Contract." *Stanford Encyclopedia of Philosophy*. https://plato.stanford.edu/entries/contractarianism-contemporary/.

Delmont, Matthew F. 2016. *Why Busing Failed: Race, Media, and the National Resistance to School Desegregation*. Berkeley: University of California Press.

Dewey, John. 1916. *Democracy and Education*. New York: Macmillan.

Du Bois, W.E.B. 1935. *Black Reconstruction: An Essay Toward a History of the Part Which Black Folk Played in the Attempt to Reconstruct Democracy in America, 1860-1880*. New York: Harcourt Brace.

Ewing, Eve. 2021. "Critical Race Theory, Comic Books and the Power of Public Schools." *Ezra Klein Show*, July 9. https://www.nytimes.com/2021/07/09/opinion/ezra-klein-podcast-eve-ewing.html

Exec. Order. No. 13950, 85 C.F.R. 60683. 2020. https://www.govinfo.gov/content/pkg/FR-2020-09-28/pdf/2020-21534.pdf

Eze, Emmanuel Chukwudi. 1997. *Race and the Enlightenment: A Reader*. Cambridge: Blackwell Press.

Fanon, Frantz. 2008. *Black Skin, White Masks*. New York: Grove Atlantic.

FitzGerald, Frances. 1979. *America Revised*. New York: Vintage Books.

Florido, Adrian. 2021. "Teachers Say Laws Banning Critical Race Theory are Putting a Chill on Their Lessons." *National Public Radio*, May 28. https://www.npr.org/2021/05/28/1000537206/teachers-laws-banning-critical-race-theory-are-leading-to-self-censorship

Foner, Eric. 2014. *A Short History of Reconstruction*. New York: Harper Perennial.

Gillborn, David. 2005. "Education Policy as an Act of White Supremacy: Whiteness, Critical Race Theory and Education Reform." *Journal of Education Policy* 20 (4): 485–505. doi:10.1080/02680930500132346.

Holden, Vanessa M. 2021. *Surviving Southampton: African American Women and Resistance in Nat Turner's Community*. Champaign: University of Illinois Press.

Irons, Peter. 2004. *Jim Crow's Children: The Broken Promise of the Brown Decision*. New York: Penguin.

Jefferson, Thomas. 1899. *The Writings of Thomas Jefferson: 1816-1826*. New York: GP Putnam's Sons.

Johnson, Lamar L., Nathaniel Bryan, and Gloria Boutte. 2019. "Show Us the Love: Revolutionary Teaching in (Un) Critical Times." *The Urban Review* 51 (1): 46–64. doi:10.1007/s11256-018-0488-3.

Jones, Martha S. 2022. "Nine Decades Later, W.E.B. DuBois's Work Faces Familiar Criticisms." *The Washington Post*, January 7. https://www.washingtonpost.com/outlook/nine-decades-later-web-du-boiss-work-faces-similar-criticisms/2022/01/07/9f9.

Kendi, Ibram X. 2016. *Stamped from the Beginning: The Definitive History of Racist Ideas in America*. New York: Bold Type Books.

K'Meyer, Tracy E. 2009. *Civil Rights in the Gateway to the South: Louisville, Kentucky, 1945-1980*. Lexington: University Press of Kentucky.

Laats, Adam. 2015. *The Other School Reformers: Conservative Activism in American Education*. Cambridge: Harvard University Press. 2015.

Leonardo, Zeus. 2009. *Race, Whiteness, and Education*. New York: Routledge.

Leonardo, Zeus. 2013. "The Story of Schooling: Critical Race Theory and the Educational Racial Contract." *Discourse: Studies in the Cultural Politics of Education* 34 (4): 599–610. doi:10.1080/01596306.2013.822624.

Leonardo, Zeus. 2016. "Foreword: Whiteness and Emo-Social Justice" In *Feeling White: Whiteness, Emotionality, and Education*, edited by Cheryl E. Matias, xiii–xvi. Rotterdam: SensePublishers.

Leonardo, Zeus, and Michalinos Zembylas. 2013. "Whiteness as Technology of Affect: Implications for Educational Praxis." *Equity & Excellence in Education* 46 (1): 150–165. doi:10.1080/10665684.2013.750539.

Lewis, Amanda E., and Michelle J. Manno. 2011. "The Best Education for Some: Race and Schooling in the United States Today." In *State of White Supremacy*, edited by M. K. Jung, J. H. Costas, and E. Bonilla Silva, 93–109. Redwood City: Stanford University Press.

Lopez, Brain. 2021. "The Law That Prompted a School Administrator to Call for an 'Opposing' Perspective on the Holocaust is Causing Confusion Across Texas." *Texas Tribune*, October 15. https://www.texastribune.org/2021/10/15/Texas-critical-race-theory-law-confuses-educators/

Love, Bettina L. 2019. *We Want to Do More Than Survive: Abolitionist Teaching and the Pursuit of Educational Freedom*. Boston: Beacon Press.

Matias, Cheryl E. 2016. *Feeling White: Whiteness, Emotionality, and Education*. Rotterdam: SensePublishers.

Matias, Cheryl E., and Peter M. Newlove. 2017. "The Illusion of Freedom: Tyranny, Whiteness, and the State of US Society." *Equity & Excellence in Education* 50 (3): 316–330. doi:10.1080/10665684.2017.1336951.

McRae, Elizabeth Gillespie. 2018. *Mothers of Massive Resistance: White Women and the Politics of White Supremacy*. Oxford: Oxford University Press.

McWhorter, Diane. 2001. *Carry Me Home: Birmingham, Alabama: The Climactic Battle of the Civil Rights Revolution*. New York: Simon and Schuster.

Meckler, Laura, and Hannah Natanson. 2022. "New Critical Race Theory Laws Have Teachers Scared, Confused and Self-Censoring." *Washington Post*, February 14. https://www.washington post.com/education/2022/02/14/critical-race-theory-teachers-fear-laws/

Mills, Charles W. 1997. *The Racial Contract*. Ithaca: Cornell University Press.

Mills, Charles W. 2007. "White Ignorance." In *Race and Epistemologies of Ignorance*, edited by S. Sullivan and N. Tuana, 13–38. Albany: State University of New York Press.

Mills, Charles W. 2014. "Kant and Race, Redux." *Graduate Faculty Philosophy Journal* 35 (1): 125–157. doi:10.5840/gfpj2014351/27.

Muldoon, Ryan. 2009. "Diversity and the Social Contract." PhD diss., University of Pennsylvania.

Myrdal, Gunnar. 1944. *An American Dilemma: The Negro Problem and Modern Democracy*. New York: Harper & Row.

Nguyen, Thu T., Shaniece Criss, Eli K. Michaels, Rebekah I. Cross, Jackson S. Michaels, Pallavi Dwivedi, Dina Huang, et al. 2021. "Progress and Push-Back: How the Killings of Ahmaud Arbery, Breonna Taylor, and George Floyd Impacted Public Discourse on Race and Racism on Twitter." *SSM-Population Health* 15: 1–9. doi:10.1016/j.ssmph.2021.100922.

Nierenberg, Amelia. 2021. "The Conservative School Board Strategy." *New York Times*. October 27. https://www.nytimes.com/2021/10/27/us/the-conservative-school-board-strategy.html

Omi, Michael, and Howard Winant. 1994. *Racial Formation in the United States*. New York: Routledge.

Pendharakar, Eesha. 2022. "Efforts to Ban Critical Race Theory Could Restrict Teaching for a Third of America's Kids." *Education Week*, January 27. https://www.edweek.org/leadership/efforts-to-ban-critical-race-theory-now-restrict-teaching-for-a-third-of-americas-kids/2022/01

Picciano, Anthony G. 1994. "Technology and the Evolving Educational-Industrial Complex." *Computers in the Schools* 11 (2): 85–102. doi:10.1300/J025v11n02_08.

Pollock, Mia, John Rogers, Alexander Kwako, Andrew Matschiner, Reed Kendall, Cicely Bingener, Erika Reece, Benjamin Kennedy, and Jaleel Howard. 2022. The Conflict Campaign: Exploring Local Experiences of the Campaign to Ban "Critical Race Theory" In Public K-12 Education in the U.S., 2020-2021. Los Angeles, CA: UCLA's Institute for Democracy, Education, and Access.

Rawls, John. 1971. *A Theory of Justice*. Cambridge: Belknap Press.

Sandford, Stella. 2018. "Kant, Race, and Natural History." *Philosophy & Social Criticism* 44 (9): 950–977. doi:10.1177/0191453718768358.

Schaeffer, Katherine. 2022. "State of the Union 2022: How Americans View Major National Issues." *Pew Research Center*. https://www.pewresearch.org/fact-tank/2022/02/25/state-of-the-union-2022-how-americans-view-major-national-issues/

Schubert, William H. 1991. "Philosophical Inquiry: The Speculative Essay."In .edited by Short, Edmund C.In *Forms of Curriculum Inquiry* Albany, NY: SUNY Press 61–76.

Schwartz, Sarah. 2021. "Map: Where Critical Race Theory is Under Attack." *Education Week*. https://www.edweek.org/policy-politics/map-where-critical-race-theory-is-under-attack/2021/06

Smith, John David, and J. Vincent Lowery. 2013. The Dunning School: Historians, *Race, and the Meaning of Reconstruction*. Lexington: University Press of Kentucky.

Tracy, Sarah J. 2019. *Qualitative Research Methods: Collecting Evidence, Crafting Analysis, Communicating Impact*. Hoboken: John Wiley & Sons.

Wood, Peter H. 1974. *Black Majority: Negroes in Colonial South Carolina from 1670 Through the Stono Rebellion*. New York: Alfred A. Knopf.

Yacovone, Donald. 2022. *Teaching White Supremacy: America's Democratic Ordeal and the Forging of Our National Identity*. New York: Knopf Doubleday.

PART III

The Racial Contract applied to educationally just methods

Too much talking, not enough listening: the Racial Contract made manifest in a mixed-race focus group interview

Bryant O. Best and H. Richard Milner IV

ABSTRACT

In this article, the authors utilize C.W. Mills' Racial Contract Framework as a tool to unpack how racial power dynamics manifested in a mixed-race focus group interview designed to understand the participants' insights on race, incarceration, and community. The focus group interview included four research participants: Two White women, one Black woman, and one White man. While the interview was framed as a collaborative, generative discussion, we observed contributions made by the Black woman to be rebuffed or dismissed by the White man, who positioned himself as the expert on the interview topic. The article concludes with implications and recommendations for researchers as they design and enact focus group interviews across racial lines in pursuit of racial justice and equity.

Introduction

In this study, centering on the pivotal work of Charles Mills,[1] we analyze how a mixed-race focus group interview focused on intersections of carceral practices and race become a potential site that enacts and reifies racial and ideological violence against a Black participant in the study. This study attempts to make contributions both to the literature on the school-to-prison pipeline and research methods, particularly mixed-race focus group interviews. For the former, the contribution revolves around the ways in which White people can work to disrupt the school-to-prison pipeline while simultaneously upholding racial beliefs and attitudes that are harmful, resulting in a net null (if not net negative) effect on systems of racial injustice. For the latter, this study is a cautionary tale in what can happen in mixed-race focus group interviews and the importance of building and practicing analytic lenses to identify when The Racial Contract manifests in the research process.

The focus group interview invited community members to share insights and recommendations about disrupting carceral practices in schools and neighborhoods. Community members participating in the focus group were selected to offer their perspectives because they lived and worked in one of the most incarcerated cities in the United States.[2] Moreover, these participants were selected because they all served at a nonprofit organization that provides services to incarcerated individuals and their families in Nashville, Tennessee. The interview was comprised of three self-identified White participants and one Black participant. During the interview, multiple attempts by the Black participant to contribute to the discourse based on her[3] lived experiences and professional background were rebuffed by a White participant who positioned himself as 'the' expert on racial justice and addressing incarceration in the community. Ironically, the neighborhood in question, located in the 37208 zip code, is almost all Black. Still, from our observation and analysis, the White man participant in the focus group positioned himself as the arbiter of knowledge, that is, the person with the most important and salient experiences and perspectives about incarcerated bodies, throughout the interview.

Our analysis uncovered and demonstrated the ways in which racial violence and racial dominance manifested through Mills (1997) conceptualization of white supremacy vis-à-vis The Racial Contract in a mixed-race focus group interview. Mills conceptualized The Racial Contract as a set of formal, informal, implicit agreements made between White people regarding social interactions with Black people. Implications of our analysis highlight areas researchers might attend to in designing and carrying out focus group interviews, particularly those focused on racial justice or those that combine Black and White participants, to prevent or mitigate potentially harmful acts. In essence, our analysis addressed the following interrelated questions: What role do researchers play in designing interview studies that potentially cause harm to Black bodies and reify The Racial Contract? How might focus group interviews, designed to address, call out, and disrupt systemic and institutionalized oppression (such as the overincarceration of Black people and other People of Color) reify The Racial Contract?

Indeed, the goal of the focus group interview as conducted by the first author was to include the voices and perspectives of White community members as well as community members of color because the project of disrupting racial injustice must include White bodies – those who benefit from, reproduce, and maintain white supremacy (Love 2019; Milner 2020a, 2015). However, even among liberal White community members who consider themselves allies or, what Love (2019) conceptualized as co-conspirators, harm and violence can emerge (Matias 2020). In *Surviving Becky(s)*, Matias argued that 'Becky' is a name ascribed to an interplay between whiteness and womanhood that subjects Black and Brown people to physical and emotional harm in often repeated ways. Becky moves include calling the police on Black and Brown people who have not committed a crime, attempting to minimize or otherwise detract from scholarship and conversations about race, and choosing not to act (i.e. standing idly by) when harm is being inflicted upon Black and Brown people. This study not only carefully analyzes the discourse and moves made among participants in the focus group interview, it demonstrates how a focus group interview about race, racism, white supremacy, injustice and incarceration can be harmful to Black and Brown people given The Racial Contract. Furthermore, it concludes with commentary on the Becky moves made by the two White women participants in the study to contribute to that theoretical base as well. The paper also concludes with recommendations for researchers as they design and enact focus group interviews across racial lines in pursuit of racial justice and equity.

A review of relevant literature

The authors rely on established bodies of literature on the school-to-prison-pipeline (which we refer to as 'pipeline') to help frame our analysis. From this litany of research, we then synthesize elements that help unpack the nexus between and among neighborhoods, schools and incarceration. Indeed, the pipeline literature can be described as pervasive, persistent, and pernicious.

The school-to-prison pipeline is a series of interconnected systems of injustice deeply steeped in racism, ableism, sexism, poverty, other forms of discrimination that push Black, Brown and other bodies out of classrooms, districts, and schools into prisons. Scholars and research across multiple disciplines have explored this topic, thus providing empirical, theoretical and practical implications about the deleterious impact of this system of oppression and societal exclusion (Blake et al. 2017; Jabbari and Johnson 2020; Milner 2013; Morris 2016; Noguera 2003). In a handbook on disrupting the school-to-prison pipeline, the pipeline was argued to be the result of a nefarious interaction that involves racial beliefs and attitudes made manifest in society, particularly in public education and criminal justice systems (Bahena et al. 2012). The pipeline is used as an analogy because it illustrates both the different systems ('pumps') that contribute to the pipeline as well as the connections between those systems ('pipes') as well. Given that context, scholarship on the topic brings to bear relationships between a student of color being pushed out of school due to a zero-tolerance policy, budgeting priorities that favor police presence in schools over counselors, psychologists, books, and broader trends in society that perpetuate racial hierarchies and inequality. In fact, some scholars suggest the pipeline does not start in school but as soon as some children are born (i.e. a 'cradle-to-prison pipeline') (Milner et al. 2019). Along similar lines, related scholarship argues that a 'school-to-prison nexus' is the more accurate description of the phenomenon (Stovall 2018). For this study, we are defining the school-to-prison pipeline as the ways in which school systems and carceral systems share a common set of racial beliefs, policies, and practices that marginalize Black and Brown students. Research shows that problems related to pushout in schools and the carceral system are pervasive, persistent, and pernicious. Given this need to understand and more deeply address incarceration in local and broader communities, our broader aim is to study and co-construct with community members strategies, insights, recommendations, and tools to address injustice and the pipeline.

The pipeline is pervasive

Our review of the literature reveals that the school-to-prison-pipeline is pervasive. Data collected by the U.S. Department of Education for the 2015–2016 school year demonstrated that over 11.3 million days of instruction (or about 62,500 years of instruction) were lost due to out-of-school suspensions (Losen and Martinez 2020). While this statistic is troubling by itself, it is further complicated by the fact that members of some student groups are suspended more than others. In 2014, the U.S. Department of Justice Civil Rights Division and the U.S. Department of Education Office for Civil Rights co-authored an open letter reminding the educators across the United States (U.S.) that 'federal law prohibits public school districts from discriminating in the administration of student discipline based on certain personal characteristics' (U.S. Department of Justice Civil Rights Division & U.S. Department of Education Office for Civil Rights 2014, 2). The letter explicitly stated that these characteristics included race, color, national origin, disability, religion, and sex.

According to the federal data, over 50% of students who were either arrested in school or referred to law enforcement were Black or Brown students, a disparity that the departments argued was likely 'not explained by more frequent or more serious misbehavior by students of color' (p. 4). In no uncertain terms, the letter stated that 'racial discrimination in school discipline is a real problem', and used the letter to offer guidance to states and districts to bring their discipline policies under compliance with federal law. Milner (2020b) argued that much of the issues or pushout and the pipeline are related to punishment practices masked in the language of disciplinary practices. In a separate report also published in 2014, the U.S. Department of Education Office for Civil Rights highlighted specific disparities in school discipline. The report noted that although Black children represented 18% of preschool enrollment, they made up 48% of those receiving more than one out-of-school suspension (U.S. Department of Education Office for Civil Rights 2014, p. 1). The report also highlighted that Black students were three times as likely to be suspended or expelled as their White counterparts, and that students with disabilities were more than twice as likely to receive an out-of-school suspension than students without disabilities. And, perhaps most alarmingly, Black students and students with disabilities were also overrepresented in terms of being involuntarily secluded or confined in school, arrested while at school, or referred to law enforcement. Scholarly research on Black and Brown boys in special education have reached similar conclusions (Artiles and Trent 1994; Connor et al. 2019; Jordan 2005). These data suggest that issues of the pipeline are not only pervasive, but they are persistent as well.

The pipeline is persistent

While many studies point to the role of schools and local communities in the persistence of the pipeline, policies play an essential role as well. Although there are records of school discipline disproportionality prior to the 1990s, laws and policies enacted by the Democratic Party, and the Clinton Administration (1993–2001) in particular, established a foundation of punitive practices in public education that has persisted for over 20 years.

The Violence Crime Control and Law Enforcement Act, also known as 'the Crime Bill', was passed in 1994, and allowed for students to be suspended or even expelled based on 'predetermined, non-negotiable' terms for certain behaviors (Browne-Dianis 2011, p. 25). These so-called 'zero tolerance policies' were adopted from the policies and politics of the U.S. Drug Enforcement Administration (DEA) which, at the time, was fighting a 'war on drugs'. Since then, several studies have demonstrated that the pipeline persists on a national (Pearman et al. 2019), state (Curran 2016), district (Skiba et al. 2002) and classroom (Milner 2020b) level.

The pipeline has persisted because it is adaptive; it can evolve and reinforce itself through systemic practices and policies – even the very practices and policies designed to disrupt or dismantle it. In 2020, Soto-Vigil Koon mapped the progress made by a national coalition in the school discipline reform industry both before and after the Obama Administration outlined 'eliminating the school-to-prison pipeline' as a federal priority. Despite the push and an influx of over one million in federal dollars to support the national coalition, Koon's study suggested that the federal priority, while well-intentioned, was likely 'absorbed, co-opted, and re-coordinated to further the interests of the education reform industry' (e.g. edu-businesses, think tanks, law enforcement agencies, psychological support specialists, and the like) (p. 401).

The pipeline has also persisted because it is difficult to address. Many schools and school districts have committed to a variety of alternative approaches to school discipline, including restorative practices (RPs), Positive Behavioral Interventions and Supports (PBIS), and Social-Emotional Learning (SEL) (Welsh and Little 2018). While these approaches have grown in popularity, the research on the effectiveness of these methods – particularly when it comes to reducing the discipline gap – is mixed (Welsh and Little 2018). In fact, a recent review on traditional school discipline and alternative approaches found a misalignment between the fact that some intervention programs are designed to shift student behavior and the fact that student misbehavior does not sufficiently account for racial discipline gaps in statistical models (Welsh and Little 2018, pp. 780–781). In other words, the pipeline problem cannot be addressed simply by changing students because students are not the cause of the pipeline problem. Given these and other areas in which the pipeline consisted, we were interested in the programs, initiatives, and wisdom community members had to offer in addressing such persistence.

The pipeline is pernicious

The research literature also demonstrates how the pipeline is pernicious. According to Annamma (2016), the surveillance-heavy, punishment-oriented system of governance we see in schools today can be attributed to a concept called carceral logic. Carceral logic drives the carceral state, whereby institutions work together to monitor, control, and punish people in society. Carceral logic, policy, and practice can be seen in some of the most common indicators of the pipeline, which include removing students from classrooms and schools through in-school suspension, out-of-school suspension, expulsion, or referral to law enforcement (i.e. arrest). Additional common indicators include the installation of police officers, metal detectors, and other forms of surveillance in schools. Attempts to 'disrupt' carceral logic have been met with mixed success.

For example, in 2010, the Obama Administration launched its Supportive School Discipline Initiative (SSDI), which prioritized 'eliminating the school-to-prison pipeline' (Koon 2020, p. 373). By 2014, a national, federally funded policy network had been established that supported personnel and programs in law enforcement, school psychology and related psychology fields, and even 'edu-business leaders' to the tune of millions of dollars. However, the network itself yielded few tangible forms of progress towards its stated goals. Criminology scholars have, in an attempt to explore the potential 'collateral consequences' of mass incarceration, designed studies that tested the effects of exclusionary disciplinary policies on non-suspended students. One such study found that sustained punitive practices in schools negatively affected the academic achievement of *non-suspended* students in reading and math classes, with the greatest effects being found in schools with more stringent discipline policies and relatively low levels of violence (Perry and Morris 2014). It is also important to note here that, despite mainstream narratives rooted in individualism and meritocracy, Welsh and Little (2018) found that most peer-reviewed articles on the pipeline do *not* find differences in student (mis) behavior to be the root cause of discipline proportionality. Taken together, these findings suggest that the mechanisms that contribute to the pipeline may be evolving to unprecedented levels. Accordingly, researchers, educators, and those who believe in the principles of social and racial justice must heed the clarion call of the generation to disrupt the pipeline in all its forms.

Conceptual framework

To make sense of and explain our analysis of a focus group interview designed to learn from and with community members about ways to understand and disrupt the school-to-prison-pipeline, we draw from 1997) Racial Contract Theory. According to Mills, The Racial Contract is 'a set of formal or informal agreements between members of a subset of humans with the class of 'full persons' (e.g. White) to categorize the remaining subset of humans of a different and inferior moral and civil status (e.g. non-whites)' (p. 11). Three claims or what we will call tenets undergird The Racial Contract: the existential, the conceptual, and the methodological. Mills explained that the existential advances the notion that white supremacy has existed for many years and continues to exist. The conceptual tenet offers that white supremacy is more than just an ideology; it is a political system as well. The methodological tenet states that the system of white supremacy can be illustrated as a 'contract' – albeit covert and hidden – between White people regarding superiority of their views and interactions with non-White people. Mills is clear that non-white people are *not* a consenting party in this agreement but are rather subject to it and are the subjects of the agreement. Further, Mills argued that 'to the extent that those phenotypically categorized as White fail to live up to the civic and political responsibilities of whiteness, they are in dereliction of their duties as citizens' (p. 14).

The Racial Contract as a theory is 'sociopolitical, moral, and epistemological' (p. 9). It is intended 'not merely … to generate judgments about social justice and injustice, but … [to] explain the actual genesis of the society and the state, the way society is structured, the way the government functions, and people's moral psychology' (p. 5). To further illuminate this concept, Mills suggested that, due to The Racial Contract, White people (generally) do not view acts such as colonialism and slavery as morally wrong; rather, such acts were simply wrong in how they were administered or executed. From this perspective, we can see what Mills refers to as the 'inverted epistemology' (p. 17) or 'epistemology of ignorance' (p. 17) that ironically precludes White people from being able 'to understand the world they themselves have made' (p. 18). As we analyze and make sense of how a White participant asserted himself as the expert on dismantling a system that whiteness has produced and sustained, Mills' theorizing becomes a necessary tool for deep interrogation.

Thus, in sum, The Racial Contract is a set of agreements made between White people that prescribe an inferior moral and civil status to non-White people through a sustained system of injustice. Second, non-White people are not consenting parties to the agreement (even in instances where non-White people are pretending to consent as a means of politics, strategy, or survival). Third, white supremacy is a political system, not merely an individual act or an institutional practice. Fourth, White people who fail to live up to the expectations of whiteness run the risk of being shamed, ostracized by others, or harmed psychologically, materially, socially, and emotionally. And fifth, the epistemology of ignorance precludes white people from being able to fully realize societal dynamics for which they are responsible for that maintain a caste system of injustice.

Grounded in Mills' Racial Contract Theory as summarized in the five principles above, we explain how a focus group interview with three White participants and one Black participant exemplified The Racial Contract. Albeit unknowingly, we argue based on our analysis that the White participants reified The Racial Contract by acting as the knowers and experts on the school-to-prison pipeline experience and how to best address it. Over the course of the interview, their subscription to The Racial Contract we argue may have caused psychological and emotional harm to the Black participant. Although we mostly only focus on one White participant and one Black participant, the remaining two White participants reify violence and The Racial Contract through their silence and inaction to disrupt the White speaking participant.

Methods

This study centers the focus group as a site of analysis as participants focused on reasons for and strategies to address incarceration in one community. 37208 is a zip code located in the northern part of Nashville, Tennessee. According to The Brookings Institution, a nonprofit public policy organization based in Washington, DC, 37208 has the highest incarceration rate per capita in the U.S. at 14% (Brookings, 2018). Said differently, one out of every three male residents between the ages of 14 and 25 in 37208 is incarcerated (Vox 2021). Further, 93% of residents living in 37208 are Black (Brookings, 2018). This community was selected for the study because the actions, initiatives, and programs created by its residents to disrupt the pipeline can serve as an exemplar for similarly situated communities. Further, the participants for the study were selected via community nomination (Foster 1997) with a particular focus on recruiting both Black and White participants to gain cross-racial understanding of the pipeline disruption policies and principles.

Researchers' positionality

We recognize the importance of overtly sharing our researcher positionality to provide readers a window into our professional and intersecting identities that bear on the topics of our research, construction of our research questions, thematic focus of our literature review, conceptual framing, data collection and epistemological stances, research analysis, and recommendations for future analyses, and implications (Milner 2007). The first author of this study is a Black man, born and raised in a community with demographics and a social context similar to that of our study of the 37208 community. For instance, similar to the 37208 community, the home community of Author One is predominantly Black, predominantly low-income, and is in the U.S. south. The second author is a Black man, born and raised in a rural, mostly Black community in the U.S. south. Both authors have close family members deeply impacted by the pipeline, and the carceral system in particular, which influence our interest and desire to study mechanisms necessary to end the school-to-prison-pipeline. Accordingly, our lens for analyzing this study is guided by an 'insider's perspective' as well as an 'outsider perspective' (Ahmed et al. 2022; Chavez 2008).

Focus group interview

Centering on assets and challenges to overcome in the 37208 community and to learn from the stories, experiences, insights and recommendations of community members, the community nominations approach (Foster 1997) was employed to recruit participants for the focus group interview. We selected the focus group interview to study and capture the views and perspectives of our participants in a group setting rather than through an individual interview process. Focus group interviews are in-depth interviews in which multiple research participants are interviewed at one time (Marshall and Rossman 2011). Originally used in marketing research, focus group interviews can also serve as valuable methodological tools to support research in the social sciences (e.g. education, sociology, criminal justice, and similar fields). Focus groups typically contain four or more participants who share a set of common characteristics, features, interests, practices and experiences connected to the research questions of the study. One of the major benefits of a focus group interview as opposed to an individual interview is that the interviewer can ask questions that can foster discussion and debate, thereby adding to the richness of the data collection. In terms of facilitation techniques, Author One adopted the transformative research practices for data collection which, among other things, acknowledges power dynamics between the researcher and the studied population (Camacho 2019).

Despite the advantages mentioned above, as we found in this study, there are also some potential challenges associated with conducting focus group interviews. Power dynamics that exist in society (e.g. dynamics across race and gender lines) are present in focus group interviews, and it is a responsibility of a researcher to attend to these dynamics in collaboration and partnership with research participants throughout the facilitation of focus group sessions. Moreover, ethical issues, such as how to protect the identities of the participants, is also important. It is common for focus group interviews to be audio or video recorded, and researchers need to make decisions regarding how they will record, store, and keep the audio and videotaped data to maintain the privacy, anonymity and where necessary confidentiality of the research topic and research participants.

Research participants

The focus group interview that serves as the focus of this analysis included one Black woman, two White women, and one White man. All four individuals served in various capacities at a nonprofit organization that supports the family members of incarcerated individuals. The focus group lasted approximately sixty minutes and resulted in approximately 7,150 words of text. The focus group interview was conducted and recorded via Zoom. Data collected from Zoom were subsequently transcribed and coded for themes using a commercial version of the qualitative data analysis software NVivo. Some of the initial codes for the present study – in alignment with the tenets of The Racial Contract – included 'inferior status', 'non-consent', 'political system', 'dereliction', and 'ignorance'.

A mixed-race focus group as a site of racial harm and emotional violence

The focus group began with the interviewer (Author One) asking everyone to speak about themselves and why they had decided to work for an organization which helped families of incarcerated people. Responses varied. Bridgette,[4] a Black woman, spoke about how her lived experiences inspired her engage in social justice work. Bridgette stated that although she was a native New Yorker, she grew up in the Caribbean islands and that working [in 37208] is really just an extension of what I think I've always done. I've always had ... this thing about giving back". In contrast Kyle, a White man, shared that his connection to the organization designed to work with incarcerated people was coincidental. Kyle mentioned that he had worked as a lawyer for decades in Nashville, and that serving for the current organization was something he did in his state of 'semi-retirement'. As questions evolved and deepened, harm and violence through the discourse of white participants intensified, beginning with Kyle classifying incarcerated people as 'feral children'.

Feral children

When asked about the high incarceration rate in 37208, and the school-to-prison pipeline in particular, Kyle shared the following:

> I was actually just thinking about the 37208 phenomena you [the interviewer] were talking about ... I [currently] have six murder one cases and five of them occurred in 37208 ... and, for want of a better phrase, and I'm not sure I want to use this phrase, but these are feral children that can function only within their own community with their own peers and cannot relate to our standard orthodox White expectations ... some of these kids literally do not know how to relate to [our] common, Southern set of expectations.

While Kyle's comments could be considered offensive or downright shocking to those who believe that children should never be compared to wild animals, Author One chose not to counter Kyle's statement for two key reasons. First, allowing the focus group interview to flow naturally without intervention from the facilitator would provide insight into just how deeply the White research participants were committed to The Racial Contract. In other words, the comment was so striking that it shifted the purpose of the interview from the facilitator's perspective; instead of eliciting feedback on how to disrupt the school-to-prison pipeline, the question now became *how does a person with that belief about Black children provide legal aid to an overincarcerated Black community?* As a site for consideration, was it the researcher's responsibility to query Kyle's comments? If so, how might the questioning derail the naturalistic flow of the participants' comments? Similar shifts in inquiry have been documented in previous studies on race (Delgado-Gaitan 1993). Second, Bridgette, the Black woman participant, was well equipped to counter Kyle's transgression, and did so with eloquence and grace.

Hedging as a form of non-consent

After Kyle's 'feral children' comment, Bridgette shared her perspective offering the following:

> You know, I have the background – just to clarify, my background after law school [was that] I clerked in Family Court. And every Thursday was [reserved for juvenile cases], so we got a lot of [moderate to serious offense] cases … and what we found a lot of times was that things like juvenile detention seemed to be the training ground for people to end up in adult court … "

Here, at this point in the focus group, Bridgette seemed to begin to intentionally establish herself as an authority on the topic at hand based on her professional and practiced experience. We also hear her using language that reflects the systemic nature of the school-to-prison pipeline, referring to juvenile detention as a 'training ground' for running afoul of the law as an adult. Bridgette further elaborated:

> The research and anecdotal evidence and what we see being reported … I think there are other factors at play like home life, poverty, a lot of things. But I think statistically, and this is not within my [organizational] experience, this has more to do with, like, me living, you know, [in the Caribbean], but we would see kids who would get into fights in school … or they would need to come before a judge for a special petition. I don't know if you've heard of it, Kyle, it's called P.I.N.S., Persons In Need of Supervision? So, these kids who are already like on this quote, unquote "bad track" if somebody didn't interrupt … "

At this point in the focus group interview, Bridgette is clearly attempting to build community – asking Kyle about his knowledge about P.I.N.S, for instance. After establishing herself as an authority figure based on her professional experience, Bridgette supplements her positioning by adding that her comments are not just based on her work but her life growing up in the Caribbean and also what she has read in literature on the topic. However, it is important to point out here that Bridgette makes no attempt to attack or ostracize Kyle, the White man participant, who made the comment about feral children, to which she is responding. Instead, she opts to 'call him in' to the conversation – to build a dialogic in hopes of co-constructing insights about why the prevalence of such profound incarceration in their community and perhaps what can and should be done about it. Kyle had no immediate response, so Bridgette continued, eventually arriving at the following:

> I'm sorry, everyone I'm just going to take two seconds for this, I think what we're seeing in the research and news is that young Black and Brown children are often seen as adults at an earlier age, and I think that if you're putting them into this punitive system, it just tends to kind of replicate. I don't know if that's the appropriate word, but it's definitely something I think that can be aborted … in elementary school. Even kindergarten. Because at very young ages, we're seeing kids [handcuffed by security officers.] First graders, you know? And where do you go from that if you're a child, and that's how you see yourself? You know I think I'm just speaking from my experience just literally watching kids [who] we had my first year as a law clerk … three years later [a kid] committed robbery of some kind, [but] I'm just like 'well, they never really got the help they needed early on, [just] my ten cents.

From our analysis, it seemed that Bridgette uses signposts such as 'I'm just speaking from my experience' as a means of giving other participants opportunities to engage in the conversation as well. She even apologizes for standing up for young Black and Brown children, presumably so as not to upset the unwritten, common rules of Southern expectations as Kyle described previously or to disrupt the Racial Contract. Kyle appeared bothered and espoused a point about 'hard data' to combat Bridgette's points.

Hard data

Although Bridgette asked Kyle a direct question in her statement, he chose not to respond. Instead, he waited until Bridgette was finished speaking, and directed his comments to the male interviewer:

> Let me suggest if you talk to somebody else here – not in this group. I'm part of [another organization] and there are several people who I can't name right now, and I don't have their information with me. But call [the organization's director] and tell him that you're interested in the school-to-prison pipeline. There is a committee looking specifically [at that] and they have *hard data*. So, I suggest you do that.

From Kyle's perspective, the conversation required 'hard data' – large scale, quantitative evidence – to be validated.

The 'hard data' comment seemed to be in direct conflict and counter to Bridgette's stories grounded in her experiences as a defense attorney and Black woman drawing from stories in the news. With this statement, he summarily dismisses Bridgette's experiences – both personal and professional – and directs Author One as researcher to speak with the director of another organization, who also happens to be a White man, and use that hard data for the purpose of the study. Bridgette and Kyle disagreed at multiple points throughout the focus group interview. When one made a statement, the other countered. Things escalated when discussing another local organization that served the formerly incarcerated. According to the research participants, [said organization] required its members to engage in certain faith-based activities, to which Bridgette objected, stating:

> I'll go [first] … I think in general we're not doing enough to address issues of mass incarceration. I think this is a topic that—somebody please stop me if you think I'm talking too much – I get the sense that here in our society, we have a lock them up and throw away the key attitude towards the incarcerated here in America. And … I think that [faith based communities] want to help and advocate but I don't necessarily agree with imposing—what I feel is an imposition of your faith on someone else because not everyone—if you have somebody who's a Muslim or agnostic or atheist who is in prison, I think it runs counter to [Christian principles] to force people—especially when you have people coming out of the prison system because they've gone through, God knows how many years of having these rigid rules and … [if the program requires residents] to go to church on Sundays … it sounds like it could be very constricting and it may lead people in the wrong direction and it may just be counterproductive. I haven't researched it, [though].

In the comments above, Bridgette seems to be asserting that even with well-intentioned mission statements and personnel, organizations and people can get it wrong in how they service communities in need. Specifically, perhaps it may be counterproductive to require those who have recently been released from prison – with all its stringent rules and protocols – to be subject to a different set of rules and protocols in exchange for having access to goods, services, and housing provided by a faith-based organization.

In response, Kyle sat up in his chair and huffed:

> You know, [that organization] is our governor's very, very favorite program! So, my advice to people going to prison is [to] become a Pentecostal Christian and get in that program and follow through with it and stay in it, even when it gets uncomfortable, and you'll have a better shot at parole.

To Kyle's comments and recommendations above, Bridgette simply responded, 'Wow...' Here, Kyle is quite literally flexing political muscle as a means of backing his point and advancing the Racial Contract. In his view, since the governor endorses the program, and the governor can pardon or commute sentences, then the program is worth participating in, even if it means a participant would have to adopt or change their religion to be a part of it.[5]

Discussion

What our analysis of the focus group interview has shown is that careful attention must be placed on designing and carrying out of such interviews particularly with mixed race participants. Our analysis and recommendation hold constant when White participants are involved even when they are community nominated and/or when they are self-identified as 'liberal', 'forward-thinking', and/or committed to social justice. Our point is certainly not to generalize based on our learning and insights from a single focus group interview – relying mostly on our analysis of the interaction and discourse between two participants, Bridgette and Kyle. Rather, our point is to build transferable lessons that other qualitative researchers should consider in the design and enactment of focus group interviews that place at their core racial justice or other topics where people have strong views that may be polarized and polarizing.

In *The Racial Contract*, Mills (1997) wrote:

> The silence of mainstream moral and political philosophy on issues of race is a sign of the continuing power of the Contract over its signatories, an illusory color blindness that actually entrenches White privilege. A genuine transcendence of its terms would require, as a preliminary, the acknowledgement of its past and present existence and the social, political, economic, psychological, and moral implications it has had both for its contractors and its victims. By treating the present as a somehow neutral baseline, with its given configuration of wealth, property, social standing, and psychological willingness to sacrifice, the idealized social contract renders permanent the legacy of The Racial Contract.

From a Racial Contract perspective, we argue that Kyle hijacks the conversation and positioned himself as *the* authority on why incarceration exists and how to get Black people out of prison. Although The Racial Contract as a theoretical project advances white supremacy and other forms of structural oppression, it does not explain what we also witnessed in our analysis of the focus group interview as the White man becomes the arbiter of knowledge and knowing over a Black woman – with a law degree.

The Racial Contract advances the idea that White people construct agreements that attempt to subordinate and own ideas about reality. Kyle, in the focus group, became visibly frustrated when Bridgette disagreed with his positions. Kyle seemed to view Bridgette's perspective as an anecdotal, unsubstantiated narrative that he viewed as inferior to his view. From a Racial Contract Theory perspective, Kyle's epistemological orientation around what datapoints were reliable advanced a 'hard data' vis-a-vis numbers and statistics that should be privileged in his view over Bridgette's ontological ways of knowing based on her own reality – historical and contemporarily as an attorney.

Mills (1997) explained that non-White people are not consenting parties to the agreement that they are inferior to White people (even in instances where non-White people are pretending to consent as a means of politics, strategy, or survival). As we examined the focus group interview, Bridgette was clearly not willing to accept Kyle's claims in classifying young people in the juvenile system as 'feral children'. Moreover, Bridgette rejected Kyle's recommendation that those incarcerated should follow a religious-affiliated program even though the governor of the state strongly supported it. Bridgette demonstrates in words and persistence that she did not accept The Racial Contract that Kyle was advancing. Kyle's reaction to Bridgette's counter to his ways of knowing in the focus group interview demonstrated that he would double down on his views at the risk of being embarrassed among others in the focus group. From a Racial Contract Theory perspective, White people who fail to live up to the expectations of whiteness run the risk of being shamed or otherwise ostracized by their White peers.

It is also telling, from our view, that Kyle was resolute in what kinds of data would and should count in deciding on strategies to address the school-to-prison pipeline. For instance, it was not clear to us that Kyle even perceived human experience as a legitimate data point as Bridgette shared her grounded view of what was necessary for disrupting an unjust system of oppression. Indeed, as Mills (1997) has stressed, The Racial Contract's epistemology of ignorance precludes White people from being able to fully understand societal dynamics for which they are responsible for constructing to maintain a caste system of injustice.

Implications and conclusion

This study attempted to make contributions to both the literature on the school-to-prison pipeline and social justice research methods. As demonstrated, White people who work in progressive positions or spaces (e.g. to disrupt the school-to-prison pipeline) can still espouse racist and other problematic attitudes and beliefs that not only undermine their efforts to advance social justice but be harmful to Black and Brown people. Simply put, doing liberal work does not equate to having liberal beliefs and practices. Author One, the focus group facilitator, is a Black man who intentionally designed a research study on the school-to-prison pipeline to call attention to systemic racism. From this perspective, the facilitator might be perceived as at least somewhat prepared to probe or ask clarifying questions of Kyle during the interview, such as why he wanted to believe in another organization's dataset over the lived experiences of his coworker. Unfortunately, this was not the case, partly because Author One was in shock. It was jarring, unnerving even, to hear a White man who works as a defense lawyer for Black people describe Black children as feral. More importantly, what *is* the appropriate response for a social and racial justice researcher in that moment? African American writer James Baldwin famously once stated, 'To be a Negro in [the United States] and to be relatively conscious is to be in a rage almost all the time' (NPR 2020). Was the appropriate response in-the-moment to: (a) continue to facilitate in as unbiased a manner as possible; (b) to push back (e.g. probe in a professional manner), or (c) to rage and potentially compromise not just a focus group interview but perhaps one's career as well? And if the appropriate response was to push back, what does it look like to push back as a social and/or racial justice researcher? We ask these questions not to excuse Author One's facilitation techniques, but to pose an important vignette for social and racial justice researchers to mentally walk through prior to conducting focus group interviews. Asking these questions are important not just for the health and safety of the researcher, but the research partici-pants as well, particularly those from marginalized backgrounds.

This analysis raises the role of the researcher in focus group interviews with mixed-raised participants. Social and racial justice researchers must be mindful of and deliberate as they make decisions about addressing conflicts that arise in studies. Author One chose to address the conflict post-interview, in the form of writing about the experience so that it might serve others. Future research could uncover what happens if a researcher chooses to address the conflict during the interview instead. It is important to note here that, after the interview, Author One contacted Bridgette via email and asked how he could support her given the way the interview had gone. Bridgette accepted an offer to meet for coffee at a local Starbucks and shared some of her frustrations with the interview and racism in Nashville more broadly. The conversation was cathartic for both parties, and Bridgette's participation in the interview was profound given that both she and Charles Mills are from the Caribbean. Unfortunately, for Bridgette, the reprieve did not last long. She eventually made the decision to leave not only the organization, but Nashville entirely due to racial battle fatigue (McGee 2021).

While this paper focused primarily on the dialogue between Bridgette and Kyle, it is important to note that the two White women participants in the study also played a role in upholding The Racial Contract. Although both initially engaged in the interview questions, their participation waned as the dialogue between Bridgette and Kyle wore on. In fact, by the end of the interview, their only contribution to the discussion was to ask Kyle to repeat his comment about parole and, after hearing it a second time, to affirm it. 'Well, it's true. That's what worked for my nephew', shared one of the White women after Bridgette muttered 'wow . . . ' in disbelief. While beyond the scope of this study, future studies could further investigate the ways in which White people acquiesce to The Racial Contract and the role gender plays. To be sure, we suspect gender and sexism played a role in Kyle's interactions with Bridgette and more studies are needed to examine these tensions and their intersections (perhaps gender, sexism, and race) in focus group interviews.

As Bell (1992) offered in his prophetic parable of Space Traders, are we to continue to sacrifice Black people to feed a system of white supremacy? Or are we going to do something about it? If the choice is the latter, we argue the path begins with calling out white supremacy, pointing out and disrupting The Racial Contract, and calling people of all races into the resistance. Conducting research on the pipeline and, more importantly, using said research to advance social and racial justice, is paramount for scholars who engage in the work of educational equity.

Notes

1. Charles Mills (1955–2021) was and still is a vital contributor in the fight for racial justice. And though he has physically departed this world, his scholarship and insights into how The Racial Contract manifests not only in global society but even within small interface group dynamics is, sadly, still relevant today.
2. According to a recent Brookings Report (2018), Nashville's zip code 37,208 is the most incarcerated zip code in the nation.
3. Throughout this article, we use pronouns that participants specified appropriate.
4. All names used for research participants are pseudonyms.

5. The program in question does not require participants to adopt or change their religion. The first author was able to interview both personnel and participants to confirm this to be the case.

Corresponding Author E-Mail Address: bryant.o.best@vanderbilt.edu

Bryant O. Best is a PhD Candidate in the Justice and Diversity in Education program at Vanderbilt University. Best's research seeks to use asset-based epistemologies and frameworks to counteract deficit narratives of Black and Brown communities.

H. Richard Milner IV is the Cornelius Vanderbilt Chair of Education at Vanderbilt University. Milner is President and a Fellow of the American Educational Research Association and an elected member of the National Academy of Education. His current research focuses on the lived educational experiences of people formerly incarcerated.

Disclosure statement

No potential conflict of interest was reported by the authors.

References

Ahmed, A., T. Vandrevala, J. Hendy, C. Kelly, and A. Ala. 2022. "An Examination of How To Engage Migrants in the Research Process: Building Trust Through an 'Insider' Perspective." *Ethnicity & Health* 27 (2): 463–482. doi:10.1080/13557858.2019.1685651.

Annamma, S. 2016. "Disrupting the Carceral State Through Education Journey Mapping." *International Journal of Qualitative Studies in Education* 29 (9): 1210–1230. doi:10.1080/09518398.2016.1214297.

Artiles, A. J., and S. C. Trent. 1994. "Overrepresentation of Minority Students in Special Education: A Continuing Debate." *The Journal of Special Education* 27 (4): 410–437. doi:10.1177/002246699402700404.

Bahena, S., N. Cooc, R. Currie-Rubin, P. Kuttner, and M. Ng, Eds. 2012. *Disrupting the School-To-Prison Pipeline*. Cambridge, MA: Harvard Educational Review.

Bell, D. 1992. *Faces at the Bottom of the Well: The Permanence of Racism*. New York, NY: Basic Books.

J J. Blake, V M. Keith, W. Luo, H. Le, and P. Salter. 2017. "The Role of Colorism in Explaining African American females' Suspension Risk." *School Psychology Quarterly* 32 (1): 118–130. doi:10.1037/spq0000173.

Browne-Dianis, J. 2011. "Stepping Back from Zero Tolerance." *Educational Leadership* 69 (1): 24–28.

Camacho, S. 2019. "From Theory to Practice: Operationalizing Transformative Mixed Methods with and for the Studied Population." *Journal of Mixed Methods Research* 14 (3): 1–31. doi:10.1177/1558689819872614.

Chavez, C. 2008. "Conceptualizing from the Inside: Advantages, Complications, and Demands on Insider Positionality." *Qualitative Report* 13 (3): 474–494.

Connor, D., W. Cavendish, T. Gonzalez, and P. Jean-Pierre. 2019. "Is a Bridge Even Possible Over Troubled Waters? The Field of Special Education Negates the Overrepresentation of Minority Students: A DisCrit Analysis." *Race Ethnicity and Education* 22 (6): 723–745. doi:10.1080/13613324.2019.1599343.

Curran, F.C. 2016. "Estimating the Effect of State Zero Tolerance Laws on Exclusionary Discipline, Racial Discipline Gaps, and Student Behavior." *Educational Evaluation and Policy Analysis* 38 (4): 647–668. doi:10.3102/0162373716652728.

Delgado-Gaitan, C. 1993. "Researching Change and Changing the Researcher." *Harvard Educational Review* 63 (4): 389–412. doi:10.17763/haer.63.4.b336053463h71081.

Foster, M. 1997. *Black Teachers on Teaching*. New York, NY: The New Press.

Jabbari, J., and O. Johnson Jr. 2020. "The Collateral Damage of In-School Suspensions: A Counterfactual Analysis of High-Suspension Schools, Math Achievement and College Attendance." *Urban Education* 58 (5): 1–37. doi:10.1177/0042085920902256.

Jordan, K. A. 2005. "Discourses of Difference and the Overrepresentation of Black Students in Special Education." *The Journal of African American History* 90 (1–2): 128–149. doi:10.1086/JAAHv90n1-2p128.

Koon, D.S-V. 2020. "Education Policy Networks: The Co-Optation, Coordination, and Commodification of the School-To-Prison Pipeline Critique." *American Educational Research Journal* 57 (1): 371–410. doi:10.3102/0002831219855338.

Losen, D.J., and P. Martinez 2020, October. *Lost opportunities: How disparate school discipline continues to drive differences in the opportunity to learn*. https://escholarship.org/uc/item/7hm2456z.

Love, B.L. 2019. *We Want to Do More Than Survive: Abolitionist Teaching and the Pursuit of Educational Freedom*. Boston, MA: Beacon Press.

Marshall, C., and G.B. Rossman. 2011. *Designing Qualitative Research. Fifth Edition*. ed. Newbury Park, CA: SAGE Publications, Inc.

Matias, C.E., Ed. 2020. *Surviving Becky(s): Pedagogies for Deconstructing Whiteness and Gender*. Lanham, MD: Lexington Books.

McGee, E.O. 2021. *Black, Brown, Bruised: How Racialized STEM Education Stifles Innovation*. Cambridge, MA: Harvard Education Press.

Mills, C.W. 1997. *The Racial Contract*. Ithaca, NY: Cornell University Press.

Milner, H.R. 2007. "Race, Culture, and Researcher Positionality: Working Through Dangers, Seen, Unseen, and Unforeseen." *Educational Researcher* 36 (7): 388–400. doi:10.3102/0013189X07309471.

Milner, H.R. 2013. "Why are Students of Color (Still) Punished More Severely and Frequently Than White Students?" *Urban Education* 48 (4): 483–489. doi:10.1177/0042085913493040.

Milner, H.R. 2015. *Rac(e)ing to Class: Confronting Poverty and Race in Schools and* Classrooms. Cambridge, MA: Harvard Education Press.

Milner, H.R. 2020a. *Start Where You are but Don't Stay There: Understanding Diversity, Opportunity Gaps, and Teaching in Today's Classrooms*. Second ed. Cambridge, MA: Harvard Education Press.

Milner, H.R. 2020b. "*Brown* Lecture: Disrupting Punitive Practices and Policies: Rac(e)ing Back to Teaching, Teacher Preparation, and *Brown*." *Educational Researcher* 49 (3): 147–160. doi:10.3102/0013189X20907396.

Milner, H R. Cunningham, H. B. Delale-O'Connor, L. and Kestenberg, Erika G. 2019. "These Kids are Out of control": Why We Must Reimagine "Classroom management" for Equity. Corwin Press.

Morris, M. 2016. *Pushout: The Criminalization of Black Girls in Schools*. New York, NY: The New Press.

Noguera, P.A. 2003. "Schools, Prisons, and Social Implications of Punishment: Rethinking Disciplinary Practices." *Theory into Practice* 42 (4): 341–350. doi:10.1207/s15430421tip4204_12.

NPR. (2020, June 1). "To Be in a Rage, Almost All the Time." *NPR*. https://www.npr.org/2020/06/01/867153918/-to-be-in-a-rage-almost-all-the-time#:~:text=In%201961%2C%20author%20James%20Baldwin,time%20%E2%80%94%20and%20in%20one's%20work.

F A. Pearman, F C. Curran, B. Fisher, and J. Gardella. 2019. "Are Achievement Gaps Related to Discipline Gaps? Evidence from National Data." *AERA Open* 5 (4): 1–18. doi:10.1177/2332858419875440.

Perry, B.L., and E.W. Morris. 2014. "Suspending Progress: Collateral Consequences of Exclusionary Punishment in Public Schools." *American Sociological Review* 79 (6): 1067–1087. doi:10.1177/0003122414556308.

Skiba, R.J., R S. Michael, A C. Nardo, and R L. Peterson. 2002. "The Color of Discipline: Sources of Racial and Gender Disproportionality in School Punishment." *The Urban Review* 34 (4): 317–342. doi:10.1023/A:1021320817372.

Stovall, D. 2018. "Are We Ready for 'School' Abolition?: Thoughts and Practices of Radical Imaginary in Education." *Taboo: The Journal of Culture & Education* 17 (1): 51–61. doi:10.31390/taboo.17.1.06.

U.S. Department of Education Office for Civil Rights. 2014. *Civil Rights Data Collection Data Snapshot: School Discipline.* Washington, D.C.

U.S. Department of Justice Civil Rights Division & U.S. Department of Education Office for Civil Rights. (2014). Washington, D.C. https://www2.ed.gov/about/offices/list/ocr/letters/colleague-201401-title-vi.pdf.

Vox. 2021. "How This Nashville Community is Turning Pain into Resilience." February 18.

Welsh, R.O., and S. Little. 2018. "The School Discipline Dilemma: A Comprehensive Review of Disparities and Alternative Approaches." *Review of Educational Research* 88 (5): 752–794. doi:10.3102/0034654318791582.

PART IV

The Racial Contract beyond

Rejecting the Racial Contract: Charles Mills and critical race theory

George Lipsitz

ABSTRACT

In this article, I explore the deep roots and long history of the attacks on Critical Race Theory in education, while at the same time savoring the equally long and eminently venerable and presently visible traditions forged by "the insights of generations of anonymous 'race men' [and 'race women] who, under the most difficult circumstances" developed 'the concepts necessary to trace the contours of the system oppressing them, defying the massive weight of a white scholarship that either morally justified this oppression or denied its existence' (1996, 131). I identify Critical Race Theory as the product of a long history of Afro-diasporic autonomous learning centers and parallel institutions as well as the producer of new ones.

Introduction

Six weeks before he died of cancer on 20 September 2021, Charles Mills responded to an invitation by American Sociological Association (ASA) president Aldon D. Morris to speak about the coordinated right-wing campaign against Critical Race Theory (CRT) in the United States. Appearing on a panel at the ASA annual meeting, Mills identified the attacks on CRT as manifestations of the concept of the 'racial contract' that he established and developed extensively in a generative series of books and articles published over the preceding quarter century (Mills 1997, 1998; Mills and Kalumba ; Mills 2007b, 2014, 2017). In those writings, Mills argues that white supremacy is not an aberrant or anomalous departure from the principles of European humanism, but the logical result of centuries of thought and action grounded in the premise that European humanism requires seeing only white Europeans as fully human, while consigning people perceived to be nonwhite to the status of sub-persons judged to be not yet fit for freedom (Mills 1997).

In this article, I argue that the racial contract as Mills theorizes it contains important yet often overlooked implications for understanding social movement mobilization as a key crucible of oppositional knowledge and as a mechanism through which the racial contract has been both implemented and resisted. I contend that along with his genius as a philosopher of race and power, Mills was also an original and generative thinker about education, about the ways in which unjust social relations are learned and legitimated but also countered and contested in dispersed learning sites inside and outside of classrooms.

This article employs a mixed methods approach. It begins with a critical examination of the importance that Mills gives to practical political action in his theorization of the racial contract. It then presents an interpretive autoethnography (Denzin 2014) of my interactions with Mills on the 2021 ASA panel and during our years working together on the Countering Colorblindness Across the Disciplines project of the African American Policy Forum (AAPF) founded by Critical Race Theorists Kimberlé Crenshaw and Luke Harris. I then contextualize and evaluate those experiences through a political critique and discourse analysis of the contemporary campaign against Critical Race Theory in education. Mills recognized the campaign against CRT as manifestly political rather than purely pedagogical or epistemological, in part because so much of his own formation as an intellectual originated in extra academic social movement mobilizations. I argue that the students who developed CRT in elite law schools in the 1980s were influenced and guided by social movements in their home communities just as Mills was. I contend that their ideas and tactics succeeded because they were based on lessons learned from popular struggles at the grass roots. I conclude by pointing to connection to contemporary struggles like these an essential part of the needed response to the attack on CRT.

The campaign against CRT in education seeks to turn back the clock and restore the racial contract to its central role as a mechanism of racist rule. It functions as a stalking horse for even more draconian efforts to expunge from K-12 classrooms specifically, and from U.S. society more broadly, access to the ideas, experiences, aspirations, and analyses of people who are not white. It portends disastrous pedagogical and epistemological consequences for all students, because it substitutes indoctrination for inquiry, kills curiosity, and leaves those it miseducates completely unprepared for living in our multi-racial, multi-lingual, and multi-national world that is augmented rather than diminished by recognition of social difference. The article deploys Mills' theorization of the racial contract to argue that the right wing social movement mobilization against CRT in education needs to be countered by an equally committed and organized social movement on behalf of racial justice.

Theorizing the contract

In all of his writing, but especially in his books *The Racial Contract* (1997), and *Blackness Visible* (1998), Mills demonstrates that the moral philosophy of Immanuel Kant and the political liberalism of John Locke hinged on deeply racist judgments about the Indigenous peoples of Africa, the Americas, and Asia. The key European theorists of morality and freedom hinged their analyses on denial of the ways in which conquest, coloniality, slavery, dispossession, and displacement fueled European global dominance. Liberal theory holds that when conquered, colonized, and enslaved people and their descendants do not experience the fairness and equality promised by western humanism, it is either their fault for being unfit for freedom or the fault of individual racists whose actions and ideas are marginal rather than mainstream (Mills 1997, 2017). For Mills, however, the liberal project that preaches universal inclusion functions in practice as a relentless generator of differential exclusion.

Mills finds seeds of white supremacy planted inside the political liberalism of the social contract – in the presumptions of a theory based on imagining what a perfectly just world would be. Contract theorists like John Rawls claim that society is held together by the quest for social relations that benefit all people and enable them to come together for mutual advantage. By making this idealized abstraction the normative rule, the concrete history of Euro-American racial subordination automatically becomes treated as an anomalous exception. Because of the denial of racism at its core, the social contract that is invoked by these theorists is for Mills actually a racial contract that makes white supremacy the 'unnamed political system that has made the world what it is today' (Mills 1997, 1). Insistence on the racial neutrality and innocence of the social contract guarantees that the critics who protest racial domination are not heard; they are like witnesses at a trial whose testimony is ruled inadmissible even before they take the stand.

The racial contract is thus also a knowledge contract based on what Mills calls an 'epistemology of ignorance' that establishes norms of cognition grounded in 'misunderstanding, misrepresentation, evasion, and self-deception on matters related to race ...' (Mills 1997, 19). Rather than identifying an already existing social contract formulated to enable people to work together for mutual benefit, contract theorists actually produce and protect a racial contract that guarantees that those who benefit most from it will be unable to understand the world in which they live. As Mills asserted in his presentation at the 2021 ASA panel, the campaign against CRT – with its claims of white injury and white innocence and its insistence on white immunity from accountability for racial subordination – is not a dangerous new development but rather only the latest manifestation of patterns of thought and action at the heart of social structures and systems that have long produced white supremacist effects without having to declare white supremacist intent. The campaign against CRT purports to be a reaction against new kinds of lessons taught and new kinds of books assigned to k-12 classrooms, but in reality it replicates a longstanding social pedagogy designed to preserve the epistemology of ignorance as part of a centuries old whiteness protection program.

Mills emphasizes that contract theory posits that implicit assumptions and tacit agreements provide the basis for not only how people understand the world but also for how they act within it. The theorists' stipulation that contracts are made by humans for human purposes enables Mills to examine white supremacy as not only a collection of ideas but also an assemblage of social practices and institutional arrangements created with intention by those who benefit from them. Mills describes the racial contract as the entity that produces 'a particular power structure of formal and informal rule, socioeconomic privilege, and norms for the differential distribution of material wealth and opportunities, benefits and burdens, rights and duties' (Mills 1997, 3). Mills explains that white supremacy is an ongoing activity rooted in concrete structures that channel wealth, opportunities, political power, and other benefits to white people, while imposing artificial, arbitrary, and irrational impediments to well-being to those designated as not white (Mills 1997). The abstraction of white supremacy acquires its determinate social impact through action. Its world view shapes the contours of a vast array of historically and socially specific practices, processes, structures, and systems. This emphasis on action opens the door to seeing the importance of social movements as vehicles for rejecting the racial contract.

Mills observes that white people do not pre-exist; it is their interpellation by the racial contract that makes them 'white'. Sara Ahmed and George Yancy (among others) have written perceptively about the ways in whiteness becomes activated at the point of contact with its designated others (Ahmed 2007, 2012; Yancy 2008). Their arguments help explain why some of the most zealously policed places are sites of inter-racial encounter: schools, stores, and streets; buses, beaches, and bathrooms; playgrounds, parks, and prisons. Mills augments this insight with insistence that interpellation begins *before* the moment of contact because the racial contract is inscribed in the ways of knowing and ways of thinking that guide the quotidian practices of everyday life. As I have argued elsewhere, the racial contract is implemented through residential and school segregation, employment discrimination and mass incarceration, and environmental and medical racism (Lipsitz 2011, Lipsitz 2018). The racial contact is thus not so much a mediator of race relations as it is a mechanism of racist rule.

In connecting the social contract as an abstraction to the workings of the racial contract as an assemblage of concrete actions, Mills opens the door to this article's exploration of the campaign in the United States against Critical Race Theory (CRT) – and of CRT itself – as products of activity by social movements. Social movements organize their constituents to identify a problem from a particular perspective, often focusing on a condition, action, or event they deem intolerable and in need of a response. They attribute the problem to particular causes and engage in actions to advance new ideas and to create collective identities. Social movements generally recognize that they cannot achieve all of their goals immediately, so they employ tactics in support of transitional demands that provide participants with transformational experiences that commit them even more deeply to future struggles. Although generally but not always located outside dominant political institutions, social movements can produce social significant social changes (Touraine 1988).

Meetings with Mills: an autoethnography

When Mills and I appeared jointly on the 2021 ASA panel, we had been working together for more than a decade as co-participants in the Countering Colorblindness Across the Disciplines Project. As Chair of the Board of Directors of the African American Policy Forum (AAPF), I joined with AAPF's co-founders Critical Race Theorists Luke Charles Harris and Kimberlé Williams Crenshaw to convene in 2009 an interdisciplinary working group to address how and why colorblindness functions as the default position for racial justice within different disciplines. Participants included (among others) legal scholars Devon Carbado and Kimberly West-Faulcon, historians Carol Anderson and Nikhil Pal Singh, economist William P. Darity, sociologist Tukufu Zuberi, political scientist Daniel Martinez HoSang, psychologist Glenn Adams, cultural studies specialists Chandan Reddy, Felice Blake, and Paula Ioanide, and education researchers Leah Gordon and Alfredo Artiles.

We selected Charles Mills to begin the 2009 meeting. His brilliant presentation distilled and crystalized our diverse experiences. It was remarkable in its erudition and insight, as well as its deft use of humor to uncrown power and embolden critique of power's predations. Mills enabled us to see that racism had epistemological as well as embodied origins, and that it relied on ways of knowing that could be upended and replaced. Crenshaw, Harris, and I had long been searching for ways to break down disciplinary silos, to prompt scholars to see that the racism they encountered in each discipline was overdetermined by its replication in others. Mills showed us how to do that job. His contestation of ahistorical and de-racialized abstractions in philosophy opened the door to similar challenges to the many different power blind and putatively raceless approaches we encountered across the disciplines.

What Mills started that day led to a project that entailed scholars offering courses on color blindness in 15 different universities and colleges, to dozens of presentations at campus colloquia and meetings of scholarly associations, and to the publication of scores of articles and books. It resulted in publication of the critical anthology *Seeing Race Again: Countering Colorblindness across the Disciplines* (Crenshaw et al. 2019) which examines how colorblind remedies came to be posited as the privileged solutions to color-bound problems in law, psychology, musicology, history, literature, and education. Participants in all facets of the Countering Colorblindness project recognized how their disciplines used ungrounded abstractions to protect and preserve racial injustice. The knowledge dispensed to us by teachers in classrooms and by scholars in research publications clashed with our embodied experiences, especially for those members of the group whose experiences entailed membership in and identification with aggrieved communities of color.

As sociologist Neda Maghbouleh notes in her splendid analysis of the continuing influence and impact of *The Racial Contract*, Mills frequently described himself as a Third World/Global South subject from Jamaica who was called to consciousness initially as a teenager by the protest campaigns and riots opposing the expulsion of Walter Rodney from that country in 1968 (Maghbouleh 2022). That early life awakening prepared Mills for the extra-academic education he received as a graduate student in Toronto where he participated in challenges to the neocolonial order by Anglo-Caribbean activists that drew him into support groups, forums, rallies, discussions, and lectures. He turned to philosophy in hopes of getting 'a big picture overview' of the injustices he observed and fought against (Philosophy News University of Toronto 2018).

Black, Asian American, and Latinx participants in Countering Colorblindness shared Mills' experiences with racial subjection and subordination. They too had come to the disciplines looking for 'a big picture overview' only to find knowledge regimes that misrepresented them and made their histories invisible. Those like me who were white no doubt missed many of the particular dimensions and injustices of these occlusions in our educations. Yet prodded and instructed by our colleagues of color, we too learned to be critical of the ingrained racism in our disciplines, sometimes sensing intuitively before we grasped intellectually how fundamentally the epistemology of ignorance distorted reality and left us with a view of racist subordination that evaded power so thoroughly that it simply did not make sense.

Crenshaw, Harris, and I grew up in industrialized cities (Canton in Ohio, Camden and Paterson in New Jersey, respectively) where the skewing of life chances and opportunities along racial lines was clearly evident. In our three hometowns urban renewal projects decapitalized and depopulated Black neighborhoods as businesses and homes were torn down to make room for highways designed to serve the needs and augment the wealth of suburban commuters. Yet these conditions provoked determined resistance from race-based social movements that influenced each of us profoundly. Crenshaw and Harris lived in communities where neighbors and siblings fixed their hair in 'natural' styles, wore dashikis, and placed photographs on their bedroom walls of John Carlos and Tommy Smith raising clenched fists cloaked in black gloves in their protest against racism at their medal awards ceremony at the 1968 Olympics. In their neighborhoods and homes, people encountered oppositional newspapers, especially *The Black Panther* and *Muhammad Speaks*. They listened to music by Gil Scott-Heron and Nina Simone. Some of them were part of the first cohorts of Black students to desegregate previously nearly all white institutions of higher learning, many of whom enrolled in ethnic studies courses, tutored inner city school children, and worked to help Black candidates win elective offices. In their communities, they were exposed to arts groups and musical ensembles that connected them powerfully to what Cedric Robinson has aptly named 'the penetrative comprehension of Black opposition' (Robinson 2000, 5).

As a white person, my experiences differed from those of Crenshaw and Harris in significant ways. My family benefited from the racist policies that oppressed them. My whiteness protected me from the mistreatment that Crenshaw and Harris received from teachers, counselors, and police officers. Yet attending an integrated high school in a city where Black activists protested constantly against police brutality and called on city officials repeatedly to compel slumlords to obey local health and safety codes opened my eyes to another part of the world. As a college student in St. Louis I came under the tutelage of working class Black activists who mounted campaigns against housing and employment discrimination, transit racism, and police killings of unarmed Black youths (Lipsitz 2015). Over the years, my teaching in ethnic studies departments populated mainly by people of color and my involvement in social movements led by Black activists fighting for health and housing justice provided me with grammars and vocabularies of opposition that have informed all of my subsequent research, teaching, and activism. My connections to Black struggle and Black study, however, have always entailed, and continued to entail, the potential to do more harm than good. White allies can be tactically useful to Black freedom struggles, but that utility always has to be judged in the context of a history where even well-intentioned white allies have reinforced rather than rejected the hierarchies inscribed in the racial contract. Desires for an exculpatory whiteness, for a redeemed white identity are understandable, but ultimately counterproductive. Soothing white psyches or saving white souls can undermine the more important imperative to save Black lives. Yet fighting white supremacy is too important for white people to leave to others; even if our tools for fighting it are imperfect. Mistakes can be corrected, but sitting on the sidelines is inexcusable.

Crenshaw and Harris found it useful to invite me in 2008 to serve as chair of the board of directors of the African American Policy Forum. In that capacity until my recent retirement I got the opportunity to work with and learn from many of the key architects of Critical Race Theory including Cheryl Harris, Devon Carbado, Sumi Cho, Mari Matsuda, Charles Lawrence, Khalid Beydoun, and Aileen Moreton Robinson. My presence as Board chair helped illustrate the arguments made by Crenshaw and Harris that racism is a current of power rather than merely a marker of embodied identity. It helped them make clear that while their agenda was race-based, it was not race-bound. My presence in an anti-racist organization challenged the disembodied universalism privileged in law and the disciplines but eschewed any narrow racial essentialism. Although we recognized strong affinities connecting the scholarship we produced, the key place where our paths crossed came from how we blended research and teaching with social movement participation. The three of us had and continue to have deep commitments to the kinds of extra-academic sites that Mills credits for his political awakening.

My presentation at the 2021 ASA panel preceded the one given by Mills. I attempted to alert sociologists to historical currents in the discipline that resonated with the racial contract. I noted that nearly a century ago W.E.B. Du Bois argued that white supremacy was a form of intellectual enfeeblement. Du Bois noted that white supremacy made its defenders become childishly furious when criticized and led them to take all disagreements as personal attacks. I noted that CRT emerged initially in the 1980s as a counter to the educational system created by that enfeeblement. It was a result of the clash between the lived experiences of law students from aggrieved communities of color and the ways those experiences were misrepresented in legal education and practice.

The interdisciplinary focus of the Countering Colorblindness project came to the fore in the presentations that Mills and I made that day, I maintained that CRT was an epistemology (a way of knowing) and an ontology (a way of being). In response, Mills joked that since I used terms from philosophy like epistemology and ontology, he had the right to locate the campaign against CRT historically. In a presentation reminiscent of arguments made frequently by political scientist Cedric Robinson (2000), Mills noted the long history dating back nearly one thousand years of the use of difference as an excuse for domination. He added, however, that a more recent history was also at work: that the hysteria about CRT was a response to the gains made by contemporary anti-racist social movements that threatened the historically privileged status of the beneficiaries of the racial contract. Reprising an argument he made three years earlier in an interview, Mills explained that precisely because contemporary white ignorance had now become more exposed and more vulnerable to critique, it had also become more belligerent and militant. Mills cautioned against paying too much attention to white supremacy's particular extremist fringes and losing sight of its existence as a knowledge and social system that secures unearned advantages for white people at the expense of their demonized racial others (Philosophy News University of Toronto 2018)

CRT as a social movement

The Critical Race Theory that Mills and I discussed on the 2021 ASA Panel was the creation of students in elite law schools in the 1980s, along with many of their family members, neighbors, and friends, they were eyewitnesses to – and participants in – a vast array of parallel institutions created by the Black freedom movement and other struggles for social justice in the 1960s and 1970s (Ture, Carmichael, and Hamilton 2014). Grassroots groups working for Black self-defense, self-definition, and self-determination built on long histories of community conservatories and alternative academies to create citizenship schools (Payne 2020), co-operative farms and Community Land Trusts (Sherrod 2010; Onaci 2020), alternative electoral systems and political parties (Jeffries 2010), medical testing and treatment centers (Nelson 2011), trade union caucuses (Georgakas and Surkin 1998), poor people's movements and welfare rights organizations (Tsuchiya 1988), community action patrols monitoring police misconduct (Widener 2010), and a wide array of self-defense and 'serve the people' organizations (Haas 2019).

These parallel institutions prefigured how a just society might work by enacting the social relations they envisioned. They filled needs that were not being met by dominant educational, economic, electoral, medical, and public safety institutions. They responded to the radical divisiveness caused by racism and poverty by establishing sites of exuberant solidarity where strangers could become friends and antagonists could become allies. By inviting participants to recognize their linked fates and to work together for change, the parallel institutions fended off resignation and despair while promoting the self-confidence and self-activity that flows from convivial collaboration. They augmented the efficacy of aggrieved groups by deepening their collective capacity for democratic deliberation and decision-making, and started to build in the present a tangible pre-figuration of the world they wished to inhabit in the future, without having to ask or wait for permission from their oppressors to do so. CRT came into being as yet another parallel institution.

The law students who created CRT challenged their teachers' expectations of how to make normative progress through three years of law school. They rejected the law's distortions of the history of Abolition Democracy and its pretensions of timeless uni-versality. They insisted that the true histories of racist subordination and anti-racist resistance be added to the curriculum. They brought with them to the law school memories of past histories of struggle against subordination that shaped their conscious-ness in the present. They sought to craft a future that could produce collective liberation as well as personal professional success. They did not see themselves living in a time of gradual yet certain triumphant progress toward a socially just future, but instead chafed against the injuries inflicted by dreams deferred.

CRT thus emerged as a parallel institution responding to the sharp contrast between the lived experiences of members of aggrieved communities of color and the representa-tions of those experiences that they encountered in law school, political discourse, and popular culture. Modest but largely tokenistic gestures toward desegregation in elite law schools brought into classrooms a small but energized cohort of students whose previous training in parallel institutions and autonomous learning centers made them critical of the curricula they encountered in professional school (Crenshaw 2011). The Third World Coalition at the Harvard Law School which included Crenshaw, Cecil McNab, George Bisharat, Glenn Morris, Mari Mayeda, Joe Garcia, and Ibrahim Gassama mounted as a parallel institution their own 'Alternative Course' in race and law by soliciting guest lectures from outside legal scholars, among them Richard Delgado, Linda Greene, Neil Gotanda, Charles Lawrence, Denise Carty-Bennia, Ralph Smith, John Brittan, and Haywood Burns (Crenshaw 2011).

These students and scholars of law had witnessed brutal repression of social justice movements by the forces of 'law and order'. Their communities suffered from state implicated assassinations and systematic incarceration of a generation of anti-racist activists. The law school curriculum addressed practically none of these experiences. It failed to deal with the limits of civil rights laws as written or with the judicial rulings that undermined enforcement even of those modest statutes. Law school education seemed oblivious to the causes and consequences of mass incarceration, and appeared indecently complacent in the face of the substantial segment of the legal community that contended that securing constitutional rights for aggrieved racialized groups perpetrated 'reverse discrimination' against white people.

Although disappointed in the shortcomings of the law school curriculum, the students were not unprepared to confront and contest it. The Supreme Court's decisions in school desegregation cases in San Antonio and Detroit in 1973 and 1974 began a steady retreat from the commitment to integration that the Court proclaimed in its 1954 *Brown v. Board* decision. Actions by the Nixon, Ford, Carter, and especially Reagan administrations enacted what Crenshaw calls the age of repudiation, a systemic reneging on the concessions granted to anti-racist groups during the 1960s (Crenshaw 1995). Decades of relentless white resistance to implementing school desegregation and resisting the fair housing and fair employment practices articulated in civil rights laws provided members of aggrieved communities with expert knowledge about what they were up against and why they had to craft their own mechanisms for recognizing and resisting what at best were merely piecemeal forms of subordinate inclusion. They drew on the kind of wisdom passed on to one young woman in Waco, Texas as she prepared to attend a previously all-white public school. Her grandmother advised her to be respectful but not overly deferential to white teachers, to 'keep your head up and back straight', and to honor obligations to the community that raised and nurtured her by making sure that when she asked a question that it was one that helped other people learn (James-Gallaway 2022). The student was counseled by her grandmother to change the system that she entered, to keep the door through which she was allowed to enter open to others, and to counter the individualist notion of education shaped by the racial contract with an understanding of education as a shared social resource and practice. This kind of collective consciousness and drawing on community cultural wealth armed the law students with the dispositions and tools they needed to create CRT

Harvard Law School students initially made modest demands for the appointment of Black scholars whose presence would begin to desegregate what was then an almost all-white faculty. They asked for courses on civil rights related issues in constitutional law. The law school Dean, one of the leading theorists of racial liberalism, dismissed their requests, telling the students that civil rights were of minor importance in the law and that there were no Black people qualified to teach law at Harvard. Had the Dean acceded to the student requests, CRT might never have come into existence. It was his resistance that compelled them to confront the limits of racial liberalism and to construct a critique of it as a manifestation of the racial contract, just as it is the very campaign against CRT today that proves the need for its existence and an opportunity for its expansion. The students responded by creating parallel institutions, initially in the form of collective study groups. They read widely in existing scholarship on civil rights and identified in that research key concepts that were absent from the law school curriculum. They discovered the existence of works by scholars with original and insightful analyses about the limits of civil rights laws. The students used those writings to create an autonomous learning center which they named the Alternative Course, an unsanctioned non-credit class to which they invited Black legal theorists to give guest lectures. Those lectures and the book of readings the students assembled for it gave rise to the key ideas that would eventually fuel CRT: 1) that civil rights laws did not meaningfully address how law itself constituted the racial structures that produce discrimination, 2) that law is fundamentally a political entity that needs to respond to struggles for social justice by aggrieved groups, and 3) that the principles of sameness/difference and single axis injury in law distorted not only demands for racial justice but also struggles for justice on the basis of gender, sexuality, language, citizenship status, dis/ability, and many other modes of social differentiation (Crenshaw et al. 1995).

The parallel institution that was named the *Alternative Course* (upper case) with its syllabus, course reader, and pedagogical successes generated a wide range of similar law school courses, but also led to a wide array of *alternative* (lower case) *courses* of action inside and outside the academy carried out by scholars, attorneys, advocates, activists, and artists in the years ahead (Crenshaw 2011). Key concepts articulated by CRT scholars spread quickly across disciplines and social contexts. These include intersectionality (Crenshaw 1989, 1991), whiteness as property (Harris 1993, interest convergence (Bell 1980), looking to the bottom of society for the most perceptive critiques of it (Matsuda) and unconscious racism (III and Charles 1987). CRT thus provided tools that added new depth and breadth to scholarly studies of social identities and power while fueling activist interventions in a wide array of dispersed community settings including fair housing councils, Community Land Trusts, reproductive justice organizations, prison abolition projects, labor union struggles, mobilizations for environmental and disability justice, community gardens, and theatre groups. Participants in these activities rarely speak specifically about the racial contract, but their work identifies its hegemony as an intolerable problem, forges a collective identity in opposition to it, and formulates ways to produce transformative experiences that commit people to future activism (Tomlinson and Lipsitz 2019).

These parallel institutions draw upon and expand what Yosso (2005, 2007, 2016) names community cultural wealth. Aggrieved groups lacking material resources must cultivate a collective capacity to be resourceful. They invent practices that nurture and sustain aspirations for success, that teach ways of navigating hostile social settings, that commit individuals to the well-being of the entire community, that rely on supporting and accompanying others, and that promote resistance to mistreatment (Yosso 2005). In the process of meeting immediate needs, parallel institutions also function as autono-mous learning centers. As deployed here, autonomy does not denote full self-rule, complete independence from state power, or freedom from corporate domination. Instead, following Gustavo Esteva and the particular strains of Indigenous thought and action that he endorses, the 'autonomous' in this case refers to the willful reorganization of society from the bottom up on the basis of practices grounded in the things people do for themselves. Esteva (2015) stresses the importance of struggles that do not settle for merely improved access to state structures but instead demand 'respect for styles and designs that surpass them' (Esteva, p.138). Autonomous learning centers do not pretend that the racial contract does not exist, but they do promote ways of interrupting its temporal, spatial and social imperatives and they generate experiences that show parti-cipants that alternative courses of action are possible.

In 'White Time' (2014), Mills explains that the racial contract compels those under its jurisdiction to inhabit the temporality of white history in which the peoples of Asia, Africa, and Latin America are presumed to have had no meaningful past before Europeans conquered them, to be lagging behind in development, and consequently to be rationally and ontologically deficient and in need of modernization. When evidence emerges that shows nonwhite people to not be free, the racial contract instructs its beneficiaries to say with condescension that their victims are simply not *yet* free, but should appreciate all that the dominant culture is doing to move them gradually toward freedom in the future. Mills notes with approval Hanchard's (1999) claim that affirmations of Black humanity have frequently staked claims to oppositional temporalities and chronologies: to a history in which deceased ancestors are still present and owed respect, to calculations about the tempos of work and leisure not tied to the labor demands of industry, and to imperatives for creating time specific improvisations that disrupt power relations in the present rather than merely accepting promises of better days in the future. Autonomous learning centers cannot free participants fully from domination by the racial contract, but they can create temporal alternatives to the working day, the life course, and narrative of historical time. When they explore multiple temporalities in music, dance, and speech, they create crucibles for living outside the clocks and calendars of their oppressors and counter promises of future freedom with insistence on a semblance of liberation now.

Mills' formulations pave the way for acknowledging CRT as a nexus of action that originated inside social movements for race, gender, and class justice. As Kimberlè Crenshaw summarizes its history, CRT was 'dynamically constituted by a series of contestations and convergences pertaining to the ways in that racial power is understood and articulated in the post-civil rights era' (Crenshaw 2011). Its emergence testifies to the accuracy of Robin Kelley's insight that 'social movements generate new knowledge, new theories, new questions. The most radical ideas often grow out of a concrete intellectual engagement with the problems of aggrieved populations confronting systems of oppression' (Kelley 2002, 9).

The campaign against CRT

In keeping with the long and ignoble history of self-serving colorblind pretensions as protective cover for unjust color-bound conditions, the campaign to ban CRT in education imagines that it is legitimate to ban overt recognition of race but illegitimate to expose racist rule. It maintains that the mere mention of race is racist. It pretends that critiques of racism are personal attacks on white people. It enforces the epistemology of ignorance by claiming that true facts should not be taught in schools if they have the potential to make students recognize the existence of whiteness as a social force and structured advantage. The campaign purports to reject the racial contract by ruling inadmissible in advance any testimony that might reveal it.

Yet in their attempts to hide whiteness, the opponents of CRT only make it more visible. The false subject created by the racial contract needs a false object. While outlawing recognition of whiteness, it deploys an endless stream of phobic fantasies rooted in representations of people of color as monstrous. In order for whites to be innocent victims, people of color need to be figured as malicious victimizers. Making whiteness synonymous with humanness relies on what Mills calls a 'contrapuntal ensemble', an interlay of opposites constructed through contrasts between allegedly innocent and virtuous whiteness and monstrous, barbarian, savage, uncivilized, and uncontrollable sub-persons who are not white. This establishes the position of white people as the primary and necessary defenders of civilization. In an inversion familiar to Indigenous people around the world, this discourse portrays its vicious aggression as frontier defense. Mills explains that the affect generated by the racial contract precludes empathy for nonwhite suffering, yet it cultivates self-pitying hypersensitivity to the point of outrage over any policy such as affirmative action presumed to diminish the over-representation and narrow the differential advantage that whites enjoy at the expense of other groups (Mills 1997). Moreover, by making people accustomed to treating aggrieved groups as subhuman, the racial contract prepares its adherents to wage war against women and people who are queer and trans, to ban books about gender non-conformity from libraries and classrooms, and to criminalize forms of marriage and medical care needed by members of those groups.

The analysis of contrapuntal ensembles that Mills presents helps explain the appeal and fervor of the attacks on CRT. As the people who have formulated and funded the public frenzy about it freely admit, they neither know nor care what CRT actually is (Hoadley-Brill 2021; Wallace-Wells 2021). One of its most visible publicists confessed 'The goal is to have the public read something crazy in the newspaper and immediately think "critical race theory". We have decodified the term and will recodify it to annex the entire range of cultural constructions that are unpopular with Americans' (Jones 2021, 4). CRT functions as a floating signifier, as a term that can be used to tap anxieties among whites, anxieties that have long been present but became exacerbated and inflamed in 2020 by the mass mobilization of the movement for Black lives that erupted in response to the killings of George Floyd and Breonna Taylor. That collective assertion of Black subjectivity and its concomitant affirmation of Black humanity struck many white people as an unforgivable offense, a repudiation of the racial contract (Matias and Newlove 2017). The only racial injury that the opponents of CRT are willing to recognize is the prospect that anti-racism will make white people feel uncomfortable, as if white feelings alone are to be protected (see Matias 2016). Thus, the opponents of CRT seek to establish as a matter of law that white vanity is to be more respected than nonwhite humanity.

The arguments against CRT in the United States advanced by the apparatchiks of conservative think tanks and their allies in politics seek to construct a social movement grounded in what can most charitably be described as a series of distortions, but which in fact are intentional lies. The campaign promotes moral panics through allegations that CRT is a form of indoctrination that defames innocent white people as perpetually guilty of personal racism simply because of their biological makeup. These charges misrepresent the actual arguments made within CRT that hold 1) that race is a social and legal construction not an immutable embodied property of individuals (Crenshaw 2019); 2) that whiteness is a socially performed, historically constructed, and legally administered systemic structural advantage perpetuated not primarily by individuals but by deeply ingrained practices and powerful institutions (Williams 1990; Carbado and Gulati 2013), and 3) that whiteness is not the same as white people, that while all white people benefit from the racial contract, not all have been, or wish to be, signatories to it (Williams 1997). CRT assumes that people do not choose their parents or their pigments. Rather, it encourages people to make better choices about their politics and their principles.

The critics of CRT project onto it the racist impulses and beliefs central to their own identities as shaped by the racial contract. They allege that CRT claims that each member of a group is responsible for wrongdoing by any member of that group, and that recognizing difference requires domination by one group over others. The campaign against CRT has led to laws, educational policies, and proposals to make it illegal for students to learn that Indigenous dispossession, coloniality, slavery, and segregation are anything other than aberrations from an imagined race-free history. A proposed bill in Kentucky mandated withholding $5,000 per day from school districts where teachers were found to be using materials which parents or the state's attorney general found objectionable (Clark 2021). They do not make the case for these policies on the basis of evidence or reasoned argument, but instead use the power of the state to make sure the argument does not even take place. They do not refute or even respond to the CRT analysis that neighborhoods, schools, and jobs remain unjustly racially segregated; that vote dilution, voter suppression, and gerrymandering artificially augment the political power of white people; and that civil rights laws offer completely inadequate remedies for the harms perpetuated by environmental, medical, and transit racism, as well as by the racist violence of police officers and vigilantes (Lipsitz 2018). Instead, they dictate as a matter of law that the present racial order must be viewed as an unquestionably just baseline norm not to be disturbed. U.S. society is portrayed as innocent of any racial injustice, and the campaign deems that saying otherwise is a criminal act. The opponents of CRT deploy state power to ban a conclusion that is based on evidence: i.e. that racism is systemic and structural rather than aberrant and incidental. They do so not because the conclusion is untrue but because its veracity makes them uncomfortable and because they worry that it threatens to make white children disloyal to the racial projects which many of their parents support and from which they profit (see McKinney 2005; Thandeka 2013).

The attacks on CRT are factually flawed and internally inconsistent. They make no sense as intellectual critique. Yet they contain great utility as a social movement strategy because they recognize the hold that fidelity to the racial contract has on individuals and institutions. Making CRT content illegal in schools is less a utilitarian project that an expressive one. It establishes that the privilege of whiteness means never having to take anti-racist arguments seriously. Exposing the lies and fabrications of the campaign will not discredit it, because it is at heart an exhibitionist exercise in white impunity. Flaunting the facts and evading accountability for implausible arguments produces its particular pleasures and accounts for its appeal. Like the claim that the 2020 presidential election was stolen from the true winner, the attacks on CRT actually *need* to treat lies as truths, because it is precisely getting away with lies and relishing the power to make others knuckle under to them that provides the movement with its deeply sadistic yet affectively pleasing allure. The meanness and mendacity of the campaign against CRT reaffirms the existence of the racial contract as an open secret, as a widely denied yet near universally applied social practice. Under these conditions, the racial contract is more than an epistemological position; it fulfills for the racial contract the performative expressive function that Segato (2010) finds in the impunity offered to killers who get away with murdering Indigenous and poor and working-class women in Mexico. She says that these unprosecuted killings function to create and sustain 'a deep symbolic structure' that teaches perpetrators to revel in their impunity (Segato 2010, 74). Moreover, like the repeated attacks on school desegregation, affirmative action, and efforts to enforce fair housing laws, the attacks on CRT, while purporting merely to correct the unwarranted excess zeal of civil rights advocates, in actuality aim at the full repudiation and repeal of the modest concessions made to the targets of racism by the legal and political reforms of the 1960s and 1970s (Crenshaw 1995). They seek not only an end to the laws and policies that might diminish the over-representation they have come to expect as a natural reward for whiteness, but they seek to enact revenge against the people whose struggles produced those reforms in the first place.

In order to sustain the concocted fictions of the campaign against CRT, the 'conservatives' attacking it violate nearly all the principles they have purported to believe in for the past half century. Conservatives have attributed their opposition to school desegregation to a principled belief in local control of schools. They have portrayed their rejection of laws protecting labor, the environment, and civil rights as expressions of a faith in small government and a manifestation of their belief that only firm family values can instill in people the capacity to solve problems by themselves. They have belittled people who point out that their membership in an aggrieved group deprives them of access to jobs, business contracts, and political representation, advising them to treat any collective consciousness or remedies as a group spoils system and instead to persevere as individuals. They have claimed that they do not 'see color' and would be colorblind were it not for civil rights laws that force them to notice race.

In the campaign against CRT, however, the self-proclaimed proponents of local control of schools use their dominance over state governments (gained through gerrymandered nonwhite vote dilution and suppression and artificially augmented white overrepresentation) to prevent local teachers, parents, administrators, and school boards from making decisions about curriculum and instruction materials. The alleged opponents of big government turn immediately to the state to declare illegal ideas that they cannot refute. They enact laws that mandate thought control, that ban teachers and textbooks from using certain words such as diversity, cultural competence, and implicit bias. In testimony before the education committees of the Wisconsin legislature, one of the co-authors of the bill to ban CRT proposed to make it illegal for teachers to mention any one of a list of 90 words and concepts including anti-racism, anti-blackness, conscious, and unconscious bias, critical self-awareness, cultural relevance, educational justice, equity, intersectionality, multiculturalism, racial justice, structural racism, and whiteness (Vetterkind 2021; Schwartz and Pendharker 2022). People who have argued incessantly that property rights are sacred now prevent privately owned businesses from choosing to provide diversity training for their work force. Claims that bans on CRT protect defenseless children fall apart when the bans are extended to deny library patrons of all ages access to books by Morrison (1994), Coates (2015), and Angelou (1970). Proclamations about the importance of family values and parental authority become exposed as hypocritical pretexts when legislators pass laws and administrators issue rulings that define as child abuse efforts by loving parents to provide gender affirming medical care for their transgender children. Claims of colorblindness disappear when the opponents of CRT assume that the colorblind children of colorblind parents will be made uncomfortable by learning about the history of slavery, segregation, lynching, and repression of the Black freedom movement, assuming that these children will automatically identify with the oppressors whose skin color resembles their own rather than with the content of the character of the freedom fighters, even though some of those were white.

The campaign against CRT thus makes clear that conservatives never believed any of the arguments they have been making for decades, that their 'principles' were mere pretexts to foment racist resentments and defend the unfair gains and unjust enrichments that white people derive from the racial contract. The campaign against CRT tells scholars, teachers, students, and parents concerned about the depths, dimensions and durations of structural racism simply to shut up and go away.

Mills shows why countersubversion constitutes the affective and strategic heart of the racial contract. The beneficiaries and supporters of whiteness are recruited perpetually to repress nonwhite resistance, to 'employ massively disproportionate retaliatory violence' against it (Mills 1997, 86). The attack on CRT deploys what Mills identities as the racial contract's core strategies of insisting on a 'sanitized, whitewashed, and amnesiac account of European imperialism and settlement' (Mills 1997, 121), and by masking its aggressions against people of color as a defense of civilization from the subversion posed demonized 'others' imagined to be subhuman (Mills 1997, 58). The attacks on CRT specifically present 'sanitized, whitewashed, and amnesiac accounts' of race relations in the U.S. They argue that anti-racism is no longer needed because the *Brown v. Board* ruling by the Supreme Court and the 1964 Civil Rights Act ended *de jure* segregation. Celebrating this version of history hides how massive white resistance neutralized the *Brown* decision and civil rights laws. It is important to remember that Bell (1980, 1987, 1992) first formulated CRT's stance on the impregnability of white supremacy precisely out of his experiences litigating cases covered by *Brown v. Board* and witnessing how its implementation was weakened to kept segregation intact (Hughes, Noblit, and Cleveland 2013).

Countersubversion plays a necessary role in the racial contract, because as Mills argues in a long but wonderfully insightful passage, white supremacy lives in dread of

> the cognizers whose mere presence in the halls of white theory is a cognitive threat, because – in the inverted systemic logic of the racial polity – the 'ideal speech situation' requires our absence, since we are, literally, the men and women *who know too much*, who – in that wonderful American expression – *know where the bodies are buried* (after all, so many of them are our own) (Mills 1997, 132).

The concept of the racial contract helps explain why censoring school books and classroom lessons is an imperative for the defenders of whiteness. It reaffirms their group's favored racial position, yet enables them to deny that they even notice race. The production, validation, and dissemination of false knowledge support the social practice of white supremacy because the mechanics of oppression distort and undermine cognition. The toxic blend of contract theory and racial subordination produces an epistemology that renders people incapable of understanding the world in which they live, an incapacity which is on full display in the campaign against CRT.

The campaign against CRT is intellectually insupportable and pedagogically disastrous, but it makes perfect sense as an efficient and effective way of mobilizing a social movement in support of the racial contract. It protects the dominant racial order without having to justify it. It portrays anti-racism as racist. It diverts attention away from the ever-increasing share of wealth monopolized by people who are rich, encourages whites fearful of falling economically or of simply not rising to the wealth level of their expectations and desires to channel their frustrations and fears against demonized racial others. It gives its adherents what seems like meaningful work to do, and it offers a sense of social connection for people wounded daily by competitive individualism and the isolation it produces. It provides the affective pleasures of vicariously wielding power to people who increasingly recognize correctly that they are otherwise powerless to influence the decisions that shape their lives.

Although, the attacks on CRT get nearly everything wrong about the premises, principles, and practices of CRT, about elementary historical facts, and about the nature of classroom pedagogy and instruction, they do get one thing right; They recognize the importance of social movements in shaping social structures and social relations. Of course their movement differs markedly from the freedom movements of the twentieth century whose gains they seek to reverse. They are a top down mobilization funded by wealthy donors whose influence guarantees them fawning coverage in the *Wall Street Journal* and on Fox News. They are coaxed, coached, and coddled by office holders from the Republican Party. Their campaign is orchestrated out of right wing propaganda 'think tanks' such as the Manhattan Institute, best known for promoting claims by Charles Murray that Black people are intellectually inferior to whites and therefore no money should be expended on their education (Hoadley-Brill 2021). Yet the campaign is not simply one of persuasion, it relies on getting its proponents to act, to disrupt school board meetings and threaten teachers and administrators, and to harass librarians into removing books from the shelves. In these ways, the campaign against CRT is being waged by a social movement, and it can be defeated only by opposition from an equally intense and engaged counter-movement.

Mills' concepts, ideas, and arguments help reveal the campaign against CRT to be an assemblage of actions rather than simply an abstraction. Yet the same holds true for CRT itself. Although most often treated by scholars and journalists as if it were merely a theoretical framework, CRT is also a nexus of actions, a product of past social movements, and a producer of present and future forms of collective mobilization and struggle. Its fate rests on the ability of its proponents to mobilize people, to offer supporters important things to do rather than merely novel things to think, to engage in collective mobilizations that deepen the capacity for democratic deliberation and decision-making among people opposed to the racial contract.

Rejecting the racial contract

The concept of the racial contract along with attendant formulations by Mills about racialized time, space, and social relations provide explanations for both the emergence of Critical Race Theory and the attacks against it. The racial contract helps explain how and why people become attached to what I have elsewhere called 'the possessive investment in whiteness', a term that references the lure of material possessions that are acquired because of the unfair gains and unjust enrichments enabled by white supremacy, but which also refers to the ways in which people privileged by whiteness come to be possessed by it psychologically, emotionally, and epistemologically, to the point of being unable to imagine themselves without the artificial, arbitrary, and irrational advantages of whiteness that they believe provide them with a floor below which they cannot fall (Lipsitz 2018).

CRT is not a narrow dogma; its advocates occupy a broad range of political positions. Some of its proponents agree with Mills that a deracialized liberalism may yet be possible and desirable (Mills 2017). Others who do not quite share that belief nonetheless often attempt to drive the law closer to that end through litigation and legislation (Carbado

2011; Ocen 2012; Squires 2012). Some seek to bring about changes through electoral politics. Educators rightfully understand the importance of resisting the attacks on CRT through innovative forms of curriculum, pedagogy, and instruction. I respect all of those stances and wish their champions well. I sometimes participate in their activities as an advocate and ally of democratic education, and as an expert witness and lecturer on fair housing issues. Yet I think that the most important victories that need to be won will be forged inside social movements and their parallel institutions and autonomous learning centers (Tomlinson and Lipsitz 2019).

The death of Charles Mills is a devastating blow to all who had the privilege and pleasure of knowing him, working with him, learning from him, of being inspired and energized by his unique blend of serious thinking and playful critique. We will miss him, yet we need to recognize that in his profound body of scholarship, he has bequeathed to us meaningful work to do and immensely useful tools with which to do it. His identification of the racial contract and his critique of ideal theory enable analysis of the contestations about CRT through the lenses of social movement theory, a lens that reveals social mobilizations and autonomous learning centers to be key sites for racial justice struggles.

Disclosure statement

No potential conflict of interest was reported by the author.

References

Ahmed, Sara. 2007. "The Phenomenology of Whiteness." *Feminist Theory* 8 (2): 149–168. doi:10. 1177/1464700107078139.

Ahmed, Sara. 2012. *On Being Included: Racism and Diversity in Institutional Life*. Durham: Duke University Press.

Angelou, Maya. 1970. *I Know Why the Caged Bird Sings*. New York: Random House.

Bell, Derrick. 1980. "*Brown V. Board of Education* and the Interest-Convergence Dilemma." *Harvard Law Review* 93 (3, January): 518–533. doi:10.2307/1340546.

Bell, Derrick. 1987. *And We are Not Saved: The Elusive Quest for Racial Justice*. New York: Basic.

Bell, Derrick. 1992. *Faces at the Bottom of the Well: The Permanence of Racism*. New York: Basic Books.

Carbado, Devon W. 2011 July. "Critical What What?" *Connecticut Law Review* 43 (5): 1593–1643.

Carbado, Devon W., and Mitu Gulati. 2013. *Acting White? Rethinking Race in 'Post-Racial' America*. New York: Oxford University Press.

Clark, Jess. 2021. "Ky. Lawmaker Wants to Make Teaching Critical Race Theory Illegal". *WKU Public Radio* June 3. Kentucky Lawmaker Wants To Make Teaching Critical Race Theory Illegal (wkyufm.org)

Coates, Ta-Nehisi. 2015. *Between the World and Me*. New York: Spiegel and Grau.

Crenshaw, Kimberlé Williams. 1989. "Demarginalizing the Intersections of Race and Sex: A Black Feminist Theory and Antiracist Politics." *The University of Chicago Legal Forum* 14: 139–167.

Crenshaw, Kimberlé Williams. 1991. "Mapping the Margins: Intersectionality, Identity, and Violence Against Women of Color." *Stanford Law Review* 43 (6): 1241–1299. doi:10.2307/ 1229039.

Crenshaw, Kimberlé Williams. 1995. "Race, Reform, and Retrenchment: Transformation and Legitimation in Anti-Discrimination Law." In *Critical Race Theory: The Key Writings That Formed the Movement*, edited by K. Crenshaw, N. Gotanda, G. Peller, and K. Thomas, 103–122. New York: New Press.

Crenshaw, Kimberlé Williams. 2011 July. "Twenty Years of Critical Race Theory: Looking Back to Move Forward." *Connecticut Law Review* 43 (5): 1253–1352.

Crenshaw, Kimberlé Williams. 2019. "Unmasking Colorblindness in the Law: Lessons from the Formation of Critical Race Theory." In *Seeing Race Again: Countering Colorblindness Across the Disciplines*, edited by K. W. Crenshaw, L. C. Harris, D. M. HoSang, and G. Lipsitz, 52–84. Oakland: University of California Press.

Crenshaw, Kimberlé Williams, Neil Gotanda, Gary Peller, and Kendall Thomas, eds. 1995. *Critical Race Theory: The Key Writings That Framed the Movement*. New York: The New Press.

Crenshaw, Kimberlé Williams, Luke Charles Harris, Daniel Martinez HoSang, and George Lipsitz, eds. 2019. *Seeing Race Again: Countering Colorblindness Across the Disciplines*. Oakland: University of California Press.

Denzin, Norman K. 2014. *Interpretive Ethnography*. Los Angeles: Sage.

Esteva, Gustavo. 2015. "The Hour of Autonomy." *Latin American and Caribbean Ethnic Studies* 10 (1): 134–145. doi:10.1080/17442222.2015.1034436.

Georgakas, Dan, and Marvin Surkin. 1998. *Detroit: I Do Mind Dying: A Study in Urban Revolution*. Boston: South End Press.

Haas, Jeffrey. 2019. *The Assassination of Fred Hampton: How the FBI and the Chicago Police Murdered a Black Panther*. Chicago: Lawrence Hill Books.

Hanchard, Michael. 1999. "Afro-Modernity: Temporality, Politics, and the African Diaspora." *Public Culture* 11 (1): 245–268. doi:10.1215/08992363-11-1-245.

Harris, Cheryl I. 1993. "Whiteness as Property." *Harvard Law Review* 106 (8, June): 1707–1791. doi:10.2307/1341787.

Hoadley-Brill, Samuel. 2021. "Chris Rufo's Critical Race Theory Reporting is Filled with Errors, and He Doesn't Seem to Care," *Flux* July 28, Chris Rufo's critical race theory reporting is filled with errors, and he doesn't seem to care - Flux | Flux

Hughes, Sherick, George Noblit, and Darrell Cleveland. 2013. "Derrick Bell's Post-*Brown* Moves Toward Critical Race Theory." *Race Ethnicity and Education* 16 (4): 442–469. doi:10.1080/13613324.2013.817765.

III, Lawrence, and R. Charles. 1987. ""The Id, the Ego, and Equal Protection: Reckoning with Unconscious Racism." *Stanford Law Review* 39 (January): 317–388.

James-Gallaway, ArCasia D. 2022. "What Got Them Through: Community Cultural Wealth, Black Students, and Texas School Desegregation." *Race Ethnicity and Education* 25 (2): 173–191. doi:10.1080/13613324.2021.1924132.

Jeffries, Hasan Kwame. 2010. *Blood Lowndes: Civil Rights and Black Power in Alabama's Black Belt*. New York: New York University Press.

Jones, Sarah. 2021. "How to Manufacture a Moral Panic: Christopher Rufo Helped Incite an Uproar Over Racism Education with Dramatic, Dodgy Reporting," *New York* July 21. Christopher Rufo and the Critical Race Theory Moral Panic (nymag.com)

Kelley, Robin D. G. 2002. *Freedom Dreams: The Black Radical Imagination*. Boston: Beacon Press.

Lipsiitz, George. 2011. *How Racism Takes Place*. Philadelphia: Temple University Press.

Lipsitz, George. 2015. "From Plessy to Ferguson." *Cultural Critique* 90 (Spring): 119–139. doi:10.5749/culturalcritique.90.2015.0119.

Lipsitz, George. 2018. *The Possessive Investment in Whiteness: How White People Profit from Identity Politics*. Philadelphia: Temple University Press.

Maghbouleh, Neda. 2022 August. "Twenty-Five Years of Charles Mills's *Racial Contract* in Sociology." *Sociology of Race and Ethnicity* 8 (4): 1–15.

Matias, Cheryl E. 2016. *Feeling White: Whiteness, Emotionality, and Education*. Rotterdam: Sense Publishers.

Matias, Cheryl E., and Peter M. Newlove. 2017. "The Illusion of Freedom: Tyranny, Whiteness, and the State of U.S. Society." *Equity & Excellence in Education* 50 (3): 316–330. doi:10.1080/10665684.2017.1336951.

McKinney, Karyn D. 2005. *Being White: Stories of Race and Racism*. New York: Routledge.

Mills, Charles W. 1997. *The Racial Contract*. Ithaca: Cornell University Press.

Mills, Charles W1998. *Blackness Visible: Essays on Philosophy and Race.* Ithaca. Cornell University Press.

Mills, Charles W. 2007b. "White Ignorance." In *Race and Epistemologies of Ignorance,* edited by S. Shannon and T. Nancy, 11–38. Albany: SUNY Press.

Mills, Charles W. 2014. "White Time: The Chronic Injustice of Ideal Theory." *Du Bois Review: Social Science Research on Race* 11 (1): 27–42. doi:10.1017/S1742058X14000022.

Mills, Charles W. 2017. *Black Rights/White Wrongs: The Crisis of Racial Liberalism.* New York: Oxford University Press.

Mills, Charles W, and K M. Kalumba. 2002. "Reply: The Racial Contract as Methodology (Not Hypothesis." *Philosophia Africana* 5 (1, March): 75–99. doi:10.5840/philafricana20025119.

Morrison, Toni. 1994. *The Bluest Eye.* New York: Plume Book.

Nelson, Alondra. 2011. *Body and Soul: The Black Panther Party and the Fight Against Medical Discrimination.* Minneapolis: University of Minnesota Press.

Ocen, Priscilla A. 2012. "The New Racially Restrictive Covenant: Race, Welfare, and the Policing of Black Women in Subsidized Housing." *UCLA Law Review* 59 (August): 1540–1582.

Onaci, Edward. 2020. *Free the Land: The Republic of New Afrika and the Pursuit of a Black Nation State.* Chapel Hill: University of North Carolina Press.

Payne, Charles. 2007. *I've Got the Light of Freedom: The Organizing Tradition and the Mississippi Freedom Struggle.* Berkeley: University of California Press.

Philosophy News University of Toronto. 2018. "Alumnus Charles Mills on Pedagogy, White Supremacy, and the Future of Philosophy," May 18. Alumnus Charles Mills on pedagogy, white supremacy, and the future of philosophy - Department of Philosophy - University of Toronto (utoronto.ca)

Robinson, Cedirc J. 2000. *Black Marxism: The Making of the Black Radical Tradition.* Chapel Hill: Univerity of North Caroliona Press.

Schwartz, Sarah, and Eesha Pendharker. 2022. "Here's the Long List of Topics Republicans Want Banned from the Classroom," *Education Week.* February 2. Here's the Long List of Topics Republicans Want Banned From the Classroom (edweek.org)

Segato, Rita. 2010. "Territory, Sovereignty, and the Crimes of the Second State: The Writing on the Body of Murdered Women." In *Terrorizing Women" Feminicide in the Americas,* edited by R.-L. Fregoso and C. Bejarano, 70–92. Durham: Duke University Press.

Sherrod, Shirley. 2012. *The Courage to Hope: How I Stood Up to the Politics of Fear.* New York: Atria.

Squires, Gregory D., ed. 2018. *The Fight for Fair Housing: Causes, Consequences, and Future Implications of the 1968 Federal Fair Housing Act.* New York: Routledge.

Thandeka. 2013. *Learning to Be White: Money, Race, and God in America.* New York: Bloomsbury.

Tomlinson, Barbara, and George Lipsitz. 2019. *Insubordinate Spaces: Improvisation and Accompaniment for Social Justice.* Philadlephia: Temple University Press.

Touraine, Alain. 1988. *The Return of the Actor: Social Theory in Postindustrial Society.* Minneapolis: University of Minnesota Press.

Tsuchiya, Kazuyo. 2014. *Reinventing Citizenship: Black Los Angeles, Korean Kawasaki and Community Participation.* Minneapolis: University of Minnesota Press.

Ture, Kwame, Stokely Carmichael, and Charles Hamilton. 1992. *Black Power: The Politics of Liberation.* New York: Vintage Books.

Vetterkind, Riley. 2021. "Wisconsin Assembly Passes Ban on Teaching Critical Race Theory." *Wisconsin State Journal,* September 29.

Wallace-Wells, Benjamin. 2021. "How a Conservative Activist Invented the Conflict Over Critical Race Theory," *New Yorker* June 18 How a Conservative Activist Invented the Conflict Over Critical Race Theory | The New Yorker

Widener, Daniel. 2010. *Black Arts West: Culture and Struggle in Postwar Los Angeles.* Durham: Duke University Press.

Williams, Patricia J. 1990. "Metro Broadcasting, Inc.V. FCC: Regrouping in Singular Times." *Harvard Law Review* 104 (2,December): 525–546. doi:10.2307/1341585.

Williams, Patricia J. 1997. Seeing a Color-Blind Future: *The Paradox of Race.* New York: Farrar, Strauss and Giroux.

Yancy, George. 2008. "Elevators, Social Spaces and Racism: A Philosophical Analysis." *Philosophy & Social Criticism* 34 (8): 843–876. doi:10.1177/0191453708094727.

Yosso, Tara J. 2005. "Whose Culture Has Capital? A Critical Race Theory Discussion of Community Cultural Wealth." *Race Ethnicity and Education* 8 (1): 65–91. doi:10.1080/1361332052000341006.

Yosso, Tara J 2007. "'this is No Slum'": A Critical Race Theory Analysis of Community Cultural Wealth in Culture Clash's Chavez Ravine," *Aztlan: A Journal of Chicano Studies* 32 1 145–179

Yosso, Tara J. 2016. *Critical Race Theory in Education.* New York: Routledge.

Charles Mills ain't dead! Keeping the spirit of Mills' work alive by understanding and challenging the unrepentant whiteness of the academy

Amanda E. Lewis, Tyrone A. Forman and Margaret A. Hagerman

ABSTRACT

In this article, we draw upon Charles Mills' powerful scholarly insights on the racial contract and epistemologies of ignorance and argue for keeping his spirit and theorizing alive through a relentless focus on the endemic reality of racism/white supremacy in our society and institutions – particularly in the institution in which he and we work, higher education. We believe that continuing Mills' legacy requires pushing back against unrepentant whiteness in the academy – the pervasive white standpoint that naturalizes so much of the inequity that transpires in our academic departments, fields, and institutions. Toward this end, we provide several examples of somewhat mundane ways unrepentant whiteness (in the form of white habitus, group interests, racial apathy, and ignorance) shows up in higher education. These examples explore Mills' concept of 'the macro in the micro', or the everyday ways that white supremacy courses through the tentacles of our colleges and universities.

Introduction

Two of us had the honor of having Charles Mills as a colleague and friend when we joined the academy, and all of us were deeply influenced by his innovative scholarship. He was not only brilliant, but as many of the earlier articles in this issue mentioned, also had a disarming sense of humor. Despite his relentless and piercing analyses of white supremacy and the macro and micro influences of racism in the world, he never seemed perturbed – always charming, relaxed, and wearing his signature faded black jeans. Whether it was on a keynote panel in front of hundreds of scholars, standing around in a gathering at a colleague's house, over beer and dinner, or at any of the dozens of the workshops, conferences, faculty meetings, or other gatherings where we shared space with Charles' over the years, he was resolutely himself. He would listen with his head tilted down and slightly to the side, chuckle at stories about predictable shenanigans of administrators or political figures or colleagues, ready with insights delivered in his graceful Jamaican accent. He was always available for intellectual fellowship, ready to listen to a story, ready to talk politics – local politics, national politics, global politics. We never saw it, but he described his apartment as overrun with the multiple newspapers he consumed daily. His office was certainly overrun with papers of every kind. When one of us met with him as part of our campus interview, he greeted him with a shy grin peeking between three stacks of paper on his desk that were approximately two feet high! Charles was a brilliant intellectual who operated with authenticity and integrity. We learned so much from him and we hope to use this essay to share some of those lessons.

Specifically, we will highlight and build on some of the key insights from previous articles in the issue and simultaneously offer a call to action to the larger educational research community for keeping the spirit of Mills' work alive. We draw attention to one of the central themes of this issue, Professor Mills' focus on the *endemic reality of white supremacy and racism in our society and institutions.* And we argue that we must continually and reflexively apply this analysis, as he did, to the institution in which he and we work: higher education. The insights Charles' offered about white supremacy, white ignorance, and the multiple levels racism operates on simultaneously are all relevant and prevalent in the academy and can make it difficult for those who want to follow in his footsteps. We argue, however, that continuing his legacy means, at least in part, that we need to take his and our own analyses seriously and not be surprised about even the mundane manifestations of white supremacy, even within spaces and institutions that somehow seem like they should know better and be better. Charles' work reminds us that the struggle is predictable, and that our job is to stay courageous and persist.

Continuing Mills' legacy, we suggest, requires actively pushing back against the often-unrepentant whiteness of the academy. As his work suggests, by 'whiteness of the academy' we mean far more than demographics but distributions of power, organizational culture and norms, the embedded logics of academic fields, and the interpersonal dynamics within organizations. Pushing back here means taking Mills' theorizing seriously and drawing upon it to challenge the pervasive white standpoint that naturalizes so much of the inequity that transpires in our academic departments, fields, professional societies, and higher education, more broadly.

Toward this end, we offer examples of somewhat mundane ways unrepentant whiteness show up in classrooms, in faculty affairs, and in debates about the boundaries of intellectual fields and the production of knowledge. Here we focus on 'the macro in the micro', or the everyday ways that white supremacy courses through the hallways of our colleges and universities. We do not mean the shaved-head, far-right boot stomping white supremacy, though there is more of that of late, but rather the political, economic, and cultural system Charles wrote about so eloquently in his work. Through these stories, we reflect upon Charles Mills' powerful theoretical contributions and his unique ability to critique and ironically chuckle about *the everydayness of racial b@!!sh#!!.* We then offer ideas about resistance, drawing on our experience and the other articles in this issue to offer some general lessons on how to proceed. As Mills would argue, we do this necessary work not just for intellectual ends but for *normative* ends. We work to describe, understand, and unveil white supremacy and ignorance with the explicit goal of trying to reduce them.

The endemic reality of white supremacy, racism, and ignorance: mills' racial contract

Professor Mills' (1997) award-winning book *The Racial Contract* theorizes how a racialized system of exclusion, what he refers to as a 'the racial contract' comes into existence. The racial contract, he suggests, is a 'set of formal and informal agreements' whose purpose is 'the differential privileging of the whites as a group with respect to the nonwhites as a group' (Mills 1997, 11). In this now classic work, Mills takes pains to carefully define white supremacy as a global ' ... system of domination by which white people have historically ruled over and, in certain important ways, continue to rule over nonwhite people'. While he takes pains to capture the global, structural, and macro manifestations of white supremacy, Mills outlines the many interrelated levels of white supremacy along with its key mechanisms. Particularly relevant for scholars are his arguments about the socialness of epistemology. He argues that '*white misunderstanding, misrepresentation, evasion, and self-deception on matters related to race ... are in no way accidental*, but *prescribed* by the terms of the Racial Contract ... in order to establish and maintain the white polity' (Mills 1997, 19). As such, white ignorance is not the same as general ignorance or lack of knowledge/understanding. White ignorance is strategic, structural, collective, and in the service of power. It is, he theorizes, an active agent or accelerant that fuels the reproduction and maintenance of racial inequity. Mills importantly adds, 'All whites are *beneficiaries* of the Contract, though some whites are not *signatories* to it' (Mills 1997, 11). Thus, similar to Bonilla-Silva (2001) and others, he reminds us both of the comprehensive functioning of the contract but also the possibility for working to undermine it. As we will elaborate on below, Mills' theoretically rich body of scholarship on the *racial contract* and *epistemologies of ignorance* provides a key foundation for scholars interested in understanding the durability of racialized hierarchy, its influence on educational settings, and how we might think about our role in resistance.

The university is not an ideal institution

George Lipsitz, in his article in this issue, reminds us of one of Charles Mills' key scholarly interventions. He notes, 'Mills counters the social contract's fantasy of an ideal society that *might* exist with the reality of the non-ideal social contract that *actually* exists: an exclusionary agreement that promotes and preserves the advantages of whiteness through structurally unjust social relations while denying justice to those of whom it takes advantage [emphasis added]'. We agree and extend this analysis to remind us that neither is the university *an ideal institution*. Over the years, we have witnessed many emerging scholars experience the heartbreak of realizing that the academy itself and their colleagues within it, in particular, often function in ways that replicate 'unjust social relations'. Especially as social scientists, humanists, and educational scholars, it can be jarring to discover that colleagues who have the language of power, race, and social hierarchy are able to analyze these dynamics in the abstract even as they replicate them in the present.

In the last two decades, scholars of race in higher education have increasingly given theoretical and empirical attention to what had been too often previously a blind spot in the literature (e.g. Cabrera 2014; Cabrera, Franklin, and Watson 2017; Chesler, Lewis, and Crowfoot 2005; Gusa 2010; Harper 2012; Matias 2015; McGee 2020). For example, Nolan Cabrera (2014, 2019) has regularly challenged higher education scholars to seriously engage with racial matters including the ways that whiteness gets normalized in colleges and universities. When this important issue is left out of the analysis, as Cabrera and colleagues put it, it 'allows [white privilege and power] to flourish' (Cabrera, Watson, and Franklin 2016, 120). Gusa (2010, 465) labels this institutional flourishing 'White Institutional Presence' or the ways that Whiteness and white cultural ideology are woven into the epistemological and cultural fabric of higher education. These scholars are helping to both describe and illuminate how the Racial Contract (Mills 2007) manifests within these institutions.

Whiteness in the graduate school classroom

An important realm of academic life in which the pervasive white standpoint and whiteness, more generally, often dominates is the classroom. While it may seem that sociology classrooms, and especially Ph.D. level seminar classrooms focused on inequality, would be immune from normative practices that reinforce white supremacy, this is not necessarily the case.

In one example from our experience, a white professor was teaching about residential segregation as part of a graduate course on inequality. The students in the course had read a book and some articles about the topic and were discussing federal policies that shaped racial patterns in where people live. During the discussion, a student in the class made an explicitly anti-Black statement: 'The reason no one wants to live near Black people is because they smell and don't take care of their yards'. When this happened, the professor did not intervene or acknowledge what had been said. Instead, he changed the topic, turning to a white student to ask them a new and unrelated question about the readings. In that moment, the professor engaged in strategic avoidance – pretending not to know that the comment was racist or pretending it had not been said, or just pretending that he could make it go away through distraction. His behavior modeled in the classroom what Forman (2004) refers to as racial apathy, an elaborate disengagement with and indifference to racial matters (see also Forman and Lewis 2006, 2015). In so doing, in this mundane way, the professor attempted to usher the class to just carry on, business as usual. When racism is smoothed over and ignored in classroom environments, we see not only the unrepentant nature of whiteness but also its social consequences.

When a Black student and a small group of white students interrupted this attempt to ignore the disparaging comment, drawing attention back to what was said and pointing out the racism of the statement, the white professor acted as if he did not know what had happened. The professor's behavior reflects what Charles Mills identified as a central aspect of the racial contract: ' . . . [whites] genuine cognitive difficulties in recognizing certain behavior patterns *as* racist . . . ' (Mills 1997, 93). Mills notes that this 'white moral cognitive dysfunction' (Mills 1997, 95) is a key pillar of the racial contract by providing many whites with a tacit ' . . . agreement to *misinterpret* the world' (Mills 1997, 18). And still we believe that this performed lack of awareness about the expression of racial bias in the classroom represents a strategic evasion of responsibility, what Mills labeled 'an epistemology of ignorance' (Mills 1997, 93). In other work, he expanded on this notion by theorizing about the power of 'white ignorance' to invalidate the moral and political significance of nonwhite suffering (Mills 2003, 2007). As he describes it, the difference between ordinary ignorance and *white ignorance* is that the latter reflects:

> a non-knowing which is not the innocent unawareness of truths to which there is no access but a self- and social shielding from racial realities ... Thus there will be characteristic and pervasive patterns of not-seeing and not-knowing-structured white ignorance, motivated inattention, self-deception, and moral rationalization. (Mills 2003, 45–46)

Certainly, the professor's clear intention was for the class to carry on as if nothing had happened and thus preserve the unrepentant whiteness of the classroom. Although Professor Mills taught us both in his writing and personal advice not to be surprised when white ignorance shows up in our own departments, networks, and organizations, it nevertheless can be demoralizing (Matias 2015).

Despite claiming to be ignorant during the class discussion that anything had happened, after the class ended, the professor offered words of 'thanks' to the white students (but, ironically not the Black student) for 'helping' him manage that difficult moment in the classroom. Of course, teachers are sometimes caught off guard by student comments in the classroom. But in this moment, the act of ignoring a harmful and racist statement illustrates how the feelings and comfort of some are prioritized over others. Mills illustrates this point in his discussion of how the racial contract places ' ... far greater value ... [on] white life, and the corresponding crystallization of feelings of vastly differential outrage over ... white and nonwhite suffering' (Mills 1997, 101). Moreover, the above example vividly illustrates the pervasive white standpoint and unrepentant whiteness that shows up and shows out in the college classroom on a too frequent basis.

The white professor performed the kind of emotional deflection that Zembylas and Matias describe in their article in this issue. As Matias writes about in this issue and elsewhere (Matias 2016), the emotionality of whiteness translates into an avoidance of discomfort and operates to ignore the costs of allowing racism to go unchallenged not only for students of color but to the community altogether. The fact that the professor and some of the other white students in the class were glad to 'just move on' from what had been said demonstrates the pervasiveness of the white standpoint in higher education more broadly – a standpoint where racism can just be ignored and everything is 'fine'. This white standpoint or 'white institutional presence' as Gusa (2010) labels it, reinforces white supremacy, brings macrolevel structural arrangements of our society to bear at the micro level, and reflects white group interests, even in a space some might assume would be more inclusive or work to undermine these practices rather than reproduce them.

We might well frame this as a small example of what Wyatt Driskell writes about in this issue as the endemic interconnectedness of white supremacy and American education. He remarks, 'I refer to my addendum to the Racial Contract as the "American Educational Contract"'. There are many layers or levels to the interconnections between white supremacy and American education – structural, organizational, and interpersonal. Fights over education are and have been key to the construction and defense of white supremacy throughout our history. As Diamond and Lewis (2022) argue:

> From its founding, the educational system in the United States was organized in a manner that supported and reinforced racial hierarchies and thus can be thought of as a white space with structures and practices that reinforce white supremacy. This is true not only structurally in the way school systems are organized, funded, and operated but also in the daily functioning of schools and classroom organizational routines within the system (p. 1472).

The above graduate school classroom example is a mundane one but one that demonstrates precisely in its mundaneness how pervasive these dynamics are (Matias 2015). They are also socially consequential – that moment was one of several that eventually led the Black student in that class to decide that the academy was not for them. These are the ways, as Best and Milner write about in this issue, racial power shows up, how white racial privilege remains invisible to those enacting it. The racial contract Mills wrote about was not just an abstract concept but is a part of everyday exchanges. These everyday moments of racial power in educational institutions exist alongside very public battles around the role of education in our society more generally. Currently, this point is only too obvious in the ongoing fights about the continued utilization of affirmative action in college admissions and the national moral panics being generated around Critical Race Theory as we will discuss below.

What is this whiteness of which you speak? Challenge the status quo

We might well think about the academy as an example of what sociologist Elijah Anderson (2015) refers to as a 'white space'. The whiteness we mean here is not just about the racial demographics or specifically those colleges and universities which are accurately described as Predominantly White Institutions (PWIs). The whiteness of this space is also about the way that white ignorance is a normative part of the intellectual life of academic fields and debates. When Charles Mills' wrote about white ignorance, he was quite clear that the whiteness being captured was not just the purview of white racial subjects but represented a broader sense of whiteness tied to white supremacy – an organized way of misrepresenting the world that is built into our structures, organizations, culture, and cognition (Mills 1997, 2007). In the present, we contend with the many reverberations of whiteness through our classrooms, departments, programs, and professional associations; we see this exemplified in the observations of earlier articles in this issue about how white ignorance shows up in the White Saviorism of teachers and human service providers (see Aviles), in Teacher Education programs (see Zembylas & Matias) and in focus groups conversations about racial dynamics (see Best & Milner).

As Mills (2007) argued, perception is mediated by social context and particularly in societies structured by domination and subordination, tends to be inflected by biases of ruling group(s). 'In all these cases, the concept is driving the perception, with whites aprioristically intent on denying what is before them' (Mills 2007, 18). This partly includes what Mills' describes as the 'management of memory' which makes possible the denial of cumulative effects of past injustices broadly and locally. As we all have experienced and witnessed, 'people' don't just deny the past but also act as if they don't know about what is happening in the present. This pervasive historical amnesia and denial reverberates in some of the core premises of our fields. For instance, one common experience we have had is coming up against hegemonic norms in our disciplines that claim we have to show evidence that racism and discrimination remains relevant and pervasive. As Tyson and Lewis (2021) put it:

> Since the 1960s, most scholars have been willing to acknowledge that White supremacist logic shaped the science of eugenics and the early science of IQ testing, but we are not always as eager to reflect on how racial logics may play a role in the unfolding of our own fields in a more proximate way. This includes, for instance, the presumption in many studies that schools function fairly until there is evidence to the contrary, rather than that schools function unfairly until there is evidence to the contrary. Fundamentally, this is about whether we assume that racism is an exception or the norm (p. 467).

Over the years, we have heard story upon story from colleagues feeling the brunt of naming racism explicitly in scholarship and in departmental dynamics. Some of this operates in particularly convoluted ways as white colleagues hear almost anything coming from a Black faculty member as a potential accusation of racism and/or discrimination.

In one example, an email was sent to the entire department asking for feedback on a draft job description advertisement for an upcoming faculty search [for the moment, let's set aside the wisdom (or lack thereof) of drafting a job description via email!]. Tyrone offered a few suggestions, including that it would be a good idea to include inclusive language beyond the typical boilerplate text that the university '. . . is an Equal Opportunity/Affirmative Action Employer' and encourages 'women and minorities to apply'. He offered the following language as an example: 'Our university values diversity and seeks talented students, faculty, and staff from diverse backgrounds. We strongly encourage applications from minorities and women'. A senior white colleague replied to 'all' with a personal and extended diatribe defensively accusing Tyrone of only wanting to hire a minority and insinuating that his proposed new language for the advertisement was somehow a personal accusation of bias against the department. The white professor in his own words:

> I don't think we needed Tyrone to come here to teach us that promoting the diversity of the faculty is important – it would and will be in this and all future searches". The professor continued: "Promoting diversity . . . is an important issue undertaken [sic] all searches, so why does this one have to be different? You cannot be saying we must hire someone who does XY&Z and is a minority (good luck getting that through any lawyer . . .). It wouldn't be . . . That said, I still think we go for the best candidate, not constrain ourselves with tons of specificity.

There are two noteworthy issues in this example. First, neither the chair nor any other faculty member acknowledged or spoke about the inappropriate, hostile, and personal attack on a colleague sent via email to the entire faculty. The late legal and critical race scholar Derrick Bell reminded us three decades ago that '. . . many whites, though not discriminating themselves, identify more easily with those who do than with their victims' (Bell 1992, 56). The silence and indifference displayed by the (mostly) white faculty to their colleague's hostile email directed at the lone Black professor in the department is a textbook case of what racial apathy looks likes today (see Forman and Lewis 2006, 2015). Mills (1997, 95–96) argues that this 'partitioned moral concern' reflects the structured reality of the racial contract that ' . . . requires in whites the cultivation of patterns of affect and empathy that are only weakly, if at all, influenced by nonwhite suffering'. Second, the white professor's comments were a dramatic misreading of language encouraging candidates from diverse candidates to apply to be 'only wanting to hire a minority'. The *unceasing significance and unrepentant nature of whiteness* in this scenario meant that a very public and exceedingly inappropriate personal attack against the lone Black professor in the department went unchecked. It likely went unchecked because many of the other (mostly) white faculty shared the colleague's indignation at a faculty member of color speaking up. As Charles Mills states in the *Racial Contract*: ' ... the white space is patrolled for dark intruders, whose very presence, *independently of what they may or may not do*, [emphasis added] is a blot on the reassuring civilized whiteness of the home space' (Mills 1997, 48). Despite this white professor's assertion that the department did not need any reminding about the importance of faculty diversity, a racially diverse pool of top-tier finalists resulted in the hiring of yet another white professor. At the time, a senior white male faculty in the department argued against choosing one of the top-tier minority candidates that interviewed because ' ... if we make them an offer, they will only stay for a couple of years and then leave'. Given the unchecked racial microaggressions and attack targeting a seemingly mundane intervention to advocate for somewhat more robust language around diversity (a seemingly uncontroversial idea) in a job advertisement there is a diabolical genius in the senior white male's conjecture.

Battles in higher education are not merely about who is in our departments and programs but about what we include in our curriculum and core courses and about what we consider to be 'good research'. This has erupted recently in very visible ways with right-wing organizers creating moral panics about 'woke' instructors and Critical Race Theory (CRT). As many have observed recently, the furor over whether schools are teaching Critical Race Theory to 'vulnerable young minds' is not about critical race theory or young minds. It is an explicit effort to push back against the growing recognition of the long-term legacies of centuries of structural racism. In his work, Mills (2007) argued that the editing of white memory was an essential strategy of white domination as it negates any requirement to address existing privilege. As he put it 'The mystification of the past underwrites the mystification of the present' (Mills 2007, 22). The most recent attack by the Governor of Florida on AP African American Studies curriculum is just another example of the management of memory that Mills theorized, a perhaps more deliberate effort to defend white ignorance than we have seen in recent years.

As with most culture wars, this furor is a proxy for something else. As Lipsitz writes about herein, CRT has been deployed by conservative social movements as a 'floating signifier'. It signifies growing white anxiety about a post-George Floyd racial reckoning and wide-scale public discussion of the endemic nature of racism in America's past and present. This deployment of critical race theory as a trope is not new and has its own history as shorthand or code language in academia too.

For instance, another of us learned these lessons a bit more publicly early in her career after the publication of her first book 20 years ago. Listening to recent news stories about 'CRT' being levied against schools as being 'biased' raised a flashback for the first author to the early 2000s. She had just published a comparative ethnography of elementary schools in which she explored how children come to understand themselves in racial terms and how their racial identity shapes their experience in schools. Both in the writing of it, and as she waited to find out whether 'people' would like it, she was earnest, hopeful, and predictably naïve for a first-time author.

Several positive reviews of the book came out after the book's publication but the only one she remembers well to this day is the one she avoided reading for years. She got several calls from colleagues one morning saying a weird and 'mean' review had just come out about her book in the discipline's flagship book review journal. The first person to call told her not to read it. As she put it, 'it's not really about your book. It is a critique of critical race theory that uses your book as an excuse to write about that'. Critical race theory? It certainly was true that the book was critical about racism and was studying the social construction of race, but it was not a textbook example of Critical Race Theory – a specific field, that at the time, was mostly in legal studies. As a sociologist, she was drawing on a long history of scholarship in the field. CRT didn't even show up in the book's index. Maybe, she thought, she could be criticized for not engaging with that work more but the field and its engagement in education was nascent then and it was not what she was doing.

Then as now, getting branded as doing 'critical race theory' was not about a serious engagement with Derrick Bell or Kimberlé Crenshaw or Jean Stefancic but was shorthand for labeling the research as ideologically driven, not good social science. Her friend who called to warn her was right in some ways: the review wasn't about the book, it was about a field trying to draw a line in the sand, about scholarly gatekeeping, and about the suggestion that work like this was a threat because it was too invested and wasn't objective. 'So what?', you might say. One bad review. And yet, this kind of gatekeeping serves multiple functions. It was that review that was put in every faculty mailbox the morning of a campus visit for a job interview. It is also the kind of intellectual gatekeeping we have witnessed innumerable times throughout our career with widespread and pernicious impact.

Conclusion: strategies of survival and resistance

So, if we are suggesting that the university is a microcosm of the larger world rather than an exception in some way, what does that mean for the future? There are a lot of good reasons people leave the academy and lots of good reasons to stay. Either way, scholars who are following in Charles Mills' footsteps need to listen closely to the lessons in his work and not be surprised when racial dynamics show up. Here, as elsewhere Charles' scholarship and wisdom is chock full of insights and encouragement about how to stay engaged and thrive without as Rockquemore and Laszloffy (2008) put it, 'losing your soul'. Charles delivered guidance directly to us all through his written words and quite often through his personal example of being. He navigated the academy on his terms: whether he was talking about the whiteness of philosophy (which he often did) or how to avoid serving in administrative roles – he once told one of the authors that whenever discussions would occur amongst the faculty about who should be the next department chair, inevitably his name would pop up. He would then gladly escort the current Dean to his office to witness the immense piles of papers strewn about making it difficult to move around. The conversation always ended there.

In his essay in this issue, Professor David Stovall shares some of the lessons he learned from Charles Mills while navigating life as an assistant professor. These can be best characterized as survival strategies for critical race scholars. A key lesson was to *be clear with yourself about 'what you are doing and why'* so that you aren't waiting around to be 'validated by the rules of the academy'. In fact, Charles might say, if you are a critical race scholar and you are doing good work, you should *expect resistance*. We cannot expect our ideas to carry the day or our graceful prose to sway all readers – if the ideas have power and challenge the status quo they will generate different forms of push back. A close colleague of ours who is now a bit of an eminence tells the story of every 'peer reviewed' article he published in the first decade of his career somehow 'requiring' review by 5–7 reviewers.

As with Stovall, Professor Aviles also writes about Charles' kindness, generosity, humor, and brilliance. She describes his influence as both intellectual and personal, and explains how, just in the way Charles always argued that his theorizing was not merely intellectual but normative, his engagement with the world lived out the liberatory possibilities of his work. One finds these tributes to Mills wide and far. Renowned Philosopher Tommie Shelby, in the foreword to the 25th anniversary edition of *The Racial Contract* writes about his deep admiration not just for Mills' work but for Mills' embodiment of professional and personal generosity. He describes meeting Mills at the American Philosophical Association Meeting in 1990. 'He was encouraging, supporting, and generous with his time, though I was a mere graduate student . . . he provided the kind of mentorship I have since sought to emulate . . . ' (Shelby 2022, p. xx). Charles' lesson to us here are multiple including the necessity of being generous, of building community, *and paying forward the help, knowledge, and encouragement* we have received to junior colleagues entering the field.

Related to this is the important advice to *find your people*. Professor Stovall describes constructing alternative intellectual communities and networks. Some have called them a 'fugitive space' or 'elsewhere space' where like-minded folks come together for support, engagement, and deep introspection. Professor Eddie Glaude (2020) elaborates on the benefits of such a space:

> I believe an elsewhere [space] can and must be found . . . That affords us the critical distance to imagine our lives . . . differently. . .We have to find and rest in a community of love. That community doesn't have to take any particular shape or form; it simply has to be genuine . . . Baldwin sought refuge among those who . . . offered him a place of nurturance to heal his wounds and an intellectual space to think creatively . . . a space to express his rage and vulnerability. . . (p.142).

For each of us, finding an 'elsewhere space' was essential not only on the path to tenure or promotion but for sustaining our scholarship and our sense of self in institutional spaces that sometimes literally marked us or our work as 'deviant' or 'difficult' for naming racism in our research or in our critique of the academy. During a discussion about a hostile third-year review process Amanda was told by her 'mentor/advocate' in the department that he was sorry for the bad behavior by some of the senior professors but 'When white guys of my generation hear the world "racism" we feel defensive'. In these moments, it is critical to have alternative epistemic communities where one's work is affirmed and valued. It is also essential to have networks that help you to navigate institutional power structures. Particularly if the work you are doing is directly challenging your field in some way, developing networks beyond disciplinary boundaries can be invaluable. While Charles Mills was always a serious philosopher, he also was simultaneously interested in interdisciplinary engagement with other critical race (and Marxist and gender) scholars. His work, in turn, has been taken up by a wide range of humanists and social scientists across fields as exemplified by the story Dr. Stovall tells of Mills traveling to receive the 2018 Derrick Bell Legacy award 'to honor scholars who advance issues of social justice, equity, and activism in education research, theory, and practice' at the Critical Race Studies in Education Association.

One quality of Charles' that we still struggle with is maintaining a sense of humor. Likely there is a great deal about his biography that helped him to keep things in perspective and to see the irony in institutional contradictions and interpersonal ridiculousness. Here the lesson we take is to *try not to get your feelings hurt when people do what they are going to do*. In their contribution to the issue, Zembylas and Matias remind us of the importance of emotion in our understanding of how white ignorance shows up. Their essay extends Mills' important work on social epistemology by layering an analysis of *affect* into Mills theories of cognition. Like the story of a graduate school classroom, we told earlier, they show how white comfort, white feelings, and white interpretations get prioritized. Zembylas and Matias remind us of the power of not just white epistemologies and white ignorance, but also of how white emotions are consistently centered, rendered more important and given more significance than the emotions of anyone else. Again, this important insight echoed for us and reminded us of the many times we have had to contend with white colleagues' discomfort with our research about racism or our attempts to make organizational processes more racially equitable.

Finally, Mills was unapologetic in his call to understand how certain structures, practices, and policies promote 'crucially flawed processes', not just for the sake of understanding but to extricate oneself and *undermine them more generally*. Herein, we have drawn on examples from our experiences in higher education to illustrate what it means to keep the spirit of Charles Mills' work alive – to *both understand and challenge* the unrepentant whiteness of the academy. As scholars we must do more than just theorize power, race, and inequality, we should also commit to utilizing our scholarly lens to describe, undermine, and ultimately dismantle the informal and formal habits, processes, and policies that reproduce white supremacy in the hallowed halls of academia. We must show up for each other intellectually and personally, hopefully with some occasional laughs, and with Charles' deep insights and commitments in mind.

Disclosure statement

No potential conflict of interest was reported by the authors.

References

Anderson, E. 2015. "The White Space." *Sociology of Race and Ethnicity* 1 (1): 10–21. doi:10.1177/2332649214561306.

Bell, D. 1992. *Faces at the Bottom of the Well: The Permanence of Racism*. New York, NY: Basic Books.

Bonilla-Silva, E. 2001. *White Supremacy and Racism in the Post-Civil Rights Era*. Boulder, CO: Lynne Rienner Publishers.

Cabrera, N. L. 2014. "Exposing Whiteness in Higher Education: White Male College Students Minimizing Racism, Claiming Victimization, and Recreating White Supremacy." *Race Ethnicity and Education* 17 (1): 30–55. doi:10.1080/13613324.2012.725040.

Cabrera, N. L. 2019. *White Guys on Campus: Racism, White Immunity, and the Myth Of"post-racial" Higher Education.* New Brunswick, NJ: Rutgers University Press.

Cabrera, N. L., J. D. Franklin, and J. S. Watson. 2017. Whiteness in Higher Education: The Invisible Missing Link in Diversity and Racial Analyses: ASHE Higher Education Report, Volume 42, Number 6. Hoboken, NJ: John Wiley & Sons.

Cabrera, N. L., J. S. Watson, and J. D. Franklin. 2016. "Racial Arrested Development: A Critical Whiteness Analysis of the Campus Ecology." *Journal of College Student Development* 57 (2): 119–134. doi:10.1353/csd.2016.0014.

Chesler, M., A. E. Lewis, and J. E. Crowfoot. 2005. *Challenging Racism in Higher Education: Promoting Justice.* New York, NY: Rowman & Littlefield Publishers.

Diamond, J. B., and A. E. Lewis. 2022. "Opportunity Hoarding and the Maintenance of "White" Educational Space." *The American Behavioral Scientist* 66 (11): 1470–1489. doi:10.1177/00027642211066048.

Forman, T.A. 2004. "Color-Blind Racism and Racial Indifference: The Role of Racial Apathy in Facilitating Enduring Inequalities." In *The Changing Terrain of Race and Ethnicity*, edited by M. Krysan and A. Lewis, 43–66. New York, NY: Russell Sage.

Forman, T.A., and A. E. Lewis. 2006. "Racial Apathy and Hurricane Katrina: The Social Anatomy of Prejudice in the Post-Civil Rights Era." *Du Bois Review: Social Science Research on Race* 3 (1): 175–202. doi:10.1017/S1742058X06060127.

Forman, T. A., and A. E. Lewis. 2015. "Beyond Prejudice? Young whites' Racial Attitudes in Post–Civil Rights America, 1976 to 2000." *The American Behavioral Scientist* 59 (11): 1394–1428. doi:10.1177/0002764215588811.

Glaude, E., Jr. 2020. *Begin Again: James Baldwin's America and Its Urgent Lessons for Our Own.* New York, NY: Crown.

Gusa, D. L. 2010. "White Institutional Presence: The Impact of Whiteness on Campus Climate." *Harvard Educational Review* 80 (4): 464–490. doi:10.17763/haer.80.4.p5j483825u110002.

Harper, S. R. 2012. "Race Without Racism: How Higher Education Researchers Minimize Racist Institutional Norms." *The Review of Higher Education* 36 (1): 9–29. doi:10.1353/rhe.2012.0047.

Matias, C. E. 2015. "I Ain't Your Doc student": The Overwhelming Presence of Whiteness and Pain at the Academic Neoplantation." In *Racial Battle Fatigue in Higher Education: Exposing the Myth of Post-Racial America*, edited by K. Fasching-Varner, K. A. Albert, R. W. Mitchell, and C. Allen, 59–68. Lanham, MD: Rowman & Littlefield.

Matias, C. E. 2016. *Feeling White: Whiteness, Emotionality, and Education.* Rotterdam: Sense Publishers.

McGee, E. O. 2020. "Interrogating Structural Racism in STEM Higher Education." *Educational Researcher* 49 (9): 633–644. doi:10.3102/0013189X20972718.

Mills, C.W. 1997. *The Racial Contract.* New York, NY: Cornell University Press.

Mills, C.W. 2003. "White Supremacy as Sociopolitical System: A Philosophical Perspective." In *White Out: The Continuing Significance of Racism*, edited by W. Doane and E. Bonilla-Silva, 35–46. New York, NY: Routledge.

Mills, C.W. 2007. "White Ignorance." In *Race and Epistemologies of Ignorance*, edited by S. Sullivan and N. Tuana, 13–31. Albany, NY: SUNY Press.

Rockquemore, K., and T. A. Laszloffy. 2008. *The Black Academic's Guide to Winning Tenure—Without Losing Your Soul.* Boulder, CO: Lynne Rienner Publishers.

Shelby, T. 2022. "Foreward." In *The Racial Contract (25th Anniversary)*, xix–xxvii. Ithaca, NY: Cornell University Press.

Tyson, K., and A. E. Lewis. 2021. "The "Burden" of Oppositional Culture Among Black Youth in America." *Annual Review of Sociology* 47 (1): 459–477. doi:10.1146/annurev-soc-090420-092123.

Index